Routledge Revivals

Historical Geography of England and Wales

First published in 1925, *Historical Geography of England and Wales* gives a picturesque account of what has come to be recognized as the 'Historical Geography' of Britain south of the Tweed. It begins by showing the geographical causes which lay behind much of the 'culture' of the Stone Ages, etc., the settlement and difficulties of Anglo-Saxon rule, and the apparent ruthlessness of the Conqueror.

The influence of the Medieval church in making the land more habitable is dealt with, as well as the responsibility of the local environment for the different staple-industries, and the change from pastoral and agricultural to industrial England. Passing from the Middle Ages to the impetus given to trade and commerce by the discovery of the New World, the narrative continues with a description of the revolutions of the Modern Period with regard to Road, Water, and Rail Transport, and the geographical evolution of the social communities from free townships with their nuclei of hamlets and villages, to the towns, cities, and 'conurbations' of the day.

This book will be a valuable resource for students and researchers of historical geography.

Historical Geography of England and Wales
South Britain

E.H. Carrier

First published in 1925
by George Allen & Unwin Ltd

This edition first published in 2025 by Routledge
4 Park Square, Milton Park, Abingdon, Oxon, OX14 4RN

and by Routledge
605 Third Avenue, New York, NY 10158

Routledge is an imprint of the Taylor & Francis Group, an informa business

© 1925 E.H. Carrier

All rights reserved. No part of this book may be reprinted or reproduced or utilised in any form or by any electronic, mechanical, or other means, now known or hereafter invented, including photocopying and recording, or in any information storage or retrieval system, without permission in writing from the publishers.

Publisher's Note
The publisher has gone to great lengths to ensure the quality of this reprint but points out that some imperfections in the original copies may be apparent.

Disclaimer
The publisher has made every effort to trace copyright holders and welcomes correspondence from those they have been unable to contact.

A Library of Congress record exists under LCCN: 26001356

ISBN: 978-1-041-12003-2 (hbk)
ISBN: 978-1-003-66482-6 (ebk)
ISBN: 978-1-041-12451-1 (pbk)

Book DOI 10.4324/9781003664826

HISTORICAL GEOGRAPHY OF ENGLAND AND WALES
(SOUTH BRITAIN)

BY

E. H. CARRIER
M.A., M.Sc., F.R.Hist.S.

SENIOR LECTURER IN GEOGRAPHY, AVERY HILL (L.C.C.) TRAINING COLLEGE

LONDON : GEORGE ALLEN & UNWIN LTD.
RUSKIN HOUSE, 40 MUSEUM STREET, W.C.1

First published in 1925

Printed in Great Britain by
Burleigh Ltd. at the Burleigh Press, Bristol
All rights reserved

CONTENTS

SECTION I. THE RACES OF BRITAIN.

CHAPTER		PAGE
I.	MEN OF THE OLD STONE AGE	11
II.	THE NATURE OF THE RECORD	18
III.	MEN OF THE NEW STONE AGE	22
IV.	THE BRONZE AGE	34
V.	THE ROMAN INTERLUDE	45
VI.	THE COMING OF THE TEUTONS	60
VII.	THE NORMAN CONQUEST	75

SECTION II. THE MIDDLE AGES (I).

VIII.	INTRODUCTION	87
IX.	ECCLESIASTICAL INFLUENCE UPON THE GEOGRAPHY OF ENGLAND	89
X.	TERRITORIAL DIVISIONS: SHIRE-MAKING	103
XI.	COMMUNITY DIVISIONS: HUNDRED, VILLAGE, BOROUGH, PARISH	117
XII.	THE INFLUENCE OF GEOGRAPHY UPON MEDIÆVAL WARFARE	129
XIII.	THE BATTLE OF LAND AND SEA: DISAPPEARANCE OF FOREST AND FEN	135

SECTION III. THE MIDDLE AGES (II).

XIV.	THE INDUSTRIES OF THE MIDDLE AGES	157
XV.	GUILDS, FAIRS, MARKETS	181
XVI.	TOWNS OF THE MIDDLE AGES	190
XVII.	COMMUNICATION AND TRANSPORT	209
XVIII.	THE GREAT AWAKENING	216

CONTENTS

SECTION IV. THE MODERN PERIOD.

CHAPTER		PAGE
XIX.	Revolution in Transport: Roadways	223
XX.	Revolution in Transport: Waterways	232
XXI.	Modern Industries	242
XXII.	Revolution in Industry	259
XXIII.	Revolution in Transport: Railways	264
XXIV.	Revolution in Village Life: Enclosures	272
XXV.	Revolution in Town Growth: Conurbations	276
	Index	289

SECTION I

THE RACES OF BRITAIN

CHAPTER I

MEN OF THE OLD STONE AGE

HISTORICAL Geography may be regarded as the Study of the Regional Environment of Human Societies, which latter, in actual fact, had already reached a noteworthy degree of development thousands of years before the beginnings of written History. Nevertheless from such records of those dim ages as remain, the story of Early Man and the life he was compelled to live may be deduced with a fair approach to accuracy.

It is now generally assumed that Man came into being as *man* during the latter part of the Tertiary Period. His home was in the hot " river drifts " or fertile flood plains, but at times he resumed the old tree-life of his far-away cousins, the Apes, or betook himself to the security of the rock crevice or cave, or constructed a shelter of branches and leaves erected on rough stakes driven into soft soil. Already he possessed the implement-making disposition, much as baboons at the present day open nuts by stones, prise up boulders with sticks, and strike their prey with stones and sticks. But in spite of this display of intelligence he was ill-equipped for his struggle against the larger and more highly specialized creatures of his environment, or the changing climatic extremes that drove him from place to place. Nevertheless, even then, when he was incontestably the hunted rather than the hunter, the germs of his glorious possibilities were present. Denied the strong, sabre-tooth of the tiger, the cunning of the wolf, the prolific breeding powers of others among his relentless enemies, he possessed a

certain quality that in the end outweighed them all—
the strength of his weakness. Not being especially
adapted to any particular environment he could and
did at will wander through all environments, flying
danger here, gaining an unexpected advantage there,
migrating southward as the ice advanced, retreating
to other localities as the climate ameliorated, always
learning, always changing, always increasing in
" mental and motor versatility . . . making good
his physical deficiency by means of mechanical appli-
ances, supplementing his powers by impelling the
animals to give him service, multiplying his individual
resources by co-operation of a kind similar to that of
the baboons,"[1] till a *habit* of progress became part
of his inheritance ; till stagnation became impossible,
till after the lapse of long ages man emerged from the
starvation and danger level to one of comparative
ease and security. His position of hunted gave way to
that of hunter, of prey to prowler, of fugitive to
domination, and finally his inheritance of " advance "
led him from matter to mind, from mere satisfaction
of the needs of food and shelter to that of observation
and introspection that underlies all mental and
physical progress.

The " Men of the Stone Ages " come into one or
other of three classifications, generally known as
Eolithic, Palaeolithic and Neolithic Man,[2] living in
the Tertiary Period, the Pleistocene or Glacial Periods,
and the Post-Glacial up to the "Age of Metals,"
estimated as from six to eight thousand years ago.
Man was no more exempt than the rest of the organic
kingdom from the successive cycles of adversity and

---

[1] Spurrel, " Man and his Forerunners."
[2] These names are derived from Greek words signifying Dawn
Eos), Ancient (Paleos), New (Neo-), Stone (lithos).

MEN OF THE OLD STONE AGE 13

extinction in the presence of a higher type. Our Eolithic and Palaeolithic forerunners have vanished completely, though the latter is said to be still represented by the Eskimoes, but the Neolithic representatives, modified by succeeding races, and raised to a much higher culture-level, still hold their own in our Western uplands and in Ireland. There was, of course, no marked date when one race disappeared and another arrived on the scene. There must have been long ages of transition when the dying and growing races lingered side by side, but that each definitely appeared, grew to its zenith of possibilities and then declined, gives rise to the thought that our position is probably not permanent and that we too may some day vanish before the advent of a superior and super-man.

Of *Eolithic Man* little can be surmised and much less known. He lived in the Tertiary drifts and river valleys and used a rough stone weapon of no particular shape, the essential quality being suitability for hand throwing, and a jagged or sharp edge. This was no doubt hurled against wild animals who ventured too near, but could not have been very effective. " Eoliths " or flints probably so used have been picked up in our chalk areas. Extensive finds of these weapons point to the provident collection of stores of suitable stones rather than to " factories." With such a weapon Eolithic man must have been mainly a vegetarian, living on fruits and seeds, and such small creatures as his simple weapon might kill. He knew nothing about agriculture, probably wore no clothing, and had no articulate speech.

Palaeolithic Man is much more important. Living in the river drifts and valleys as " drift man," and later in caves and rock crevasses as " Cave Man,"

Palaeolithic Man is estimated to have covered a period of approximately two hundred thousand years! The Cave-men of the second hundred thousand years are distinguished as belonging to the Mammoth and Reindeer Periods.[1]

As "drift man" Palaeolithic man apparently wandered into Europe during the fourth Interglacial Period. The advancing ice made him take to the caves. Naturally he did not live on the ice-sheet, but regions far to the south of it necessarily felt the influence of the Arctic climate and the icy winds. The hills of England were much higher than at present, being in fact ranges of low mountains rising to nearly 2,000 feet. Our eastward-flowing rivers were then tributaries of a large stream flowing northward up the centre of what is now the North Sea, and collecting also the waters of the Rhine, the Scheldt, and the Elbe. Ireland and England were joined to Europe by a land passage, and great rivers to which at the same time English and Irish, English and French waters were tributary ran westwards over the present continental shelf.[2]

In England "drift man" settled in the valleys of the South-east and West, especially in what are now the submerged Channel lands. His mode of life was similar to the earlier human type. His food was still mainly vegetarian—different sorts of nuts, wild fruits and berries, edible fungi (cp. French truffles), roots, honey, snails, frogs (a French dish to-day), fish alive and dead, shell-fish of various kinds, and especially oysters, seaweed, snakes, insects, caterpillars (still

---

[1] These somewhat fanciful divisions are named after animals typical of the two periods of the Old Stone Age.
[2] The north-western limits of this ancient Europe may be reconstructed by making France, the Low Countries and Scandinavia stretch across the English Channel, North Sea and British Isles to the Atlantic limit of our continental shelf.

MEN OF THE OLD STONE AGE

eaten in China) and carrion obtained in times of exceptionally good fortune (note how the taste for putrid game still survives). He smashed up bones with a stick, and made a thick, gritty paste of jelly. Thus early Palaeolithic Man was still in the "collecting stage." However, adversity was about to overtake him, adversity with its scorching fires of progress. The increasing cold forced him to master his fear of the dark—a fear which had kept him from the dim forest, and drove him to seek refuge in caves. The woolly mammoth, the cave lion, cave bear, Irish elk, his contemporaries, forecasted the oncoming of glacial conditions, restricting the possibilities of food-getting for all forms of the animal creation, and teaching man this much at least, that his weapons must be improved. And under the spur of this new necessity man's improvement made rapid strides. Inhabiting a chalk and clay area, that is to say within reach of iron pyrites and flint, he was bound sooner or later to discover and become a master of fire, an acquisition that made his cave more secure from the tigers[1], wolves, etc., that at one time had disputed its possession with him, and the moral benefit accruing from the success of this new method of waging war upon his hitherto over-powerful enemies must have been incalculable. The new freedom given encouraged group life in the caverns and man became more social. Unable to grow a coat of fur like the woolly mammoth, he began to wear clothes, the dried, scraped and fire-cured skins of his one-time foes.

This new advance was accompanied by another. The natural vegetable food was being produced in increasingly smaller quantities as the great cold

[1] "Sabre-tooth" the tiger—foe of Cave Man, was allied to but not identical with the tiger of our modern world.

became still greater. Birds' eggs, grubs, wild fruits and seeds, besides being less in quantity, had not sufficient warmth-giving qualities to support man under his Arctic conditions of life. To survive at all he was bound to become a hunter, and the new weapons, lances and javelins in flint, harpoons and borers in bone, show a marked advance in tool-making. Given fresh meat and fire, cooking soon becomes inevitable, and from heating between stones and baking in clay, the art of pottery making was bound to follow. Permanent possessions may be marked for ownership, and the marking often developed into intricate and beautiful ornamentation. Drawings, and even good drawings, became quite common on cave walls, on horns, on ivory, on wood, even on slate, though as has been already noted the pictures of human beings are poor, crude and grotesque. Finally the mammoth gave place to the reindeer, and with this substitution man's subsequent taming of the animal kingdom is foretold.

Yet with all this, Palaeolithic Man had advanced little judging by modern standards, perhaps he cannot even be said to have been "civilized." His struggle for existence was still too fierce to afford that leisure which, together with the strenuous work making it possible, may result in real intellectual progress, and he disappeared before the oncoming of a higher race before which he was naturally bound to "go down." Perhaps the new peoples, men of the New Stone Age, herdsmen and agriculturists, drove him from his poor steppe to the forest, and the exile to an unaccustomed climate for which he was unfitted effected his destruction. Perhaps he had come to rely too much upon the reindeer which went back to Arctic latitudes with the retreat of the ice.

Yet the memory of his ineffectual struggle with the conquering Neolithic invaders is still kept alive by certain "legends" handed down to us from the remotest limits of history concerning a small, dwarfish race of beings living "underground" and the savage orgies of uncouth, sharp-teethed ogres!

CHAPTER II

THE NATURE OF THE RECORD

THE " Record " left of the early culture of Man consists in objects of necessity or luxury, indestructible by nature, or carefully preserved in some special manner to be presently described, and which can be examined to-day. They are collectively known as "remains," and remains of a very primitive people are fairly wide-spread, especially in the regions south of the Ice Sheet limit. By virtue of the nature of their weapons, these people are generally put into one or other of two classes, and thus designated as men of the "Old" and of the "New" Stone Ages. Remains belonging to the first class—weapons made of roughly chipped flints and chert—have been unearthed from the drift or gravel beds of old rivers, and the floors of limestone caverns. Weapons of the New Stone Age were more finely wrought and of polished flints or stone ; they occur in the beds of ancient lakes, the débris of refuse heaps, coast forests, earthworks, rude sepulchres and early stone structures. In our own country there have been famous excavations at Crayford and Galley Hill in Kent, Kent's Cavern, Torquay, at Glastonbury and Wells in Somerset, Piltdown in Sussex, etc. Early man settled as far north as the Peak District, but apparently failed to reach Scotland or Ireland ; probably the climatic conditions were adverse. The remains left to us to deduce both his extent and his habits of life may be divided roughly into five classes—human, food, weapons and tools, buildings, art-work.

THE NATURE OF THE RECORD 19

Of the *Human Remains*, the most important is the skull, which tells a man's size and build, his race (from its shape), the food he eats and method of eating (jaw, teeth), while the shape of the forehead and brain capacity gives a clue to his instincts, intelligence and character. By examining the graves and modes of sepulchre of a people a guess can be made as to its beliefs, hopes, customs. Sometimes bodies are found burnt before burial, either to prevent the return of the " ghost " or for reasons of sanitation. Some graves contain food jars, cups, ornaments, coin, probably to make the ghost feel at home and therefore disinclined to haunt his living relatives, though the motive may be more altruistic. Coin is obviously to pay the passage to the other world (the spirit or ghost world) and is not found in the graves of very primitive man. The earth mound erected over the sepulchred remains of the New Stone Age peoples will be considered later. Clearly the nature of the ornaments found in these graves, jewellery, pottery, etc., indicates the skill of the people and the standard of their art.

Remains of Food have been found extensively in the great refuse heaps flung by the cave dwellers outside their houses. Denmark, America, Scotland and Ireland give many examples. Bones and teeth of animals, shells of molluscs, seeds, cooking pots, indicate the kind of animal contemporaneous with cave man, and his strength and skill in hunting and fishing.

Remains of Weapons and Tools occur in refuse heaps, under the stalagmitic floors of caves, in river beds and drifts, sands and gravels, sometimes fifteen to twenty feet below the surface, and the material is generally flint. The London and Hampshire Basins have given a plentiful yield and some of these finds have been so great as to suggest a primitive "factory" (e.g., Brandon and Piltdown in Sussex.) The weapons are whole or broken and consist of "scrapers" (for scraping skins for clothing), needles, axes, hammers, knives, arrow-heads, swords, spears, etc., sometimes rough and jagged, sometimes beautifully cut and polished.

The Remains of Prehistoric Buildings are mostly connected with religion—stone circles, tumuli, dolmens, cromlechs. Stonehenge, for example, was a Neolithic structure probably connected with Star Worship. Avebury was another such temple of even greater antiquity. Some of the buildings were really dwellings, e.g., small round huts on Dartmoor, underground dwellings in Ireland (now, of course, attributed to the hosts of Elf-land), pile dwellings on lakes whose foundations have more than once been discovered when the lake was drained, or much reduced through abnormal drought (e.g., lake-dwellings at Glastonbury). The architecture of the Swiss "Chalet" appears to be a descendant of that common to "lake villages."

Remains of Art-Work. The earliest cave-men were good artists and filled the walls of their caves with drawings—a habit lingering, perhaps, in the modern custom of wall-papering. He also made drawings on bone, wood, slate, etc. These "pictures" are generally of animals, telling us therefore much about contemporary types, and executed with great spirit. Here and there the human form has been attempted, but always in hideous caricature, probably through a superstitious fear lest the "ghost" of the subject after death might return to "haunt" the lifelike pictured image.

Later on man made a rough pottery, possibly led thereto through the accidental discovery of the action

THE NATURE OF THE RECORD

of fire upon clay, and as increasing skill in the making led to greater permanence of the made, leisure, perhaps combined with pride of ownership, resulted in increasing skill of ornamentation.

Bronze objects mark the last advance of earlier Man before the present Age of Iron.[1]

At this moment there is no self-respecting country, county, or town that does not possess its collection of prehistoric remains, and it is from these and similar sources of knowledge that attempts, gradually increasing in wealth of detail and accuracy, have been made to reconstruct the life of Primitive Man.

[1] Though we are apparently passing into a Steel Age.

CHAPTER III

MEN OF THE NEW STONE AGE

TOWARDS the close of the Palaeolithic Age the land to be called Britain underwent great climatic and structural changes. The retreat of the Ice drew after it the flora and fauna of Arctic conditions leaving the newly released territory a land of swamps and spreading forests. To this land, depopulated of so many of its preglacial and glacial species, the flora and fauna of her present continental neighbours passed without much difficulty, though much less succeeded in getting so far as Ireland. But whether the weight of the Ice had set seismic forces in operation, or whether the cause lay quite outside this, the connection between the " Low countries " and Eastern Britain began to be severed, until that great river, once gathering the Thames and Rhine, Ouse and Elbe as tributaries was merged in the waters of an encroaching sea, and the eastern hills (the Dogger Banks) themselves had fallen below the newly admitted ocean. Southwards similar changes were in progress. A renewal of pressure carried still higher the chalk and the wealden uplift, and no doubt the " complementary depression " was the first cause of the invasion of the Atlantic into that area now known as the English Channel. Rivers cutting gaps through the chalk upfold had eroded the barrier which the Wealden Uplift presented to the inflowing waters, until it was quite cut through and " North Sea " met " English Channel " where lie the Straits of Dover.

To this period, therefore, must be assigned that

MEN OF THE NEW STONE AGE 23

"Rising from the azure Main" which has had its economic no less than its poetic value, and with the new Island must be associated a new people.

From this time onward the remains of early man change in character, notably in his common weapon—still of flint, but better shaped, carefully polished, and altogether capable of doing very effective damage. Nor was this "New Stone" or "Neolithic" man his Palaeolithic predecessor grown wise and wary in southern and therefore more favoured lands. Quite the contrary; he was slighter in build, swarthier in complexion, with dark hair and eyes, and possessed a more upright carriage, and "longer" head.[1] These people adopted an outdoor life, as their "remains" testify. Bone awls and needles point to the sewing of strong material—clothing and tent making. Saws, hammers, grinding stones, drills, knives, daggers, bolts, pins, needles, spindle-wheels of stone betoken their more domestic arts, while children's toys bear witness to a parental tenderness, and personal ornaments in jet, shale, and amber show a development of a certain phase of personal pride or vanity.

The finding of the remains by the ignorant—for they are being continually turned up during ploughing, or come to light through the action of rain upon the soil—has given rise to strange legends, the neolithic celt (a species of chisel) being often regarded as a "thunderbolt," and the small, polished, but deadly arrow-heads as "elf-shot"; spindle-wheels are regarded as "fairy millstones" or "pixie's grindstones," helping, no doubt, to perpetuate the legend of a diminutive people. The fact that some of these people did

---

[1] A "long" head indicates that the measurement from the bridge of the nose to the nape of the neck is long relative to the breadth across the forehead.

live in natural caves has aided in the imaginative construction of much that deals with elf and gnome-life.

The " buildings " of this period were often very large as at Stonehenge and Avebury in Wiltshire.[1] They consist of single or multiple stone blocks. The single stones (megaliths or menhirs, from Celtic *maen* = stone, *hir* = high) were similar to the still standing " Blind Fiddler " at Penzance, and marked either the grave of a chief, a " tablet " commemorating some great trival event, or simply the " totem " of the tribe. Dolmens (Celtic *dawl* = table) are generally composed of three or more stones, one of which, long and flat, is supported in a more or less horizontal position by two or more others. The dead body, or jar of ashes, was placed in the chamber so constructed, this " mausoleum " then forming the centre of an artificial mound, often of great extent and elliptic in shape, and known to us as " long barrows." To-day these dolmens are frequently discovered in lonely places with the covering earth all worn away; the bared structure is often erroneously taken to be an altar preferably of the Druid religion. " Kit's Coty hole " is an example of such a one found in Kent.

Stonehenge and Avebury show the outlines of stone circles and avenues of wide extent, and are clearly the result of a great and organized co-operative effort. Perhaps they were " meeting " houses or rallying points for trade or religious services, to which " Neolithic Jerusalem " the tribes at certain periods repaired. The presence of gigantic stones foreign to the neighbourhood and placed in present position by agencies

[1] It is frequently asserted that Stonehenge and Avebury in existence to-day are remains of constructions erected by the Celts of the Bronze Age upon older, or Neolithic foundations. The point is still under dispute.

MEN OF THE NEW STONE AGE 25

undoubtedly human have led some enthusiasts to claim for these people a great engineering and transporting skill which they were unlikely to possess. Probably these alien stones formed part of the terminal moraine of some long-vanished glacier, travelling so far south much in the way that modern glaciers push their tongues considerable distances below the ice-line. Ignorance of their mode of locomotion thither would invest these blocks with a peculiar, superstitious sanctity very suitable for temple use.

The tombs of these people, and they are of frequent occurrence, have yielded many skeletons, showing that the human body had become more graceful, the shape of the forehead, jaw and teeth denoting at once a higher intelligence and a better food. The life they led as early as 8000 B.C. was much the same as that of the peasants in out-of-the-way places all over Europe at the beginning of the 18th century.

The race home seems to have been in northern Africa which was then more humid and fertile than at present, and under such climatic conditions that this primitive man was merely swarthy, and not black. From this race home he wandered north into a region to-day known as the "Mediterranean Region."[1] Here he found nature conspiring to favour his early development. A transition area between the trade and the anti-trade winds, it partakes according to the swing of the sun and the wind system of the climate of both. The heat minimized the necessity for shelter, summer drought made irrigation necessary, and irrigation—quite apart from its psychic and economic value, requiring exercise of intelligence, careful work abundantly rewarded and its consequent leisure—necessitated family and even tribal co-operation providing

[1] His "southward" wanderings do not here concern us.

both a small and a great unit of social life. On the other hand, the mere fact that rain came in the winter, or "resting" season, and the greatest heat at the time of the greatest dryness, would produce a "grass" or a "park" land eminently suited for a people who could not clear extensive forests except by the rather dangerous use of fire. In a transitional area of this kind neither flora nor fauna could form any real barrier to the introduction of a new-comer with his flocks and herds, and his grain-producing grasses.

A pause must be made at this place, however, to consider how this acquisition for pastoral and agricultural enterprises was effected. The process was probably lengthy.

In his latest stage palaeolithic man had been a great hunter, and his successor practically began where he left off. Somehow the dog, once his competitor in the great struggle of the chase, became his friend and assistant, and other roaming beasts his "subjects." Possibly wounded or young, strayed creatures were first kept as pets but soon their emergency value as food would be patent. Once the conception of taming animals evolved, man no longer contented himself with hovering on the outskirts of the herds of wild cattle and sheep. Aided by his new ally, the dog, he learnt to turn them when they seemed about to go too far from his hunting ground, to pen them in valleys and later into folds, or at least into well-defined areas where he could be sure of finding them as need should arise. When one area was exhausted he led them to pastures new, and no doubt becoming exceedingly adept at "cattle-lore," eased them when they were hurt, fed them in times of scarcity and so mastered them.

Established as a pastoral people[1] other gains soon

---

[1] The "Itali" were "Cattlemen."

MEN OF THE NEW STONE AGE

accrued to this early man. His pasture must bear strict relation to the needs of his flocks, and as these later increased the herdsman was obliged to wander far afield. But however far his day's journey, he must have some way of returning at night. Eventually he would recognize the relation between the heat of the sun and its position in the heavens, and also presently understand that if he faced the sun in his morning wanderings he must also face it on his return. He thus developed elementary ideas of direction (east and west). For a long while he would be content with the sun as guide, especially as he must have reverenced it for the heat and light it gave, but at last he would discover that there were other and surer guides. In the clear evening skies of the southern land the stars shine out magnificently, and the warm, rainless nights must often have led him to open-air slumberings and even journeyings. Finally, not only would the sun and stars guide his wanderings but give him some idea of the times when it was propitious to undertake this or that operation, especially when he later became an agriculturist.

Sun worship and star-gazing thus form the beginnings of primitive religions aided and diversified by man's ignorance and therefore intense veneration for the operations of natural phenomena. He knew that when he slept his soul passed into a region in which men and things moved confusedly, and that whereas he afterwards returned from these wanderings upon awakening, it was not always so. His growing knowledge of the mystery and grandeur of life made him respect the sleeper who would not awaken, and from his own experience he knew that in the sleeping state men did strange and sometimes terrifying things. He often heard the "sleeping" soul moaning in the storm and howling in the tempest; it mocked him in the rocky gorges and steep places, and could be felt, rather than seen in the extraordinary appearance of land and water when a cold breath blew and clouds blotted out the sky. Further, the soul of the sleeper who would not awaken could pass through thick walls, closed doors, all material objects. For reasons both altruistic and egotistic he desired to preserve the body in the possibility of the " ghost's " power to make it again its material home, but he did not wish to come into personal contact with the reanimated corpse. The cold and lonely exile, the loss of home, possessions, or power, were causes sufficient to kindle a great and disastrous anger. Hence the stone chamber as burial place, and the earth mound or tumulus above increasing in size and weight with the prestige and hence avenging-possibilities of the dead man. Jars containing food and drink, personal ornaments cherished in lifetime, were often placed in the tomb, and may have been offerings of friendship, pity or remorse. As societies become more organized and possessions greater in consequence (as Nature became better understood and therefore less terrifying) the possible return of the dead *in corpore* becomes less and less desirable, and the custom gradually arose of destroying the body by fire before burial, the ashes being placed in an urn with the customary oblations, no doubt for the purpose of providing a place which the ghost might " haunt " in preference to its one-time comrades.

So much for the beginnings of the religion of primitive man. Change in customs and their recognized meanings necessarily accompanied man's developing intelligence, but even in those early times their simple superstitions had other and far-reaching results. At first the herdsman or perhaps his wife "caught" the crops that grew in a wild state in his neighbourhood. Later he cut, dried, and housed graminiferous grasses as fodder for his flocks. Presently he realized that the seed of these grasses could be made to furnish a very acceptable food for himself. He determined that his sleeping comrade in the great earth mound should likewise partake of this food, and the more especially as if deprived of an accustomed diet he might return to ask the reason why. Thus began the custom of flinging some of the grass seed over the grave. The newly turned earth, the freshly aerated soil, were influences he did not at first understand; but one thing he could not fail to notice, that where seeds were flung grasses grew superior to the "grasses" that grew wild. Thus was made the first discovery in agriculture and associated—for obvious reasons—with death and burial. Even in the present day primitive man associates his seed-time with sacrifice, though a human victim is nowadays rare.

By some such developments as have been outlined above Man of the Neolithic Age became an agriculturist, growing cereals (barley and wheat) and vegetables, fruit (apples), carrots, peas, flax, etc., thus providing food for his present as well as his future needs. The tending of flocks, the harvesting of crops, requires co-operation of effort to which the mere hunter is entirely foreign. To this co-operation must be added well-disciplined organization, in order that the best may be obtained from it. On the other hand, many co-existing heads weaken the tribe, just as little salvation is found in overmuch advice. Hence disciplined obedience to a recognized authority becomes eminently desirable, because in the long run the most disciplined tribe will outdo the weaker one.

Thus Mediterranean Man had travelled far along the road of civilization when the great emigration began that should lead him from his sunny, fertile home in the Mediterranean lands to travel by way of Spain and France to the colder shores and cloudier skies of Northern Europe. The cause of this epoch-making journey is still in dispute. It has been suggested that the "faulting" or "falling in" of the rock mass between Ceuta and Gibraltar exposed the whole vast area of the Middle Lands to the slow flooding by the Atlantic.

The operation took time, even centuries, but quietly and irresistibly the ocean poured in, till much of the great fertile region lay buried under water and the populations inhabiting it had been obliged to seek new homes. To the South lay the Race-home, already in the throes of that dessication that changed a great inland sea into a Sahara; in front were the barriers of the Alps and the Balkans with passes here and there leading to vast forested areas with which "Neolithic Man" at his present stage of tool development could not cope. The stronger tribes naturally retained their hold upon the lowlands now bordering this great and ever increasing inland sea; the weaker were driven away to wander in lands so far undreamt of, rounding the corners of the Pyrenees, and so by way of Maritime France to Northern Europe. The halts upon the journey were many and long, the invaders stamping their customs and culture upon previously occupied territory, and founding Iberian, Basque and Berber Settlements which have persisted to this day. Always the cruder, weaker members of the tribes would be driven in front of the main advance, till the final goal was reached and a period put upon the great emigration.

MEN OF THE NEW STONE AGE

Near Dover the channel narrows to twenty-one miles and must have been adventured upon many times in the course of fishing expeditions. Individual pioneers may have landed upon those distant shores and returned to report a land not greatly differing from the latest home. At length the passage was resolved upon and was effected in coracles, a light structure of skins stretched on a wooden framework. The land, as we have seen, was not empty, but its inhabitants were as inferior to the invaders as in a later day the Celts were to the well-disciplined Romans. So the Neolith drove the Palaeolith from his poor steppe, and took his place.

The settlements of these people in England are easily traced. They lived near the *foot* of the chalk hills where springs and wells occur through the meeting of clay and chalk. They pastured their flocks upon the short sweet grass of the downlands, and they cultivated their crops in such ground as did not support trees or which they could not clear by fire. The deep forests in the Vales and especially of the Weald still harbouring the stag, the great ox, the bison, the wolf, became their hunting grounds, and the hills their refuge in times of intertribal warfare. These latter they converted into veritable forts, piling huge earthworks on the lower levels (not forgetting a "wolf" platform) erecting emergency huts on the summits and guarding against want of water by the construction of dew ponds. Into these forts, many of which are quite easy to trace[1] the people of the settlements and their cattle were driven in times of danger, but the usual residence was still near the foot of the downs, or on the grassy plains.

---

[1] e.g., Old Sarum "Camp" near Salisbury, the so-called "British Camp" near Southampton, Martinsell Hill Camp, on the Wiltshire Downs, etc.

Cattleways, sometimes a trenched, sometimes a mere
beaten track, led upwards into these forts, and when
journeyings were done from one place to another the
safest "roads" were obviously upon the crests of the
treeless hills which often still show the broken earth-
wall through which the "ridge ways" passed. The
chalk ranges of Sussex were for hundreds of years a
centre of commerce, a great trade being carried on in
flint weapons, which are found in such quantities at
Brandon as to point to the existence there of a factory.

From the chalk areas, these men of the New Stone
Age passed to the equally healthy oölite limestone and
the heathlands once bordering the Wash. Finally
they spread to the granite moorlands of the Western
Peninsula, into Wales, Scotland and Ireland, where
their descendants still showing the marked Neolithic
features once suppposed to result through the mingling
of the Irish peasantry with the wrecked Spaniards
at the time of the Armada adventure, are found to
this day. Here and there a small colony of these people
chose a new method of living, building their wooden
houses upon "islands" surrounded by marsh land,
or upon platforms erected upon piles driven into the
soft mud bottom of a lake. Their flocks, pasturing
on the "mainland" were probably housed in time of
danger or in winter in the partially open space under
their dwellings. In England "lake dwellings" were
not so common as on the Continent, though evidences
of such a community have been discovered at Glastonbury, at Ulrome near Bridlington and in "Lake"
Pickering.

On the bleak Yorkshire moors another method was
chosen. Here "pit dwellings" were constructed, a
great hole being dug in the ground and the excavated
earth piled round the margin. A long pole was fixed

MEN OF THE NEW STONE AGE

in an upright position through the centre of the cavity and fashioned with a roof of boughs round it, sometimes covered with turf. Remains of similar pit dwellings are found on the Yorkshire Wolds near Bempton, and on the moors behind Whitby.

The individual and community life went side by side. There were definite places for the exchange of commerce in kind or in tools and weapons, and temples such as Stonehenge and Avebury to which the tribes could repair for religious celebrations or official census. The still enduring earthworks testify to great endeavour, great perseverance, and great co-operation.

To-day almost pure types of Mediterranean Man are to be found in our Western Highlands and in Ireland. The next invaders conquered for a time but were presently absorbed in the existing population. These conquering intruders are known as Celts or Kelts, and accordingly the later Neolithic aborigines[1] are designated pre-Celts or pre-Kelts.

[1] These aborigines are also called Ivernians, a word akin to Iberia, Hibernia, Spain and Ireland respectively, countries partly peopled with these Mediterranean men and their descendants.

CHAPTER IV

THE BRONZE AGE

CELTIC INVASION OF OUR ISLANDS

THE change in the material of which man fashioned his implements marks a change in culture though not necessarily in race. The men of the New Stone Age passed insensibly from the use of stone to that of metal, the two being long co-existent. The discovery was bound to take place sooner or later and perhaps one may wonder that it was so long deferred. Copper occurs native in many parts of the world and by virtue of its great malleability can easily be hammered into any shape desired. Copper is then the material of which the first *metal* implements were made. Accident would ultimately reveal the fusing action of fire upon it, and hammering would be replaced by casting in moulds. But the metal is too soft for a cutting tool, and its use in this direction is consequently restricted. However, copper in its ores is often associated with tin from which the rough metallurgy of those times would not always succeed in freeing it. Soon it would be established beyond doubt that the presence of this impurity (tin) gave the copper a new colour and hardness (bronze) and bronze would and did become the material of which tools and weapons were made. Bronze was probably first used in the East Mediterranean, but by trade and intercourse the secrets of finding, smelting, and casting the metal were spread eventually over the whole of the then-known world. The Chinese appear to have been acquainted with it about 4,000 B.C., and the Egyptians soon after. The " remains " of this age show very definitely the lines upon which man's needs were increasing: swords, spears, knives, hammers, fish-hooks, of course; but needles, razors, necklaces, brooches, hair-pins, combs, bracelets, bronze vases and pails, prove that personal possessions were rising above the mere necessity level. The "imitation" stage of the Bronze Age passed insensibly into the "beautiful stage" in which objects made were ornamented with delicate patterns and not infrequently inlaid with gold.

Before 1000 B.C. *iron* was used in Asia, and soon afterwards in Egypt. Its use spread rapidly by sea and river routes especially to Greece and Italy at what is sometimes called the dawn of the historic period. The last three thousand years, therefore, cover the "Iron Age."

Bronze came to Britain about 2000 B.C., though it was long before the people as a whole gave up their weapons of stone. The new material was of incalculable utility in their building operations and both Stonehenge and Avebury seem to have been "rebuilt" under the influence of the Bronze Age upon their earlier sites.

The Neolithic inhabitants of our islands (Ivernians) were still making weapons of stone when a new race appeared in Central Europe (the so-called Alpine region) whose most notable characteristic was its "broad" or "round" skull. This race, fighting the difficulties of its "highland" environment, grew cunning in warfare and adventurous in temperament. About 600 B.C. Eastern Europe was subject to the invasions of Asiatic nomadic tribes from the Steppelands, driven west in search of pasture and water for their flocks under the influence of a progressive "dessication" that was overtaking their continent and which culminated between the years 400 B.C.-600 A.D.

Under this pressure from the East there was an outward movement of the existing peoples in Central Europe, who ultimately came as far west as the Atlantic borders of Scotland and Ireland (about 500 or 400 B.C.). These invaders were warriors in search of new homes and possibly in search of gold. They buried their mighty ones in round instead of oval mounds of earth (in popular parlance—round instead of long "barrows") and were skilled in the art of working in bronze. They easily conquered the stone-weaponed aborigines (Ivernians) but though they imposed their government, customs, religion and speech, they do not seem to have very materially influenced the subject populations—at least to judge by the small proportion of "broad" heads existing in our Islands at present. Occasionally a "round" head is found in a "long" barrow, and a "long" head in a round one, but old customs are not obliterated in a day, and possibly then as now native merit may rise to hold a great position even among a conqueror-people.

These "Alpine races" generally known as Celts, came to us in three great waves of invasion. The first "wave" broke on the Atlantic shores of Ireland and Scotland, which therefore marks their most western frontier. The "Ivernians" or Hibernians living in these regions were, as has been said, the descendants of the Neolithic people who built Stonehenge but were later known to the Romans as Picts.[1] The Celts gave to the people of these remote districts the languages now modified to the Erse of Ireland, the Manx of Man, and the Gaelic of Scotland, so that the areas of their domination may be roughly established as including all of Ireland (with the exception of the North-East corner still held by the Picts), the part of Scotland

[1] Because they painted their bodies. Lat. Pictor.

THE BRONZE AGE 37

between the Firths of Forth and Clyde and the Mounth district of the Grampians, and parts of the Isle of Man, Erse, Gaelic and Manx are collectively called the "Goidelic" group of languages, and from the initial sound of K or Q in many of their place-names (kin = headland; Kintyre, Kinsale), they are sometimes called Q Celts.

The second invasion of the Broad-heads brought the intruders no further west than the coasts of Wales and Cornwall, and no further north than the River Earn in Perthshire. They are known as the Brythons or Britons. From the occurrence of P as initial letter in their place-names (pen = headland; Penzance, Penrhyn) they are called P Celts. These Brythons were workers in iron.

The "Ivernians" ultimately came to adopt their conquerors' weapons and while accepting and continuing their culture, eventually absorbed them as a race (for their strength lay only in weapons and not in numbers). It thus happens that the Cymric (Celtic Wales) and Cornish languages do not really belong, or are not "native" to the people who now speak them, and who therefore defend their present use and continuance by reasons obviously based on ignorance or mistaken sentiment.

Shortly before the dawn of the Christian Era a third Celtic invasion swept into our land. This people may have been a last Brython wave, or a quite distinct third wave, but they differed from previous intruders in that they practised agriculture. They were originally raiders from Belgic Gaul, and in Caesar's time they still retained their Belgic tribal names. They inhabited the English lowlands and part of Southern Scotland. They very assiduously worked the native iron and some other metals, but imported their bronze from Gaul.

The Goidels and the Brythons named most of the physical features of the country. Thus it may be said that the names of rivers and most other physical features are of Celtic origin throughout the British Isles. In Ireland, Scottish Highlands, Buchan Promontory, Wales, the " village " names are Celtic, but it must not be forgotten that these *names* do not betoken the present-day survival of the Celtic peoples but rather the subsequent fate of the indigenous peoples who, after they had fought and lost the great struggle between themselves and the " Teutons," finally found a refuge in those uninviting " Lands of Difficulty," those " Homes of Lost Causes " where they could practise their customs and maintain their individuality almost down to modern times. The Roman interlude brought them Christianity to which they clung even when the greater part of " Lower Britain " fell under the pagans from the Northern Sea. Their Christian preachers and martyrs and saints were not forgotten and their renown is perpetuated to this day in the names of many a " holy " well and many a village. St. Enedoc, St. Austell, Merthyr Tidfil and the numerous " saints " of our highland or moorland villages bear witness to the constancy of these people and to the torch they still kept burning through the dark hours of the pagan night.

As regards geographical features most of the names for our rivers, mountains, headlands are Celtic or contain elements of a later stage grafted on to a Celtic stock. Thus the river-names Ouse, Esk, Axe, Avon, Thames, Severn, are all Celtic, as are also Pennines, Penzance, Kintyre, in which Pen or Kin signifies a mountain or headland. Durham is a hybrid, built up of Teuton ham (home) and Celtic dur (water). Anyone who has seen the hill upon which now stand

THE BRONZE AGE 39

the castle and cathedral of Durham will realize the early significance of this hill site, nearly surrounded by the river, as an impregnable " home on the water." Another hybrid is Oxford, the first syllable of which represents a modern descendant of the ancient Celtic Oich or running water, and which equally gave rise to the names of the rivers Ouse, Aisne, Oisne.

Under the Celts, especially the Belgic Celts, with their agriculture and innovations from the "continent," the people of these islands gathered very generally into settlements, or little clusters of houses with small fields, each cluster possessing its own name which often later became the name of the Parish. These settlements, however, must not be confused with the large " open field " village of the Saxons.

The Roman historian Tacitus has left an account of the climate and resources of Britain at the period of the Roman invasion and domination:

"The climate is disagreeable from the constant rains and fogs; great cold, however, is unknown. . . . The soil is suitable for cultivation and is fertile, though the Olive, Vine, and other fruits of warmer climes will not thrive in it. The crops are early in starting and late in ripening, and in both cases from the same cause, viz., the extreme wetness of the soil and climate. Britain offers a prize to the conqueror in her gold, her silver and other metals; the ocean also yields its pearls, but they are dark and bad coloured. . . ."

The silver came from the galena or lead ore found in the Mendips and in Derbyshire, gold was possibly obtained in Cornwall or Wales; and the pearls in question were extracted from a species of fresh-water mussels.

Of the industries of Celtic Britain Pytheas of Marseilles, visiting Britain about 330 B.C., mentions the British chariot and weapons of war, from which the art of smelting and working tin, lead, and iron may safely be assumed. Tin was a necessity for Europe in the Bronze Age and Britain supplied tin to North Europe in the later Celtic Age with perhaps more regularity than at the time of the much earlier Phoenician trade. The "tin commerce" moved along the Jurassic or Chalk Escarpments from West to East, towards Essex, Suffolk and Norfolk, to be exported from Camulodunum (Colchester) to the Baltic where terminated the land caravans between the north and south of Europe. The Baltic furnished that "amber" in such great request as the favourite ornament of prehistoric times, and which accordingly provided a "return cargo." When the land route through Gaul was established tin went across the English Channel to Normandy. The Isle of Wight was a suitable entrepôt for the coasters meeting the ocean trading ships, and Brading was a port of shipment.

The tracts of many of the old prehistoric or Celtic "roads" of England can still be traced, especially in the chalk districts. They were of course unpaved, and were formed by the "treading" action of myriads of feet and vehicles; bringing the tribes to the national meeting places at Stonehenge or Avebury; bringing tin and lead from the Western Peninsula to the Eastern Quadrant; carrying back the Continental bronze or bars of iron from the sand measures of Sussex and Kent; or bearing the heavy, broad-wheeled chariots in time of war. The main part of pre-Roman Britain was forested lowland or swampy morass through which the "Celts" could neither cut a way nor artificially drain a path, and their roads therefore followed the short-grassed chalk or limestone ridges above the forest line. A glance at the relief or geological map

THE BRONZE AGE

will show the probable routes. Five ridges of chalk or oölite limestone converge on Salisbury Plain (a low plateau) and possibly Stonehenge drew its importance from this convergence of natural *high* ways. Of these routes the " Ichnield Way " from the Fens along the Western Slope of the Chilterns, and the " Old Road " along the North Downs to Canterbury are the best preserved to-day though both have entirely lost certain sections of the ancient way.

The " Old Road," by virtue of its position was always the most important. Along it went the iron from Gloucester and the Severn Valley to reinforce, as an article of trade, the iron from the red stone of the Sussex Weald ; along it travelled lead from the Mendips and tin from Cornwall, and homeward to the West journeyed also—not only manufactured commodities in exchange, but ideas of culture and progress received from a people akin in religion, language, and blood living across the dividing waters.

This " Old Road " therefore may be regarded as perhaps the first of such forms of pre-Roman national enterprise in our islands. Everywhere an observer, placed upon the crest of the chalk or green-sand ridge could view in the morning the entire course for the day's journeying, with its guiding line of hills cut by flat-bottomed river gaps.

From Salisbury to Farnham there is no definite ridge, but a water parting on the high downs makes an easy route. From Farnham the " road " follows the southern side of the range of hills till it reaches the sea above the Portus Lemanis inlet which now covers the marshy plain below the site of present Lympne. The sections from Stonehenge to Farnham, and from Farnham to its later terminus of Canterbury, are known respectively as the " Harrow " (or Hoar, that is Ancient) Way and the "Pilgrim's Way." The section from Stonehenge to Farnham was early abandoned as trade was drawn to Winchester as a more useful distributing centre, while its eastward extremity which was to serve a coastal port for Continental trade came to end at Canterbury, a place of Roman origin and inland.

This early importance of Canterbury arose from the effects of the tides and winds in the Straits of Dover, rendering it impossible to foretell with certainty at which one of the five or six neighbouring ports debarkation or embarkation might be effected. This doubt rendered it necessary to have some point inland upon which all routes from the coast could converge, and which might serve equally as a central depôt for trade and a military base. Canterbury was not quite in the centre of the circle of which the ports of Ramsgate, Richborough, Sandwich, Dover and Folkestone lay on its circumference, but the river Stour, by virtue of its inland communication and water supply, drew this " central depôt " to its banks, and at a situation just above the tide limit of the river, and yet sufficiently inland not to fear the sea-pirates of the coast.

The early importance of Winchester was due to similar factors. Boats crossing from the continent opposite the Solent here make the shortest possible " cross channel " journey out of sight of land, aided, moreover, by the direction of the prevailing wind. The horizon of Barfleur Hill on the Contentin Peninsula, and of St. Catherine's Head on the Isle of Wight are not very distant from each other. To this must be added the effects of the tides which, with a failing wind, would greatly help the entry to the Solent and Southampton Water. Like Canterbury, Winchester, on the Itchen, is out of the way of invasion by sea-pirates.

THE BRONZE AGE

Various "roads" led along unforested heath or chalk from the south-west and west into Winchester, including the road from Southampton, and at one time various short-cuts led from Winchester to the Harrow Way, but these, like the Harrow Way itself, were finally abandoned, and in its last form the Road went eastward from Winchester up the vale of the Itchen to the watershed, and then down the vale of the Wey, passing through Alton to Farnham. Shortly after leaving the latter place it struck the range of the North Downs, and continued along them to the valley of the Stour where a short addition led it on to Canterbury. Both termini came to have their Saint—Canterbury, St. Thomas (à Becket), and Winchester, St. Swithin.

So much of the Old Road as remains owes its preservation to the Canterbury pilgrimages for the purpose of worshipping at the shrine of St. Thomas the Martyr (1272). At the dissolution of the monasteries (1536) the shrine was violated and the pilgrimages ceased. The Turn-pike system of the 18th century caused the old roadway again to come into requisition by the indigent "pack riders" who could not afford the tolls paid on the new roads. In addition to this the old road has been preserved by the nature of the chalk itself, which is not so marshy as to lose all impressions made upon it, nor so hard as to resist the impression of feet and vehicles, nor hitherto sufficiently valuable to be wanted for building operations.[1]

A few words on the importance of pre-Roman London might be in place here. Though not the focus of organization before the Roman occupation the territory around present-day London was evidently the nucleus of a small empire. Here dwelt the allied

[1] "The Old Road," by Hilaire Belloc, gives these and further particulars concerning this ancient way.

tribes of the Catuvellauni and Trinobantes, protected eastwardly by the Fen Marshes—the great marsh bordered the Thames Estuary and the Forest of the Weald, in which refuge natives sheltered, ready to be aggressive if attacked. The tribes of the Iceni, Cantii[1] and Belgae occupied the open ground between these barriers, alike isolated from the Catuvellauni and from each other. The Celtic Stockades of Camulodunum (Colchester) and Verulamium (St. Albans) bear witness to the early recognition of the value of "Lyndun's" strategic position.

[1] Celtic Ceint—open ground, or unforested ground.

CHAPTER V

THE ROMAN INTERLUDE

THE third great wave of Celtic invaders had barely spent itself when a new conquest of the country became imminent. On the Continent a mighty power had arisen which, governing all the Mediterranean lands on both sides of the Great Sea had at last thrust its northern frontier along the borders of the Rhine. The lands in France, inhabited by Gauls or Celts akin to the Belgic Celts of Britain, did not meekly submit to that military aggression which was destined to bring them under the benefits of the "Roman Peace," and their sympathizing brethren across the Straits lent their aid against the all-conquering legions of the Caesars. This occurred about the year 55 B.C. and resulted in a Roman Road at or near Hythe, of which the object was to strike a wholesome terror into the hearts of the British interferers. The next year (54 B.C.) Julius Caesar returned and landed men near Sandwich. The expedition was so far successful that the Romans were able to cross the Thames at Brentford, and reach Verulamium (St. Albans). The native submission was sealed by the levying of a yearly tax probably in metal (tin). The aim of this second invasion was much more serious than the first, being nothing less than the addition of a new province to the Roman Empire, and a province which was regarded as being rich in mineral wealth. Camulodunum (Colchester) was soon occupied and the Britons were driven towards Wales. In Mona (Anglesey) there was a great slaughter of native priests or druids.

While the Roman soldiers were busy in the West and East, under Boadicea, "the British Warrior-Queen," who had been publicly flogged for resisting unjust taxation,[1] there was a final but unsuccessful attempt to throw off the Roman yoke. The Roman centres of Camulodunum, Londinium and Verulamium (Colchester, London, St. Albans) at that time "civil" towns and but lightly fortified, were burnt, and the Roman officials massacred. The return of the main army put down the insurrection and the "Queen," widow of the chief of the Iceni, committed suicide by poison (A.D. 61).

Between the years A.D. 78 and 85, the "legatus," or governor Agricola effected the conquest and settlement of the south and centre and then marched north of the Tay. Great military camps were established at Deva and Luguvallium (Chester and Carlisle). A relief map shows the importance of these two places as natural "gates" of the routes leading to the unsubdued Brythons of Wales and Picts of the Galloway region. In A.D. 120, further revolts among the native tribes resulted in the visit of the Emperor Hadrian to Britain. Eboracum (York) was made a great military base and the wall or barrier from the Tyne to the Solway was begun. This fortification, known as "Hadrian's Wall" was continued and completed under later Emperors, notably the Emperor Severus (A.D. 208). Parts of it are still in existence and a brief summary of its construction is interesting as an example of the patient thoroughness these great peoples put into their work.

The isolated forts of Agricola built in the north and across the lowlands and uplands of Scotland may be regarded as the first step in the "building of the wall"

---

[1] The governor responsible was recalled to Italy; the Roman emperor desired the conquered Britons to be treated fairly.

THE ROMAN INTERLUDE 47

which extended from Wallsend near Newcastle to Bowness near Carlisle, a distance of fully eighty miles. South of the Wall ran a flat-bottomed ditch, the Vallum, seven feet deep and thirty wide, the excavated material being piled up to serve as ramparts. This vallum may have been used as a means of protection for the workmen engaged in the actual building. The first wall—the true "Hadrian's Wall" was built of turf sods packed closely together with a V-shaped ditch forty feet wide and twelve to fifteen deep on the north side. It was afterwards replaced or perhaps strengthened by a stone wall (completed under the Emperor Severus) eight to ten feet thick and two hundred and twenty feet high. From Tyne to Solway there were about a score of stations or fortified camps in which markets were held and the ordinary life of Roman villages carried on, but which were under martial law. Castles or square tower forts were erected every mile, with four smaller fortified "turrets" in addition between each pair of towers. South of the Wall Roman civilization developed in security, but though Agricola and his successors penetrated as far as the Mounth district of Caledonia (Scotland) they never succeeded in making their rule effective in this region.

Roman Britain may be said to have lasted three and a half centuries (till A.D. 410) but the real rule was confined to the Plain or land below the 500-foot contour. This region was appropriately known as "Lower Britain" while the only nominally subdued uplands were designated "Upper Britain." At the opening of this period the native inhabitants were chiefly living in settlements upon the hill slopes isolated from each other by a vast wilderness of forest, marsh and moor. However, they had certain well-defined centres of tribal organization, which included Old Sarum, Exeter, Winchester, Chichester, Silchester, Caerleon, Cirencester, Leicester, Caistor, Lincoln, as their Roman names clearly demonstrate. Thus Winchester was well-known as "Venta Belgarum," the tribal centre of the Belgae, Exeter as Isca Damnoniorum, in which Isca is from Celtic oich, water, and Damnoniorum the genitive of the tribal name of the Damnonii; Caerleon was Isca Silurum, and of the two holiday towns of Aquae Sulis and Aquae (Bath and Buxton) the first contained hot springs dedicated to the British goddess Sul, and was early connected with the British, that is pre-Roman, Prince Bladud. The British centres were merely reorganized on the Roman plan and then linked together by roads, but it is noteworthy that the Romans themselves could not have chosen better or more natural positions.

The Britons kept cattle and their main food was milk and flesh, but not cheese. They grew some corn; they mined tin in Cornwall, lead in the Mendips, and iron especially in Northamptonshire, and they used bars of iron as money. The metal or its ore was exported to Gaul in exchange for ivory bridles, chains, amber, glass and metal goods. The Romans showed them how to improve their agriculture and other industries, initiating such developments as poultry-keeping, brick and glass manufacture, pottery and embroidery making. Certain stretches of woodland were cleaned, valleys cultivated and fens drained; life began to move downwards from the hill-slopes towards the plains. Mediterranean plants were brought to Britain and took kindly to their new home—walnut, vine, cherry, peach, pear, fig, beech, the common elm, chestnut, sycamore, box, laurel, holly. Pheasant, deer and hornless sheep were also introduced.

THE ROMAN INTERLUDE 49

The mineral-producing areas were greatly extended—the Weald and the Forest of Dean for iron—there was an armoury at Bath—and the Peak district for lead. The Tyne district yielded surface coal, Wales and Anglesey copper and gold, Worcester and Cheshire salt. The exports were still, however, of raw material, corn, tin, cattle, gold, silver, iron, skins, slaves and hunting-dogs. British life gradually became Romanized—courts of law, market places, temples and (later) churches, gladiatorial arenas (of which latter there are remains at Silchester, Caerleon, Cirencester, Richborough and Dorchester), all attest the spread of Roman civilization, which did not stop short at this point. The aim of the Roman conquest was acquisition of new subjects, in whom it was desired to "create an earnest and brave spirit," and the establishment and furtherance of commerce. So well did the Romans achieve the task that the historian Tacitus was able to eulogize the peaceful disposition of the native Briton and the cheerfulness with which he paid his taxes which, in fact, were not oppressive. The land belonged to the State, that is, the Empire, the natives being retained as cultivators and organized into colonies. The rule resembled the British rule in India—imperial with the focus at the centre of the Empire. There was no real mingling of the peoples, the one working the resources of the land, albeit under good and equitable auspices, for the benefit of alien governors who regarded themselves as living in exile and looked forward to a return to Italy once their work was accomplished. To-day there are few traces of this Roman occupation left on our language or race, and though we owe a great deal to them—thinking in Roman forms, reasoning on Roman principles, and governing largely in accordance with the standards of Roman law—we received this legacy, not from the peoples of Roman Britain, but much later and from quite other descendants of the Great Empire.

We have seen that the extent of the Roman Conquest of Britain was roughly delineated by the 500-foot contour. The Empire was a system based mainly on agriculture and there was little attempt to extend its rule over barren hill districts or difficult mountainous regions. Thus the Roman Province of Britain actually consisted of the English plain, well watered, crossed by limestone and chalk ridges with convenient gaps, and extending to the marginal highlands of South Wales and the Pennines. This fertile triangle was easily garrisoned. Eboracum (York) became the great military capital on an easy route from London, with bridges at Doncaster (Danum), Castleford, Pontefract, etc. Many of these Roman bridges were still good in Tudor times (1485-1603). To rule the Welsh[1] was difficult, and as the country possessed little to attract them, the Romans contented themselves with establishing forts at Deva (Chester), Viroconium (Wroxeter) and Glevum (Gloucester), thus " shutting off " these unattractive uplands and at the same time minimizing the danger of raids upon the prosperous lowlands from these lands of difficulty. About A.D. 70 Viroconium ceased to be a great military base ; Isca Silurum (Caerleon-on-Usk), the head-quarters of the Second Legion, was perhaps regarded as sufficient, though some accounts refer to a destruction of Viroconium by the upland tribes.

The south-west promontory of Britain was long neglected, but eventually the attraction of its minerals

---

[1] In this chapter Roman names of sites are freely used. The word " Welsh " is Teuton, and originated much later.

THE ROMAN INTERLUDE

made itself felt. The country was loosely settled and worked to this end.

The Pennines, including the hills of the Lake District and beyond the Solway, comprise a wedge of uplands valueless in itself in Roman estimation, but in view of the fertility of the lowlands of York, Lancashire, the Eden Valley and Central Scotland, it was bridged with roads guarded by permanently fortified ports which kept in awe the unconquered uplanders so long as Roman power was felt. The length and straggling character of the Pennines coupled with the fact that the rivers cross from west to east made holding difficult. A route was constructed with Bremetennacum (Ribchester) as Western base, and which followed the Aire gap to Olicana (Ilkley) and then the Wharfe to Skipton and Tadcaster (Calcaria), ultimately to join the great North Road at York. Pontefract, commanding the crossing of the Aire in the plain, was obviously the key to this junction of routes. The wall on the Tyne was eighty miles or four days' heavy marching north of this east-west route, and the road to the Peak, for the rounding of the Pennines, was nearly as far distant. Two other east-west roads were accordingly constructed, one on each side of the Aire gap, the northern, or the Tees-Eden route over the gap by Kirkby-Stephen, and the southern, or Manchester-Slack route leading down the Calder valley. The Peak district was secured by two roads converging on Buxton, the natural belt of marsh along the Mersey preventing hostile raiders rounding the Peak and so penetrating into the Lancashire Plain. On the south side of this marsh lay Deva (Chester), the head-quarters of the 20th Legion, on the north, the military fort of Mancunium (Manchester), which had been established on an outcrop of firm rock where the outlying hills of the Pennines came down to the plain.[1] At Stockport a neck of firm ground never more than three and generally less than two miles wide led through the marshes, and here the Romans erected a causeway as they did elsewhere where the roads had to cross marsh-banked rivers.[2]

In considering the position of the Roman road (to-day mainly followed by the principal railways) there are three important guides upon which reliance may be placed.

The first roads were for the military, affording " good going " for an advancing army. We may look for them, therefore, as linking military bases or fortresses. Later, trade and commerce would use the same routes. Next we have the nature of the Imperial conquest which involved the continuance where possible of native centres of population—hence the numerous roads that do not lead to ports. Lastly there are the many short roads, converging from the West on Canterbury or Winchester, the two great depôts in connection with landing arrangements from the Continent and external trade.

These people from Italy were a " land " people, who had made their great journey up the Rhone valley and not through the stormy waters of the Atlantic. Their landings were therefore effected where the sea passage was comparatively short—at Portus Magnus (near Porchester—later replaced by Portsmouth) and on certain " ports " on the Dover Straits. Of these latter Regulbium (Reculver) and Rutupiae (Richborough) were at the north and south issues of the Wantsum Strait, thus severing the Isle of

---

[1] This site is now called Castlefield.
[2] Round these old Roman causeways across rivers " ford " towns have since grown up, *e.g.*, Stamford, Stratford, Stretford, etc.

THE ROMAN INTERLUDE 53

Thanet from the mainland: Portus Dubris or Dubrae (Dover) on the Dur (Dour) estuary was a third landing-place in this region, and like the other two was connected with Durovurnum (Canterbury) by a road. From this latter place—which served these ports as inland depôt—the celebrated " Watling Street " ran by way of Londinium (London) to Deva (Chester). There was another landing-place at Portus Lemanis, at or near present Lympne, on the edge of the Romney marsh ; Anderida (Pevensey) south of the great Anderida Silva (the forest of the Weald) and west of the still submerged Pevensey Level, was perhaps of later date, being purely a fortress used against the Saxon pirates who began to infest the " Saxon Shore " about the 5th century.

The Colne creek received reserves from Londinium or the south-east required for maintaining the military station of Camulodunum (Colchester). This place was connected by road to Venta Icenorum (Caistor), the eastern terminus of the ancient Ichnield Way. A road led from Portus Magnus (approximately Portsmouth) to Venta Belgarum (Winchester), the great depôt for this region.

The chief " towns " may be grouped as military bases, commercial centres, route towns or reorganized ancient British centres of population. The first of these were necessarily on the frontiers of Roman Britain, Yorkshire and the Welsh Border and on what became known later as the Saxon Shore. Eboracum (York), Deva (Chester), Glevum (Gloucester), Viroconium (Wroxeter), Isca Silurum (Caerleon-on-Usk), Luguvallium (or Caer Leul = Carlisle) are examples of frontier stations against hostile Britons. Branodunum (Brancaster, in Norfolk), Burgh Castle in Suffolk, Orthona (Bradwell, Essex), Regulbium (Reculver), Rutupiae (Richborough), Dubrae (Dover), Portus Lemanis (Lympne), Anderida (Pevensey), Portus Magnus (Porchester) were nine stations fortified against the Saxons, and of these nine Dover and Richborough alone were fortresses under the Romans before the Saxon invasion.

The commercial centres and route towns are to be found at the heads of estuaries for sea navigation, Durovernum (Canterbury), Deva (Chester), Venta Belgarum (Winchester), etc.; or where roads crossed rivers as at Pontes (Staines), Bremeternacum (Ribchester), Durobrivae (Rochester), etc.; or at the junction of Roman roads, Venonae (High Cross), where Watling Street crosses the Fosse Way, Calleva Atrebatum (Silchester), a veritable "Swindon" of Roman roads; or where roads crossed hills by passes, Lindum Colonia (Lincoln); or on the coast, serving both for commercial ports and the coming or return of troops. Among the latter are Rutupiae (Richborough), Portus Lemanis (Lympne), Portus Dubrae (Dover). All the Roman ports have vanished as such either by silting or submergence. Dover is now of stategic consideration only, and Portsmouth is a naval station not exactly on the site of the former Portus Magnus. (See page 139.)

It is customary to consider all towns whose names to-day end in some form of the word castra (camp) to have been in existence during the Roman occupation. This is not always the case. In naming their villages the Anglo-Saxons used the affix castra (as chester, caster, cester, eter)[1] to denote a site previously occupied by a Roman town, or upon which were found Roman

[1] Compare Wroxeter and Exeter, formerly Wroxcester and Excester; the "c" and "s" have been lost through phonetic and Norman influences respectively. These towns lie in the territories governed by the Norman Lords Marcher.

THE ROMAN INTERLUDE 55

remains of some kind, were they of military forts (castles and camps) or country mansions (villas).

On the other hand the Romans did not *originate* the sites of many new sea-ports or towns on large navigable rivers. And when they did as in the case of London, Richborough, Wroxeter, Rochester, and Canterbury, they were guided by reasons either strategical or indirectly connected with the traffic in minerals, Britain's great industry during the Roman occupation as before. Thus Silchester (the " capital " of the Atrebates) was on high ground along which British waggons could travel, a conveyance for routes from Cornwall with tin, from the Mendips with lead and copper, from Gloucester and South Wales with iron, while from Silchester radiated other natural routes to the east and south coasts of England. Thus the mineral wealth, and trading interests giving direction to the early British " Ways," combined with military considerations to give directions to the Roman roads that succeeded them.

The object of the Roman roads was therefore to connect the Continent with the military ports of London, Colchester, Chester, Wroxeter, Gloucester, Winchester, Silchester, Porchester and Brading (Isle of Wight), and the chief trading towns with each other. At suitable positions on or near them military camps were placed to protect the centres of the metal industry and the roads leading to them. This policy thus enhanced the transport conditions of the country as a whole, and was carried out in accordance with a well-planned system which may be regarded as being conducted on quite " National " lines.

Speed in transit and avoidance of ambush were attained by the arrow-like straightness of the roads ; and where deviation was necessitated by the softness of the ground, or presence of some village or " town " off the straight line the road was constructed in a series of zigzags. Thus the site of Peterborough causes a deviation in Ermine (or Erming) Street, the forests of the Weald (Anderida Silva) and of the Midlands still impeded cultivation though Roman roads were plentiful in the much less dense woodlands of Hampshire.[1] The Roman roads have the reputation of topping hills, descending great hollows, or driving straight through swamps rather than deviate from the original alignment. But in actual practice the Roman roads are not so obstinate, frequently skirting great shoulders of hills and excessively marshy areas. Thus Stane Street, a purely military road, from Chichester to London, makes at least four sharp angles in the route.

From military considerations only it is a simple matter to establish the position on the map of at least the chief of these arteries of communication. They must radiate from the landing-places or some inland depôt, and they must avoid dense forest and very wide extended swamps unless a fairway can be found or made through them.

(a) From the landing-places near Sandwich, Dover and Hythe, actually Reculver, Richborough, Dover and Lympne, roads led to the central site of Canterbury, and from Canterbury a road (the famous Watling Street) led to London. This was the first great Roman road of the Conquest.

(b) From London three great roads led north-east, north-west and south-west. The first left Londinium (London) in the neighbourhood of the present Marble Arch and proceeded to Camulodunum (Colchester) and then round the western border of the Fens to Lindum (Lincoln), after which, skirting the marshes of

[1] Stane Street, however, ran across the Weald.

THE ROMAN INTERLUDE 57

the Isle of Axholme and Hatfield Chase, it leads to Eboracum (York). This road, Ermine, Irmine, or Erming Street,[1] was subsequently extended south from Lindum to Londinium. Its northern extension crossed the Tyne and Hadrian's Wall to the Firth of Forth. This London-Lincoln-York-Newcastle route is now known as the Great North Road.

The second of the great roads, later known as Watling Street, crossed the Colchester Road near the present Marble Arch, and passing north-west through Verulamium (St. Albans) cut the Ichnield Way where Dunstable now stands, and the Fosse at Venonae (High Cross). At Viroconium (Wroxeter) on the Severn, it sent out a branch, also called Watling Street, to Isca Silurum (Caerleon on Usk) and Deva (Chester). Thus Watling Street connected the south-east ports with Canterbury, London and Chester.

The Colchester Road and Watling Street may be regarded as among the earliest of Roman roads in Britain.

The third of these great "London Roads" crossed the gravel of West Middlesex and the Thames by the great bridge at Pontes (Staines), built upon the *stony* islands in the river. Wallingford was avoided because of the great forests of Buckinghamshire and Oxfordshire. From Staines the road passed over Bagshot Heath to Calleva Altrabatum (Silchester), from which junction four branches were sent out to Aquae Sulis (Bath), to Corinium (Cirencester) and Glevum (Gloucester) to Sorbiodunum (Salisbury) and Isca Damnoniorum (Exeter) and to Venta Belgarum (Winchester), Portus Magnus (Porchester) and Regnum (Chichester).

(c) Of the "Lateral Routes" there is first and fore-

[1] Latin stratus, straight.

most the Fosse Way, from Lindum (Lincoln), through Ratae (Leicester), Venonae (High Cross), Corinium (Cirencester), Aquae Sulis (Bath) and Isca Damnoniorum (Exeter). Another important road connected Eboracum and Deva (York and Chester), the great legionary head-quarters, either directly through the Midland Gate, or making use of portions of other roads. There was also a road from Segontium (Carnarvon) to Deva, with an extension through Mancunium (Manchester) to Luguvallium (Caer Leul=Carlisle). Lastly Akerman Street, in the basin of the Upper Thames (Tamesa), connected the Ichnield Way to the Fosse Way at Corinium (Cirencester).

The decay of the Roman roads is due to two connected causes. In the first place the Anglo-Saxons, unlike the Romans, regarded the rivers as the most important "Ways" and no doubt the Roman draining of riverine lands made this inland navigation much easier towards the end of the Roman occupation than it had been in the earlier days. It is interesting to note in this connection that for the Romans the rivers were frontiers, not ways—whereas the reverse was the case with the Anglo-Saxons, who settled round the rivers and frequently used the "roads" as frontiers; thus Watling Street became a shire boundary between Leicestershire and Warwickshire. After A.D. 410 the river-loving invaders had no power to mend the roads when they fell into disrepair, and when roadways again became common, the bad roading was necessarily avoided and villages and towns began to spring up at some distance from the one-time main ways. Much of the Roman pavement too had been broken up and used for building purposes.

The prosperity of eastern and south-eastern Britain drew upon it various pirate raids of certain peoples of

THE ROMAN INTERLUDE

north-west Europe whom the Romans denominated collectively as "Barbarians," or "Saxons." These invaders, a seafaring folk, easily penetrated up the estuaries of the tidal rivers and carried on their work of plunder inland. They gave the rulers of Britain much trouble, and an official known as the "Count of the Saxon Shore" was appointed to superintend the defences of the coast from the Wash to the Channel which was most affected. Nine stations were garrisoned against these invaders, of which seven were at this time newly equipped as fortresses.

However, these "Saxon Barbarians" were not the only foes with whom the Romans had to deal. The Vandals and the Goths were attacking the great Empire nearer to its centre, and the Emperor was obliged to call his overseas legions to its aid. Clearly the last conquered and the most remote of all the Imperial provinces should be the first to be abandoned in this desperate rally round Rome, and by A.D. 410 the last of the legions had gone. In answer to the appeals of the subject race, unable of themselves to withstand the now triumphant raids of the "old" barbarians from the British uplands and these new barbarians from beyond the British seas the Roman generals promised to return when "Rome was secure," a promise, as it afterwards proved, entirely vain.

CHAPTER VI

THE COMING OF THE TEUTONS

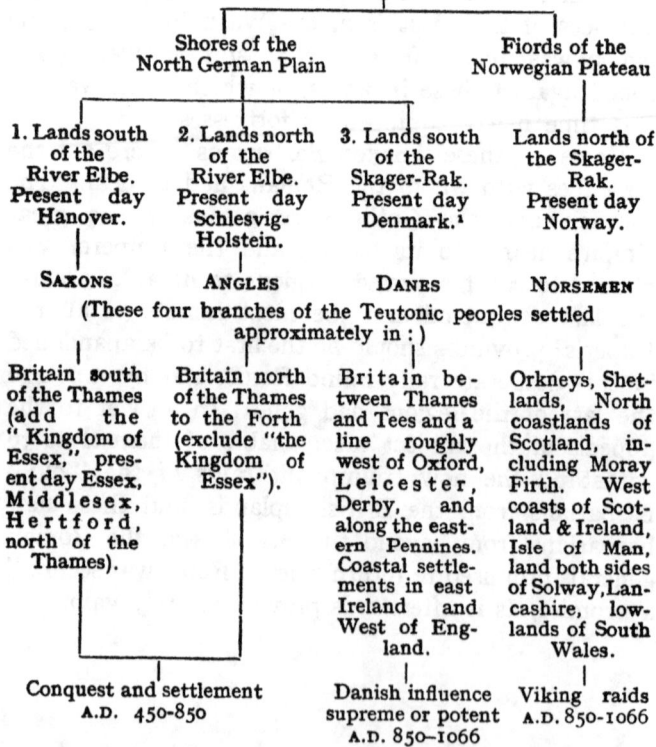

INVASIONS OF THE SAXONS, ANGLES, DANES, AND NORSE COMING FROM

- Shores of the North German Plain
  - 1. Lands south of the River Elbe. Present day Hanover. → SAXONS → Britain south of the Thames (add the "Kingdom of Essex," present day Essex, Middlesex, Hertford, north of the Thames).
  - 2. Lands north of the River Elbe. Present day Schlesvig-Holstein. → ANGLES → Britain north of the Thames to the Forth (exclude "the Kingdom of Essex").

  Conquest and settlement A.D. 450-850

- Fiords of the Norwegian Plateau
  - 3. Lands south of the Skager-Rak. Present day Denmark.[1] → DANES → Britain between Thames and Tees and a line roughly west of Oxford, Leicester, Derby, and along the eastern Pennines. Coastal settlements in east Ireland and West of England.

  Danish influence supreme or potent A.D. 850-1066

  - Lands north of the Skager-Rak. Present day Norway. → NORSEMEN → Orkneys, Shetlands, North coastlands of Scotland, including Moray Firth. West coasts of Scotland & Ireland, Isle of Man, land both sides of Solway, Lancashire, lowlands of South Wales.

  Viking raids A.D. 850-1066

(These four branches of the Teutonic peoples settled approximately in:)

LONG before the evacuation of Britain by the Romans the Teutons had begun to raid the East coasts. Possibly hunger-pressure drove them so far across the sea;

[1] The Jutes also came from Jutland or Denmark, A.D. 480 *et seq.*

THE COMING OF THE TEUTONS 61

possibly the Dogger and other fishing banks invited some of them to adventure; but no doubt sea-piracy on the Roman trading vessels and the rich loot of the prosperous coastal towns were great incentives in the first stages of the invasion. The " Count of the Saxon Shore " must have found his duties increasingly arduous, and when the protection of the Roman legions was finally withdrawn the " Romanized Celts "[1] of Britain, for all their " groanings " fell an easy prey to the pagan hosts. The ashes found among the Roman ruins of various towns such as Old Sarum, Caerwent (or Venta Silurum), show the methods of the conquest.

Before long mere raiding gave way to the more serious task of colonization, the new-comers bringing their wives and families with them, desiring to take absolute possession of the land and to make permanent homes. The completeness of this operation is obvious from the universal " blondeness " of the English of the British lowlands; only in parts of Yorkshire, notably in the Forest of Elmet, and in the neighbourhood of London (Hertford and the Chilterns), do unexpected " outcroppings of nigrescence " in the population prove that here and there, where the forests were thickest, or the energy of the invasion weakened, were the Britons able to maintain their independence.

The methods of Anglo-Saxon warfare were as ruthless as effective, but time inevitably cooled the initial exterminating zeal, so that in the more remote parts of Britain, after conquest, the native population was granted life on promise of payment in service or in kind. The clash of English and British arms can to-day be traced by the number of saints and martyrs

[1] It should not be forgotten that these Celts were "Celticized Ivernians," or the descendants of the Neolithic peoples.

where blood spilt by pagan hands watered the ground
now known by their glorious names. In much of the
West, therefore, the native language and customs were
retained, and of course the Anglo-Saxons, no more
than the Romans, could break down the steadily
maintained independence of the difficult mountainous
districts.

THE KINGDOM OF KENT FOUNDED

Despairing of obtaining assistance from Rome
the Britons of Kent invited certain Jutes to settle on
Thanet Island and help them against the Saxon
pirates. The Jutes "settled" to such good effect
that using Thanet and Sheppey as military bases,
they presently succeeded in occupying the territory
of the Cantii as far as the Medway. A little later
history repeated itself further west. A second body of
Jutes, this time as part of a great Saxon invasion,
took possession of the Isle of Wight, then crossed to
the mainland and working north and east round the
Weald secured the Cantii territory west of the Medway.
This river, whose name is Teutonic and signifies a midway, is a very appropriate frontier between the two
Jutish settlements now marking the Men of Kent,
and the Kentish Men, respectively, east and west
of a medium or dividing *way*. The "Kentings"
attempted further expansion north, but the great
Briton-held fortress of London was still sufficiently
powerful to bar progress in this direction.

THE KINGDOM OF SUSSEX FOUNDED

While these two operations of the kindred Jutes
were in progress a body of Saxons effected a landing on
Selsey (then an island) and presently conquered the
territory north and east as far as the South Downs,
thus as South Saxons occupying the "Kingdom of
Sussex."

THE COMING OF THE TEUTONS 63

The Kingdom of Essex Founded
There was another invasion of Saxons, this time up the Thames Estuary, also frustrated by London. They then entered the marshland north of the Rivers Colne and Chelmer; Colchester and Maldon became the centres of their kingdom, which included the present Essex, Middlesex and Hertford.

The Kingdom of Surrey Founded
Later these East Saxons made a further and successful attack on London, and then crossing the Thames founded a " Southern Realm " or perhaps " island " of East Saxons between the Jutes of Kent and the Saxons of Wessex. Their kingdom is called Surrey. This invasion of Surrey from the north seems attested by the great number of -tons (tuns = fortified places) in the Thames Valley, and of -hams (hams or homes of peaceful settlement) further south among the village names.

The Kingdom of Wessex Founded
The Saxon invasion of the Hampshire Basin initially involved Jutish landings and settlements, but such of the Jutish population as had not penetrated to West Kent became conquered or absorbed by their one-time allies. The Itchen led these Saxons to the neighbourhood of Winchester, but further progress north was barred by the great chalk ridge in its rear. At first (A.D. 500) the Kingdom of the West Saxon comprised present Hampshire and Berkshire (Berk = Box tree). Fifty years later Wiltshire was incorporated, and later still Dorsetshire, Somerset and Devon. Beyond lay Cornwall, theoretically Wessex, but still Celtic in language and customs.

It is worthy of note that " Middlesex " was never a kingdom. King Alfred the Great gave this name to a piece of territory between the East and West Saxons from which he had beaten back the Danes (about 781 A.D.).

THE KINGDOM OF EAST ANGLIA FOUNDED

The Angles effected landings from the Rivers Stour (Suffolk), the Orwell, Waveney, Yare, Great Ouse, etc. Present-day Norfolk and Suffolk approximately cover the Kingdom of East Anglia.

THE KINGDOM OF MERCIA FOUNDED

The geographical conditions of our Midlands made it a region very open to invasion and correspondingly difficult to defend. Up the long rivers—the Great Ouse, the Nen, the Welland, the Witham, the Trent—swept the galley boats of the invaders, good waterways down which they might take flight when the chances of battle were temporarily adverse. When strength of numbers made it possible to leave the rivers for the roads, even these routes, diverted by the Fen Marshes and the Humber, led inland to the centre.

Lindum, on the " Isle " of Lindsey (former Lindum Colonia) was first occupied. The Roman road, then, took the Angles to Leicester, and here, as at Nottingham, they made settlements in the Roman forest clearings. The Trent-way carried them to Lichfield, whose name commemorates the fierceness of the battle fought against the Britons (Lichfield = field of corpses) and to Stafford.[1] Crossing the watershed they seized Shrewsbury and Warwick and finally robbing the Hwicca tribe of the West Saxons of some outlying settlements at Hereford, Worcester and Gloucester, they reached the westward frontier of their Markland or Mercia, right up against the Welsh border. Kindred tribes who had settled in the valleys of the eastern rivers ultimately accepted the " Mercian of Lichfield " as their chief, so that, at its zenith, the great kingdom of Mercia

---

[1] Where the river was fordable by aid of a staff.

THE COMING OF THE TEUTONS 65

spread from Lincoln to Gloucester, from Bedford to Chester.

THE KINGDOM OF NORTHUMBERLAND FOUNDED

Finally, a third body of Angles sailed up the Humber and northern rivers. The great basin of the Ouse, naturally centred at York, became the kingdom, afterwards the sub-kingdom of Deira, while Bamburgh (Bamborough) a rock fortress of a very massive type supplied a capital to Bernicia which extended from Durham to the Forth. All this territory—Humber to Forth—was collectively known as North Humberland or Northumbria.

The progress of the "colonization" of England can be traced by the place-names of the localities concerned. Their *doings*, however, are very little known, but two dates at least stand out clearly. In 577 the West Saxons won a great victory over the Britons at Derham (near Bristol) and thus obtained free access to the Bristol Channel. This victory effectively separated the Britons of Cornwall and Wales. The Saxon name for these people was Welsh or "foreigner," a word akin to Walloon, and from which "Wales" is derived. The Southern Britons of "West Wales" now became known to them as "Welsh of the Horn" (from the shape of the country) and their territory as Horn Wales or Cornwall. Some of these Britons fled across the Channel and joined the Celts (Alpines or Broad Head people) already settled there. The exodus of Britons from devastated Caerleon resulted in the founding of the kingdom of Leon in North Brittany, a name which began to be heard from this time.[1]

The second date is 607 (or 613). About this time the

---

[1] Hence the French names of Bretagne and Grande Bretagne, or Brittany and Great Britain.

E

Angles of *Northumbria* repulsed the Britons in the Battle of Chester and so got through to the Irish Sea. This victory separated the Britons of Wales and those of English Strath Clyde (Cumberland). Later Chester became Mercian and was incorporated in the diocese of Lichfield.

THE ESTABLISHMENT OF THE DANELAW

During the succeeding two centuries there was much tribal warfare and certain changes, to be considered later, inevitable on the reintroduction of Christianity, but about the year 850 *England* began to experience the same troubles and dangers as *Britain* had experienced more than four centuries earlier. The Danes and Norwegians, often collectively designated as Norsemen, other tribes of the Teutonic branch of the Aryan family, but at this period as fierce and pagan as the former raiders of the Saxon shore, began their epoch-making migrations from their homes. In these latter days the story of the 5th century was repeated, even to the preliminary settlement on Thanet Island, and capture of the Wantsum trading vessels. The heathen Norsemen were also tempted by the treasures of the monasteries, many of which were built on or near the coast; Lindisfarne, Yarrow, Peterborough, were all sacked and burnt. The once warlike Anglo-Saxons had become peaceful followers of the plough; farmers, disinclined for military enterprise and weak adversaries for these new antagonists. The Danes met with no great difficulty in seizing York and establishing a great kingdom round it. North of this tribute only was exacted, the people being left unchanged by any admixture of Danish blood, so that between Tyne and Forth the English race is purer than elsewhere in our islands. Further south the Danes held the land

THE COMING OF THE TEUTONS 67

by means of the five confederate "boroughs"[1] (or fortified places) of Lincoln, Stamford, Nottingham, Derby, Leicester, all natural strategic centres. It is said that in no part of England did the Danish Invasion work greater changes than in Leicestershire. Beside the above-mentioned boroughs, other localities, such as Bedford, Huntingdon, Cambridge, etc., hitherto only villages, were made by the Danes into small military fortresses, until the conquest was made secure from the Thames to the Tees. In East Anglia a second Danish Kingdom, that of Gunthrum, was established by agreement with King Alfred (about 874) and all this occupied territory, the two kingdoms and region of confederate boroughs, was known as the Danelaw. Its northern and westward boundary may be defined as follows : The Thames from the Estuary to the River Lea—the River Lea to its source—an artificial boundary to Bedford, and then by the Bedford Ouse to Stony Stratford, and thence Watling Street to Chester. The northern boundary was the Tees and Lune.

The English reply to this creation of Danish "Boroughs" consisted in the revival of certain hitherto deserted Roman towns whose walls gave hope of repair for military needs. The former name of these old fortresses having fallen into disuse, or oblivion, they entered into a new life as the -casters, -chesters, -cesters, -sters of the Teutonic nomenclature. These "Burghs," as the English equivalent for the Danish "boroughs" were named, were supplemented by some new burghs, such as Wallingford, the great Saxon burgh of Berkshire, Eddisburgh, etc. St. Neots, Bury St. Edmunds, St. Bees, etc., record a repetition of martyrdom afforded by the pagan invasion of a Christian country.

[1] Sometimes called bergs or burghs as well as boroughs.

During the Danish supremacy in eastern and middle England Wessex was able, more or less, to hold its own, and to this the geographical features of the country south of the Thames—the absence of long rivers—was partly due. It fell to King Alfred the Great (A.D. 871-901) and his immediate successors to wrest the conquered lands, bit by bit, from the conquerors, and to *add* it to his own heroic kingdom. The result was highly important for us, because England emerged from the struggle no longer parcelled out into petty kingdoms, but mainly united under one head. At the same time it is distinctly worthy of note that Alfred did not win back " England for the English," but Angleland for Wessex.

Our eastern shores were not the only scenes of Scandinavian activity. Sometimes alone, sometimes together, Danes and Norwegians, beating round the remote north and western coasts, continued their work of sack and plunder and then of settlement. In this way were " colonized " the Orkneys, Shetlands, and the Western Islands, the lowlands round Moray Firth, Caithness, Sunderland, the country either side of the Solway, the Isle of Man, Cumberland and much of Lancashire. In the case of the Moray Firth the people to-day are English—that is Teutonic—not Gaelic, and in Lancashire the Norse occupation flowed through the Aire gap into the West Riding district of Yorkshire. In these districts of Scotland and in part of Yorkshire Norse river-names denote the completeness of the invasion, and this grafting of Danish and Norse upon Angle blood may account for the special " burliness " of the Yorkshireman. In England the first Norse settlements on the west coast were in Cheshire. Hither vikings from Dublin established themselves a little after A.D. 900, where Ethelfled, the

THE COMING OF THE TEUTONS 69

Lady of the Mercians, and King Alfred's sister, gave them land. There are numerous Norse names to be found in the Wirral Peninsula.

The lowlands of south-west Wales shared the fate of the lowlands of north-east Scotland, and such place-names as Uxwick (Oxen creek), Milford (a fiord in Norse estimation), Freysthorpe (Freya, a Goddess in the Norse Valhalla), Fishguard, Gateholm, Swansea (Sweins ei or Isle of Swine) testify to the strength of the Norse settlement in Pembroke and the Gower Peninsula. This territory, known later as "Little England beyond Wales" and as the "Englishry," was subsequently by virtue of the language, customs and traditions of its people a valuable military base against the Welsh of the uplands.

It should be noted that Norse settlements in England are not included in the Danelaw. This may be because they originated in the 10th rather than in the 9th century, though it is possible the Norse did not like to be under the Danish sway. However this may be, it is noteworthy that "hold" was a Norwegian title, and Holderness or promontory of the Hold may refer to a Norse raid and temporary settlement of territory already occupied by the Danes (East Riding).

With the favour shown to the Norse on the west, it was unlikely that the Danes of the eastern England would keep strictly within the limits of the Danelaw, and resulting hostilities culminating in a massacre of Danes on St. Brice's Day (1002), paved the way for the accession to the English throne of the Danish King Canute a few years later. Here the Danes and Norse were again working in concord, and the intermingling of Danish and Norse life in and about London is shown by the numerous Danish names. Moorgate, Aldersgate, Aldgate, Ludgate, Greenwich, Woolwich, etc., the six churches dedicated to the Norse Saint Olave, the throwing up of an earthwork of Scandinavian origin (Southwark) and the Parochial Church of St. Clement Danes just outside the City (1000—1100).

In Ireland the Danes founded Dublin, Waterford and Wexford, but though they wasted the riverine lands of the north and west, the native inhabitants were able to take refuge in the forests or the mountains, and the raiders could not hold the country.

THE VILLAGE LIFE OF THE ANGLES, SAXONS AND DANES

The Teutons, whatever their origin, preferred rivers to roads, and though they could and did on occasion use the Roman routes, these latter nevertheless fell gradually into decay. The Anglo-Saxons had no skill to mend them and naturally as this need became greater their utility diminished. The villages were therefore far away from the roads, probably because of water requirements (the Romans had often taken water to places unprovided with this commodity by means of aqueducts), but a wish to avoid piracy may have been a contributory motive. The Roman houses with their separate rooms, their baths, their heating apparatus, were alien to the Anglo-Saxon ideal of a "country life." The villages were really a collection of homesteads clustered together. If small, it supported all the members of one class or tribe, and became their "home" or "ham." Thus Horsa, a Saxon chief, gave his name to the ham or village of Horsham. Sometimes the settlement was near a ford, and the subsequent name recorded the name of the family who lived in it, as when the kindred of Beda settled near or at a ford on the Ouse (Bedford). Sometimes the village was placed at or near one of the great Roman streets—Streatham, Stratford, and so on. The village name subsequently designated the tribe

THE COMING OF THE TEUTONS

collectively—as Hastings, the "ing" recording how the German chief Hasta settled with his kin at this particular place. Similarly the family of the Dorkingas settled at Dorking. Clearly combinations were possible, giving a series of -inghams, -infords, such as Sheringham, Wallingford.

A village or home given the dignity of an earthwork rampart to keep out wild animals (or as a fortification against the natives in the earlier years of the conquest) was known as a tun (to-day, ton). Some chief, of name unknown, placed his "ton" in a suitable position on the banks of the Wily (Wilton); a tribe of the line of Kensa fixed their tun at the locality to-day known as Kensington.

This tribal or family organization may account for the practice of communal farming so characteristic of Anglo-Saxon life. Each man in the village had a homestead of his own and several separated strips of arable land in an open field, yearly re-arranged. This was to ensure that each man might have his due share of good and bad land, but clearly the temporary ownership was not conducive to careful farming. The unploughed boundaries between the strips were known as "balks" and in places they may be recognized to-day. Beyond the arable land was pasture and wood common to the whole village or township, each villager being entitled to drive his cattle or pigs into them according to rules laid down by the community.[1]

The shape and position of the village is often instructive. For example, in certain parts of Hampshire the villages are long and narrow—by waterways; elsewhere they are wide and almost circular, because of a great sufficiency of room.

[1] This matter will be dealt with more fully in a later chapter.

Sometimes there is a string of villages upon a river, sometimes in marshy districts the villages have been relegated to the surrounding hills where to-day the spires of their flinty Anglo-Saxon churches stand out clear against the sky-line; sometimes they lie one after another at the foot of a chalk or other rock ridge, where clay and chalk, or clay and sand meet, producing a line of springs.

In the east of England the cottages of the villages were clustered together, with arable land round them. The native Britons were here either exterminated or enslaved, or had evacuated the soil. In the west the scattering of the cottages into little groups of two or three through a wide extended village shows the continuity of British life. To-day these scattered dwellings, these portions of a "home," are known as "hamlets."

The houses in which the Anglo-Saxons lived were wooden barns with small shuttered windows. When the great fire burnt upon the hearth the room filled with smoke and this defect may have aided the desire for "outdoor" life.

Each village was self-contained, growing, often with difficulty and at a great disadvantage, all it required. The markets were therefore local and large-scale production was impossible.

The agricultural nature of the work carried on in these villages is easily recognized by the number of Teutonic words handed down to us describing their occupation. Thus acre, plough, furrow, rake, hoe, harrow, seed, rye, wheat, barley, oats, beans, grass, hay, ox, cow, sheep, hive, honey, mead, beer, quern (a hand-mill for grinding corn) are Anglo-Saxon, though spade and mill are Roman. Before the re-introduction of Christianity crop-growing was effected

THE COMING OF THE TEUTONS 73

in a cycle of three fields, of which two were always fallow. Later the cycle only required one fallow field; perhaps some simple method of crop rotation was devised or taught by the priests.

The Danes introduced some distinct changes in village life. They did not favour "communal farming" and preferred their homesteads scattered. Their influence tended to break down the "patriarchal" system, the different branches of the same clan becoming quite independent of one another. The Norse influence was, of course, in a similar direction, their mode of life in Norway being based upon equality of sex and equality among all the working units of the same family. In the township each man had his homestead which, as in Denmark, was called "Toft," and besides this he had his share of land or "Croft." "Toft and Croft" is the usual expression. In the Danish village the cultivated part of the land was fenced, and known as a "Yang." In the Yang each peasant had his lot or share which was measured by a rope.

We shall now consider very briefly the actual position of the Anglo-Saxon, Danish and Norse villages—the -hams and -tons. It is interesting to mark on a map place-names of Teutonic origin, and by these means we can often estimate the strength and extent of the invasion according as the settlements or colonies are scattered or condensed into a small area—the physiographical environment of marsh, forest, river and in some cases even the direction from which the invasion had come. Originally the invaders used the tribal name; in later and more peaceful times and when their numbers had greatly increased, recourse was often had to accidental circumstances of the presence of a wood, a river, a colony of beavers, etc.

74 ENGLAND AND WALES

The British natives seem to have very soon given up the coast land to the fierce, oversea warriors, and accordingly initial homes or hams abound in these regions. Later British resistance or the enmity of kindred tribes resulted in the erection of the fortified (earthwork) tun further inland, and other terminations too were used to denote strong or military positions. Numerous "hams" in a district bearing names other than tribal will imply a later and peaceful settlement, and where British place-names are quite absent there was probably extermination or emigration of the original Romano-Celtic inhabitants. Where British (Celtic) and Teutonic names exist side by side the wave of invasion was weakening or methods of occupation were becoming more humane. Where Teutonic nomenclature is absent, British independence was either never threatened or victoriously preserved. Physical features, military necessities, the nature of the woodland and its denizens have also contributed largely in providing the names of villages originating in this period.[1]

---

[1] e.g., Dun, a hill fort; Lyn, a pool (both Celtic) Lyndun (or London). Worth or Wark, a protected place (Teutonic) Bosworth, Oakworth, Southwark. See also pp. 54f, 69, 146-147, 150f, 151, 153, 201, etc.

CHAPTER VII

THE NORMAN CONQUEST

THE Normans brought us no infusion of Gallic blood, for they were Norsemen who had settled in Normandy before the "Conquest." Hence they possessed the energy and strength of the other branches of the Teuton family, but during their sojourn in France they had acquired the military discipline and orderliness common to the Romance countries, their great inheritance from Imperial Rome. And it was just this element of the Empire in the adventure which accounts for the speed of the Conquest and the completeness with which England settled down under it. It is also worthy of note that the period covered by the Norman Conquest and kingship of William and his descendants down to 1485, when the accession of a new dynasty also ushered in a new historical epoch, represents roughly the length of the Roman Conquest and subsequent occupation of Britain.

At the time of this, the latest of the Teutonic invasions, England was divided into great Earldoms, of which it may be said that those in former Wessex remained loyal to Harold as their natural overlord, while those in the northern part of the realm were distinctly hostile, never having become wholly reconciled to the Wessex conquest of the Anglian kingdoms. This internal dissension naturally weakened Harold's cause and perhaps he himself was weak if we are to believe that he had promised, albeit hypocritically, to cede his future possibilities of kingship for a " mess of pottage."

Duke William's March on London.—Duke William prepared for invasion as soon as he heard of Harold's coronation, alleging claims to the throne of which the most reasonable might be the right of " might." His first step was to collect a large fleet at the mouth of the Somme and to incorporate among his forces various " nobles " from far and near who owed him no feudal duties, but who desired both the joy of the adventure and the rewards that seemed likely to follow its successful accomplishment. On the 28th September, 1066, William landed at Pevensey, the Roman port of Anderida. Meanwhile Harold had gone north to quell an invasion of Danes in favour of his exiled brother Tostig. The Danes—who now had many blood alliances among the North-Humber-lands—had effected a capture of York, but Harold, encountering their forces at Stamford Bridge on the 2nd October, won a signal victory over them and then hurried south to meet his other foe. In barely five days he was back in London, having covered a distance of 200 miles, showing that the Great North Road, by which he made his journey, still afforded a good routeway. Unfortunately for him his speed was too great for the large levies of the northern shires to accompany him, and in consequence the troops he commanded on " Battle Hill " at Senlac were small compared to what they might have been had he but waited longer. Yet at first sight his precipitancy seemed legitimate—an endeavour to save London, the key to the whole kingdom, from the grasp of the invader!

However, he need not have feared, for William had no intention of marching inland as yet, desiring the rather to keep in touch with his fleet, which for the time being was his base for supplies and which could give him a refuge should the misfortunes of the day so require. All he had done was to proceed along the shore to Hastings, cause his fleet to be beached

THE NORMAN CONQUEST 77

there, and his engineers to fling up earthwork defences in front of the " town."

After the fateful battle in which Harold lost his life William still refrained from pressing his conquests inland. He was a great leader and he knew how to wait. It was military strategy rather than the barrier of the Weald that led him to take the coast-road east, skirting the lagoon of Dungeness and so on to Dover, which he easily reduced, thereby providing a second line of communication between himself and his Continental base.

At Dover he took the Watling Street to London, passing over Shooter's Hill and down the Old Kent Road. At Southwark the defenders of the capital denied him the London Bridge crossing. Duke William did not argue the point. In an immediate contest he would probably have been victorious, but his victory would have been local and a succession of such contests at the various defended entrances round the great walled town would have resulted in heavy losses among his own followers and probably destruction of the city with its large supplies and military conveniences. He desired London, but by surrender, not assault. He therefore contented himself with burning the suburbs in pursuance of a certain plan, and if he travelled west as far as Wallingford before he crossed the Thames, he took this long détour of free and well calculated choice.

Avoiding the numerous fords or bridges from Brentford onward, a little south-west of Staines he came to the Roman road from Silchester to Gloucester and followed it to its crossing of the Kennet. All along his line of march, and far south at each point into Surrey and Berkshire he harried and burnt the country —not through wanton destruction but with the intention of cutting off or isolating London, the great strategic and political centre of the kingdom. His road now lay through the Wallingford gap between the Marlborough Downs and the Chiltern Hills. At Wallingford itself there were two portents of great moment. Here, the only Saxon "burgh" in Berkshire, witnessed the surrender of a Saxon thegn, Wigod, who made no attempt to defend the burgh or ford, and here also Stigand, Archbishop of Canterbury, came to offer him the submission of the Church. Duke William now crossed the corner of Oxfordshire and central Buckinghamshire, probably using the old pre-Roman Ichnield Way until he came to the Berkhampstead Gap. This "Way" through the Chalk Ridge is to-day used both by the London and North-Western Railway and the Grand Junction Canal. This fact alone sufficiently testifies to an easy route to the Capital, and it is characteristic that at this point the hearts of the Londoners became filled with fear. The strategic ring of wasted land which had commemorated each step of William's march so far had isolated the great city from all but one corner of the rest of England. Moreover William was but a day's march from the Great North Road, and but two hours from Watling Street. The danger pressed heavily. Therefore, instead of fortified Berkhampstead offering him any resistance he was met by a deputation of great earls, clergy, and citizens of London. The throne was offered and accepted, and the Norman Duke was crowned King of England at Westminster, on Christmas Day (1066).

King William's March on North-Humberland.—King William met with no serious national resistance. He brought to England a feudal system, perhaps a little stricter, but still of a kind to which she had become

THE NORMAN CONQUEST 79

accustomed. Following, whether consciously or no, his Roman predecessors, he did not seriously interfere with the purely domestic details of the national life. Of course it was necessary to reward those who had helped him up the steps of his throne, and it was equally necessary to deal with the most prominent Saxon nobles so that they should be rendered powerless to injure him. The Thegns and local Ealdermen were replaced by Norman "Lords of the Manor," to whom the villagers rendered corvée and tribute just as they had done in Saxon times. The Shires, now governed by the Norman " Counts " became known as "Counties" and these and other administrative offices were filled by men upon whom the King believed he could rely. But otherwise the operations of the " Feudal System " on the Continent and in England were too alike for the Conquest to make any fundamental changes—only were its operations made more efficient—from the King's point of view.

After his coronation in London, all King William's subsequent troubles with his new subjects were divided between the personal ambition of a few powerful feudatories, who saw no reason to suppose their claim to supreme authority—save in the matter of the accomplished fact—in any way inferior to his, and to the opportunities for brigandage which an invasion necessarily supplied. There was, no doubt, some irritation caused by the government administration being conducted in a foreign tongue, but it was probably of small moment. The "Counties" near London maintained their loyalty to the new King, even raising large levies to serve under the Conqueror's banners. The countries far from the centre, especially the borders and marches of the hill countries, with the independence created by their environment, were bound to give trouble, and here again, by the nature of the disease and its remedy, there is an obvious analogy with Roman methods.

The Romans, to guard the northern extremities of the fertile plain of " Lower Britain " had erected forts and linked them by military roads. By these same roads King William marched forth intent upon the similar purpose of guarding this frontier. In other times we expect other manners, and William's plan of frontier guard was to harry and waste a wide strip of territory to act as a no-man's or a buffer-land between the danger zone and the dwellers in the plain. This accomplished, he crossed the Pennines probably through the Skipton Gap and reaching Chester established there a well-garrisoned castle. The military camp at Deva had been erected to meet the same danger—alien raiders by land and sea; in King William's time Welsh and Irish were Scandinavian.

King William and the New Forest.—It is more absurd to speak of the New Forest than of Newcastle. The circumstances giving rise to the latter took place nearly nine hundred years ago, but the New Forest was forest-land (or woodland in the English sense of the word " forest ") when the Romans came to Britain.

So far the destruction of existing hamlets and villages in the neighbourhood of London and in the North seemed to William the necessary accompaniments of his great work of conquest, and these two of these " cruel deeds " are not the ones that generally rise to the popular remembrance. In the case of the New Forest, however, royal relaxation and not military necessity was the motive force, and this element of personal pleasure may be the factor that has rendered the fame of this operation immortal.

But facts are facts in spite of the distorting capabilities of sentiment. A glance at the geological map of this district shows that much of it consists of infertile sand, and even to-day woodland glades alternate with large stretches of barren heathland, which with all our modern knowledge of farming supports only a sparse population. It was William's intention to enclose a certain area for the Royal Chase, to promulgate strict laws enforcing its proper maintenance for this purpose, and to recompensate the dispossessed owners of the isolated clusters of cottages which had grown up in certain favoured positions. No doubt his agents were unnecessarily harsh in carrying out his orders, but it is probable that had it not been for the tragic death of William Rufus, little or nothing of William's "cruelty" in regard to the New Forest affair would have found such favour with certain exponents of history.

THE RESULTS OF THE LESSONS OF THE INVASION

The ease with which Duke William came, saw and conquered must have taught him its lesson. What he had done another might do; and *at once*, on the morrow of his coronation, he set to work to guard against that possibility.

To begin with, he had encountered no difficulty in his march from Hastings to Dover. Therefore he would make a difficulty for any future would-be emulation of his glory. In Roman times the danger of invasion had come at the northern frontier—a danger met by the erection of Hadrian's Wall with its fortified towers and turrets. William's invasion-frontier was along the southern coast, which he protected by a line of castles, none of them more than one day's march from its nearest neighbour. These castles were heavily garrisoned and were supplied with food and ammunition so that there was not a river-way, not a

F

gap through which a hostile force could proceed unless the castle were friendly, unoccupied or reduced. From Dover to Southampton, at Saltwood, Rye, Winchelsea, Corfe, Hastings, Pevensey, Lewes, Bramber, Arundel, Chichester, Porchester, and a number of other places, the castles kept grim guard. This line of defence was backed by subsidiary fortresses at Rochester, Reigate, Guildford, Farnham, Salisbury and Winchester.

Next, there was the ease of his march on London, and his great strategic détour. Castles at Windsor, Reading, Wallingford, Oxford and London (the Tower) would adequately prevent any repetition of his own triumphal progress on the part of a future would-be " conqueror."

In the neighbourhood of the Great Road to the North by which he had travelled to York, castles at Stamford, Grantham, Newark, Lincoln, Gainsborough, Doncaster, Pontefract and York secured this route for him.

In the Midlands he had met with practically no resistance, the native population even following his banners gladly. But it was well to take as few risks as possible. The " dispossessed " Saxons were inclined to resent the loss of their former grandeur, and occasionally a " rebel " might count on much local enthusiasm. Castles were therefore raised at Northampton, Bedford, Towcaster, Huntingdon, Warwick, Nottingham, Leicester, and a host of other places.

The Welsh Marches, troublesome now as in Roman times, were guarded by a line of castles passing through Newport, Chepstow, Monmouth, Hereford, Ludlow, Shrewsbury, and so to Chester. Indeed, it may be said that wherever there was a market town with its supply of provisions and ammunition, or an important river-crossing, or well-placed mountain pass, there presently stood a Norman castle with its duplicate

THE NORMAN CONQUEST 83

and even triplicate walls with moat and ditch and well-equipped in the necessities of mediæval warfare.

When first erected the castles were the property of the government, and since its continuance depended upon the power of the garrison and the loyalty of their chiefs, the appointments were not hereditary, resting in the King's own hands, and removable were treason or half-heartedness suspected.

Their chief feature was a Keep, or donjon, standing in a courtyard, often designated as the "bailey." Round the courtyard was a high wall, generally supplied with turrets, and pierced by a gate-house or barbican. All this was surrounded by a ditch, or moat, crossed by a drawbridge, beyond which there might be other walls. The early Norman castles were not infrequently perched upon a mound. Many of them were of wide extent, capable of holding a large garrison for months. Even the smaller castles could check an enemy's advance for a few days. Their function was fourfold, "a refuge for armies in the field, a base for excursions, a depôt and an obstacle."[1]

The first castles were of timber and constructed on an earthwork mound—advantage sometimes being taken of the artificial "barrows" raised by the primitive peoples. Between the Battle of Hastings and the issue of what may be called the first great ordnance survey—the Domesday Book (1085), no less than eighty keeps were constructed, a feat impossible in those days of poor freight transport had the castles been of stone. The Bayeux Tapestry shows beyond the possibility of doubt that the first castle erected at Hastings was of the mound and timber variety. Stone castles were not built until the time of Henry I. Bamburgh Keep dates from the reign of Henry II

[1] Belloc, "Warfare in England."

Alnwick from 1153, two fortresses erected to deal with Danes and Scots. Other timber castles of 1068 were—Warwick, Nottingham, York, Leicester, Huntingdon, Cambridge. The immediate danger to be apprehended here arose from the power of the two " Mercian " earls, Edwin and Morcar. The 1070 (e.g., Stafford and Chester) castles were likewise of timber.

Since one object was to defend the towns from Danes and Scots the castles were constructed outside the town wall, and often where it struck a river or ford important to the town. Castles merely intended to overawe the Saxons were generally placed " low down " among the populace.

It should be borne in mind that the possession of a castle added considerably to the importance of a town, in times of peace attracting the great of the land to its neighbourhood—defending and often securing its safety in times of war. Some of these " castle towns " (often written Castleton) owe their entire development to the presence of these fortresses, hence they cannot be neglected in dealing with the geographical aspects of our country. In particular the castles rising on the boundaries of the two great areas " laid waste " by William assisted materially in drawing back such prosperity to these regions as they had lost.

Finally it should be carefully noted how the geographical importance of a place often makes itself felt through all the varying phases of its existence. The Norman castle at Winchester replaced the fort of the old Saxon burgh, and the Saxon burgh replaced the walled town of Venta Belgarum, enclosed by the Romans round the locality, clearly the geographical centre of the Celtic tribe. Rochester and Chester, Roman Durobrivae and Deva respectively, repeat the same story.

SECTION II

THE MIDDLE AGES

I

NOTE.—In the following pages the presence of square brackets [ ] indicates that the inserted narration refers to a historical introduction or conclusion considered desirable, but outside the general time-limits of the section involved.

CHAPTER VIII

INTRODUCTION

IT has already been pointed out how greatly the nature of the environment guided man's mode of life and general activities in the earlier stages of social development. Caves and rock shelters of the very remote past, huts and "highways" above the forest line or on the hill-tops, lake villages and a commerce of flints evidence an extreme simplicity of living extending over uncountable centuries, and prove the dominance of the environment over the doings of man.

Later we saw our island invaded by a highly civilized people and its inhabitants tamed beneath the Roman yoke or in refuge in those unenviable lands not worth the attention of so practical a nation. Here will be found the descendants of those refugees, still governed by the environment, proudly preserving their customs and traditions, acquiring the narrow outlook of isolated regions, and all those qualities of bravery, perseverance and devotion to old ideals which are pre-eminently fostered in "Lands of difficulty."

We have also seen the more local effects of river and forest localities of settlement and domestic concerns. But the change is already at hand. The gradual winning of the land from fen and forest begins to teach man that environments need not be permanent, that defects may be rectified, and a better understanding of transport methods show him that if his environment does not supply all his requirements he can get them elsewhere. He ceases to be at its mercy, and the whole history of the development of trade and commerce is witness of each step in his progress to its mastery.

In this and the following section the history will be carried through those long centuries conveniently designated the "Middle Ages." No definite year marks their beginning though the triumph of the Goths and Vandals and the fall and sack of Rome (A.D. 410) give a sufficiently approximate date. No definite circumstance marks their close, many of their characteristics lingering well beyond the historic date of Henry VII. The Dissolution of the Monasteries (1536) terminated Mediæval Ecclesiasticism with its hold upon the life and industries of the people; the rise of modern ports dates from Henry VIII's statute with respect to harbours (1545). Modern draperies first appear in the reign of Elizabeth; mediæval iron-smelting lingered till 1720, when pit-coal largely replaced the use of char-coal. We shall therefore consider in detail those factors of the Geography of England and Wales as, during the period under review, were influenced by and themselves influenced ecclesiastical and social organizations, industries and trade developments with their relative associations for the furtherance of commercial enterprises.

CHAPTER IX

THE ECCLESIASTICAL INFLUENCE ON THE GEOGRAPHY
OF ENGLAND

THE CONQUEST OF CHRISTIANITY

DURING the latter part of the Roman occupation Britain had become Christian, and Christianity, by means of the Britons of Cumbria, had found its way to Ireland. Under the heathen invasion of 410-550 Christianity for the time being was very generally "wiped out." Only in the untamed West, and in Ireland was the torch kept steadily burning, but it must be conceded that in Ireland, at any rate, the flame was as hot as it was steady. From the northeast corner of that country it spread to Iona, which became the great rallying centre of what was later called the Christianity of the Romano-Celtic type. From Iona and Ireland Christian missionaries were sent out to various parts of pagan Britain, sometimes to sustain and encourage a Christianity which had not died, sometimes to convert pagans, who later professed themselves as extremely anxious to be converted. From St. Columba's great monastery on Iona missionaries arrived in due time on Lindisfarne (Holy Island) which ultimately became the head-quarters of English Christianity, with St. Cuthbert as the patron saint. The Bishop's seat, or see, was therefore on Holy Island, where the ruins of St. Cuthbert's Cell or Church on the little outlying rock of St. Cuthbert's Island are still to be seen. The diocese, or area under St. Cuthbert's ecclesiastical government would originally not extend beyond the Farne Islands, of which group

Lindisfarne or Holy Island is a member. But in course of time missionaries were sent from Lindisfarne to pagan Northumbria which, however, long resisted their persuasive tongues.

In 685 St. Cuthbert visited Carlisle, which was added to the Diocese of Lindisfarne.

Irish missionaries made their way to Cornwall to help in the conversion of the pagans who had invaded it or to support the enfeebled Christianity of that remote region. St. Columb, St. Gwithian are two place-names recording the labours of these Irish saints, but probably not a few of the "Saints" in Cornwall (St. Agnes, St. Erth, St. Just, etc.) refer to martyrdoms of Christians by pagans.[1]

But help was already at hand. Far back in the 6th century pirate Saxons were raiding the coasts of Angle Northumbria, carrying off men, women and children to sell as slaves, and a little previous to A.D. 597 some fair-haired boys from Deira, the kingdom carved out of North Humberland, were exposed for sale in the slave market at Rome. A certain Gregory, taking compassion on them, and learning they were "Angles," is reported to have said, "not Angles but Angels." Later this good Gregory became "Bishop" of Rome and sent St. Augustine to "Angleland" with forty monks for missionary purposes.

THE ESTABLISHMENT OF BISHOPS' SEES. THE DIOCESE

About this time King Ethelbert of Kent married a Christian princess and expressed himself as desirous to be converted by the Saint's eloquence, with the

---

[1] There is always some confusion between the early British martyrs and these English ones, due to the later Danish and Norse invasions. St. Bride, St. Tudwals, may denote Christian martyrs. Merthyr Tidvil recalls the martyrdom of Tidvil, a British Princess. On the other hand, St. David and St. Asaph, as in the case of St. Cuthbert, refer to Bishops who founded sees.

ECCLESIASTICAL INFLUENCE 91

result that St. Augustine became the first Bishop of Canterbury, his diocese extending over the "East Kentings." A little later Rochester was also made the seat of a Bishopric, of which the diocese extended over the "West Kentings." It will be remembered that Kent had suffered two distinct invasions of Jutes, from the West and from the East, and though they had settled down under one king, the Medway seems to have preserved from extinction some obscure, yet distinct difference in their tribal or "national" life. The "Mother-church" of Canterbury, as the first of the English as distinct from Celtic or British, Bishoprics, still holds the ecclesiastical supremacy.

The East Saxon king in due course installed a bishop at London, whose diocese, corresponding to the then "Essex" embraced the present Essex, Middlesex and Hertford. The See established at Elham serving the East Anglian kingdom[1] and another at Chichester, for the kingdom of Sussex, shows how Roman Christianity on the new plan was spreading onward from the south-eastern gate of England.

Like Kent, the kingdom of Wessex possessed two dioceses, Winchester (a place of no importance till the dangers of the 9th century revived its recognition as a strategic centre) for the territory occupied by present-day Hampshire and Surrey, showing incidentally how early Surrey passed from the East to the West Saxons; while Salisbury served as see for the three West Saxon colonies of Berkshire, Wiltshire and Dorset.

Somerset, somewhat isolated, was the diocese of the Bishop of Bath and Wells, and Exeter served the south-west peninsula.

[1] Elham was the bishop's see in Norfolk at the time of the Conquest. It was moved to Thetford 1075, and to Norwich 1096.

The Hwicca territory of the West Saxons, occupied to-day by the counties of Hereford, Worcester, Gloucester and south Shropshire, was early conquered by the Mercians and became divided between the dioceses of Hereford and Worcester. The diocese of Lichfield (to-day the counties of Derbyshire, Staffordshire, north Shropshire, Cheshire and south Lancashire) and the diocese of Lincoln (East Midlands from the Humber to the Thames at Oxford) made up the remaining two of the four bishoprics of Christian Mercia.

It will be remembered that Northumbria received its Christianity from Holy Island, that is to say, it was of Romano-Celtic origin. The diocese of Northumbria was ultimately centred in the See of Durham, whose bishop may be regarded as the survival or successor of the bishop of Lindisfarne. Northumbria and even Carlisle in the then Celtic kingdom of Strathclyde, thus became the "Patrimony of St. Cuthbert" in its ecclesiastical affairs. In 664 the two types of Christianity, the Romano-Celtic, and Romano-English[1] found it necessary to effect a compromise regarding matters of ceremonial and ritual, if Christian harmony was to be preserved between them, and a Synod or Conference was called at Whitby for that purpose. The outcome was the absorption of the "Celtic" into the "English" Church.

Finally must be mentioned the bishopric of Sodor and Man[2]—which is a remnant of the Viking sovereignty centring in later times in the historic island of Iona.

Christian England was thus parcelled out into the great ecclesiastical divisions of Canterbury, Rochester,

---

[1] Of course this word was not then in vogue in its modern sense, and perhaps "Teuton" would be a better denomination.

[2] Sodor = South Islands, namely Iona and the surrounding islands to the south of Sudrey or the Outer Hebrides. Sodor and Man were Norse till 1296, and then handed over to Scotland.

ECCLESIASTICAL INFLUENCE 93

Winchester, Salisbury, Bath and Wells, Exeter, London, Norwich, Lincoln, Worcester, Hereford, Lichfield, Durham including Carlisle, and Sodor and Man. With the exception of the " Viking " Bishopric, the divisions go back to the Saxon Heptarchy and are older than the civil divisions into shires and counties.

After the Norman Conquest certain changes were necessarily made in them. With the exception of Northumbria (and Sodor and Man) all these ecclesiastical districts were united in the " Episcopal Province " of Canterbury, whose bishop became the chief or arch-bishop of the system. But Domesday Yorkshire, mainly occupying former Deira, and once a strong Danish kingdom, together with Nottingham, became the diocese of York, with a separate " arch-" bishop. The ecclesiastical diocese of Durham became the civil territory of the old Earldom of Northumberland from which that section of St. Cuthbert's Patrimony, later to be called the County of Durham, was already incipiently separated in 1066.

The diocese of Carlisle was founded by William II, and made to include that southern region of the old Celtic kingdom of Strathclyde known as " English Strathclyde " (Cumbria). In this same reign the See of the East Anglian bishopric at Thetford was removed to Norwich. The diocese of Ely was severed from that of Lincoln by William I.

By the nature of its relief, Wales is divisible into three regions. The first, Northern Wales, was formerly inaccessible to " English " invasion by land on account of its uplands and protecting forested marshes. This territory, consisting of the counties known to-day as Anglesey, Carnarvon and Merioneth, corresponds very closely to the diocese of Bangor. The second region, to the east of the first, lay open to the English

Plain with only marsh and forest for effective frontier. This is the ecclesiastical diocese of St. Asaph. These two dioceses approximately correspond to the principalities or "kingdoms" of Gwynedd and Powys. The rest of Wales was anciently known as Dinefawr; less secluded than Gwynedd, less exposed than Powys, it became ecclesiastically the large diocese of St. David and the small one of Llandaff, the latter occupying the civil district of Gwent and Morganweg, that is, approximately, Monmouth and Glamorgan.

PARISHES

A diocese was subdivided into parishes. Tradition ascribes their formation to Theodore of Tarsus, Archbishop of Canterbury, 669. The same tradition declares that the township was taken as the basis of the parish, but some parishes included more than one township, e.g., the parish of Ripon, which owned thirty-two townships, and the parish of Ronaldkirk, which owned seven; while on the other hand, the city of York, in the time of Henry V, had no less than forty-one parish churches. Probably the parishes were not all formed at one period, but grew up irregularly.

In its origin, a local landowner—thegn—might get a priest to live on his estate, erecting a church for his use, and probably building him a house. To support the priest the thegn would dedicate to the church a strip, or strips, of land in the common fields—glebeland. In later times the assignment of the limits of a parish became much more complex, owing to certain other factors which had to be taken into account, and the matter will be dealt with more fully in a later chapter.

CATHEDRALS

Cathedrals were at first constructed of wood. The first church in England is that of Glastonbury and

ECCLESIASTICAL INFLUENCE 95

was of wattle and wood. The Druid tradition may have invested wood with a peculiar sanctity. The foundations of the present Winchester Cathedral were laid in 1202, and Lichfield Cathedral dates from 1200-1325.

ECCLESIASTICAL ORDERS IN ENGLAND

The re-Christianization of Teutonic England was effected by means of missionary monks sent hither for that purpose by some powerful ecclesiastical " order " on the Continent. The establishment of a Monastery[1] or Monkish house, in any part of the country meant, at least in the earlier period, the introduction of a centre of civilization in an area otherwise barbarian. Apart from this in general the establishment of a monkish house in any locality drew a population to this spot and made for the better exploitation of the surrounding neighbourhood. It will be useful to note the different ecclesiastical orders that came to England and the date of their coming.

THE BLACK MONKS

The Black Monks, comprising the Benedictines (A.D. 597) and the Cluniacs (A.D. 1077) were so called because of their black garments. The Benedictines, the oldest and most popular order, came first with St. Augustine's Mission in A.D. 597. They established " houses " at Glastonbury, Peterborough (then known as Meadhampstead), Bury (later known as Bury St. Edmunds) and Reading, etc.

---

[1] Monasteries were called Abbeys or Priories according as their head was an Abbot or a Prior, though an Abbot usually had a Prior under him. Benedictine houses attached to a Cathedral had Priors only, the Bishop of the Cathedral being regarded as a " Mitred Abbot." The Cathedrals thus served by monks were Canterbury, Rochester, Winchester, Ely, Norwich, Durham, Gloucester. A Minster is really the Church of a Monastery, but it is often applied to a Cathedral Church, as in the case of St. Mary's Church, or York Minster, and Westminster Abbey, both really Cathedrals, and from possession of which "Cathedral" the two " Cities " of York and Westminster have been evolved.

The Cluniacs were founded to reform the older order or " rule " which had become rather slack. The " houses " were governed by Priors chosen by and responsible to the Abbot of Cluny in France. They came to England in A.D. 1077, but because they were a " reforming " order, more anxious to reform themselves than to live on familiar terms with the people, they never obtained a great hold in this country. The only Abbey of their congregation was at Bermondsey, then an island of firm ground in the Thames marshes. There were " houses " in Lewes (1077), Sussex, and at Pontefract (St. John's) and elsewhere in Yorkshire, mainly upon districts controlled by the De Warennes, who gave estates and buildings to this order.

THE WHITE MONKS (The Cistercians, 1127.)

The White Monks received their name owing to their white garments. This order was founded in Citreaux in 1098 and came to England in 1127. It was the " rule " of the Cistercians to build only " in places remote from the conservation of men," hence their houses were placed in lonely spots far from the neighbourhood of towns. The order became very popular. The Cistercians may be regarded as the " Puritans " among the monks. To them we owe the Abbeys of Fountains (1132), Waveney (1219), Tintern, Melrose, Walden, Kirkstall, Woburn, Furness (1127, founded by King Stephen), Buckfastleigh, Beaulieu, Jervaulx and Rivaulx (that is Ure Vale and Rye Vale) which latter was regarded as " a place of loneliness and horror," but whose Abbot was the head of the Cistercians in England. Between the years 1127 and 1152 no less than fifty houses had been established.

The Cistercian monks devoted themselves to practical farming of which they became the " managers " with the lay brethren as labourers. They prescribed penance in terms of farm labour so that if the delinquent obtained pleasure from his sins the monasteries obtained useful work out of his atonement!

Originally austere, their early churches were as simple as their lives, but this simplicity of architecture and living was not permanent. As the order became prosperous, rich, ambitious, these Abbeys became dainty, ornamental, beautiful—models of design which greatly influenced men's taste in quite different types of building.

THE GIFT OF MONASTICISM

The gift of monasticism was very great and in widely diverse spheres. Here we are concerned with its valuable work in the cultivation of waste or forest land, and influence upon the growth of national industries.

Perhaps of foremost importance was the tilling of the fields belonging to the monastery, whereby much of its food was supplied. The new and useful methods, often brought direct from France, did not fail to set a good example to lay landowners. In this connection may be mentioned the engineering works for the draining of the Fens about Crowland[1] and other places.

To this reclaiming of the land must most certainly be added the work done by the monasteries in vanquishing that " wasted North " resulting from King William's celebrated " harrying." Historians tell us that this was so complete that in the devastated area no attempt was made for nine years to till the ground, and that between York and Durham every town stood empty. " Not till the dawn of modern trade did Yorkshire recover her old position."

These criticisms of the methods of the great Con-

[1] See page 151.

queror have been formulated without due consideration of the geographical position and resources of Yorkshire —its proximity to the rather wild regions of the forested Pennines, its wide extent of forest and bog, its distance from the South-Eastern lowlands of England which was the centre of mediæval civilization, and especially to the undoubted fact that for long centuries after the infliction of King William's severe punishment the country was disturbed by perpetual bands of Scottish raiders bent on marauding and "harrying" expeditions of their own.

But even in William's time the restoration of Yorkshire was begun, and later continued as the combined work of the barons, churchmen and monks. On a height above the Swale, Alan of Brittany built the castle of Richmond, round which subsequently grew up the town of Richmond, now naming the shire. Ilbert de Lacy built his castle near the Aire where William I had found the broken Roman bridge, a nucleus for the later town of " Pontefract " (Broken Bridge). The first Norman Archbishop, Thomas of Bayeux, rebuilt the ruined church of York. Clearly "devastated" and untilled Yorkshire was eminently fitted for the establishment of Cistercian monasteries, whose monks presently introduced sheep and allied pastoral industries into Holderness—indeed, the monks were the first to keep large flocks of sheep in Yorkshire.

The City of York soon regained its early importance as Capital of the North, obtaining a charter from Henry I enabling the citizens to manage their own affairs. Beverley obtained a similar charter from Archbishop Thurstan (c. 1128) and became the earliest centre of the woollen trade in Yorkshire.

As regards industries the monks were skilled in many trades, frequently through their connection

ECCLESIASTICAL INFLUENCE 99

with the Continent. Thus they introduced into this country the art of window glass making (Bishop Bisop, 675), of weaving vestments, of collecting and "illuminating" books. Among the less "monkish" trades they taught the people methods of quarrying and smelting iron-ore, of quarrying and transporting stone for ecclesiastical buildings; while the influence of the Abbey buildings in educating the national taste in architecture must have been very great. The monasteries, further, set the example in the English manufacture of "woollens" (really worsteds) though the material was neither of the finest quality nor suitable for export. Many of them, however, sent *wool* to the Low Countries and to Italy.

During the Middle Ages the monks generally held themselves responsible for the preservation and repair of such roads as there were. This work was regarded as "a pious and meritorious work before God, of the same character as visiting the sick and caring for the poor," and therefore highly suitable as a means of gaining indulgences hereafter for present misdeeds. Thus Richard de Kellawe, Bishop of Durham (1281-1316) granted a forty days' indulgence to contributors to the Road Repairing Funds, and it became a custom for rich men to bequeath money, lands, cattle, to the monasteries in exchange for their upkeeping of roads and bridges, and for the payment of the bridge toll for the poor.[1] In the reign of Edward III, hermits (ranking among the "religious") were allowed to keep the roads in order and to put toll-bars across them so as to facilitate the collection of a fixed amount in

---

[1] Hence existing ruins of mediæval "Chapels" built on bridges in order to collect the toll from passing travellers, and which to-day remind us that much of the department of "Roads and Bridges" was once largely in the hands of the Church. Such a "Bridge" Chapel may be seen at Wakefield.

some cases, and a voluntary offering in others, for the use of the road.

We have seen that it was the monks who gave the impetus to church building. Anglo-Saxon churches are still in existence at Hexham, Jarrow, Monkswearmouth, Ripon, Wittingham, Dorchester (Oxford), Faversham (Kent), Colchester, Stoke d'Abernon (Surrey), Deerhurst, Stretton, Daglingworth (Gloucester), etc., while portions of many churches such as Corhampton (Hants), Wickham (Berks), etc., show Anglo-Saxon features. St. Aldhelm's Cathedral, Sherborne, Wilts, contains the bones of King Alfred's brothers. Along the valley of the Nen the number of early and stately churches is very great. The stone was near and of good quality, while barge transport was comparatively easy.

It sometimes happened that where a religious house was founded a town grew up round it on the monastic lands, the townsfolk being tenants of the monks, just as monastic institutions were often tenants-in-chief of the King. On one of the " Manors " or estates of the monks of Ramsey Island, in the Fens, there was a little village on the Ouse called " Slepe." Here, while ploughing, one of the villeins turned up a skeleton which the monks of Ramsey declared to be the body of Ivo, a missionary bishop from Persia, who came to England in the 7th century. The sacred relics were enshrined in a Priory built for that purpose and the town that grew up round that Priory became known as " St. Ives " in place of its former village name of " Slepe." Higher up the Ouse was the village of Enolfsbury, which upon receiving the bones of a Cornish *hermit*, exchanged its name for that of the hermit-saint, becoming known as St. Neots. At the time of the Danish invasion, Edmund, the Christian

ECCLESIASTICAL INFLUENCE

King of East Anglia, was put to death by the pagan Danes and his "martyred" bones were subsequently transferred to Beodericsworth, where a shrine worthy to receive them was constructed (1020). This shrine gave rise to the monastery and town of Bury St. Edmunds (Bury).[1]

Monasteries, as well as kings, suffered heavily at Danish hands, their wealth marking them out as attractive prey. At the end of 869 a Danish army marched southwards from York and burnt Meadhampstead Monastery, slaughtering all its monks. After the Wessex conquest the ruined walls were repaired by Bishop Ethelwold of Winchester, and the revived Abbey dedicated to St. Peter.

In its earliest days the Cathedral Monastery of Ely made no nucleus for a city. The disadvantages of the undrained fen round about more than outweighed any advantages the monks could offer.

The reign of Henry VIII brought an abrupt conclusion to the monastic system. In general it had outgrown its usefulness, and save in exceptional places where the monastery was still the guiding star of a somewhat unfortunate peasantry, the Act of Dissolution probably did little injury to the people at large or to the wishes of their founders and benefactors, which in many cases had been abused for centuries.

In the midst of the general destruction of the churches, the nave, which previously the laity had been allowed to use, was often spared[2] and its functions continued as the Parish Church. Thus many of our present

[1] Bury probably refers here to an earth hill or mound of some kind. The connection does not lie between the "martyred" King and his deferred funeral rites.
[2] This partial destruction has often been erroneously ascribed to Oliver Cromwell, whereas the orders for the defacement were issued in the name of his remote ancestor, Thomas Cromwell.

parish churches once formed part of a monastery. In some cases a payment saved the Abbey Church. The burgesses of Tewkesbury, for instance, purchased it from the King for their parish church, while the Church of the Monastery of Pershore (Worcester) was never in danger, the people having the right to use it for their parish.

CHAPTER X

THE TERRITORIAL DIVISIONS: SHIRE-MAKING

THE division of England into counties and hundreds as we know them to-day may be generally attributed to King Alfred, who, if he did not originate "shire-making" certainly put method and extension into a system already unconsciously begun. The Shires of England, also called "Counties" since the coming of Norman William, fall into three well-defined groups.

SHIRE-MAKING—GROUP I

Shires occupying the open high ground adjacent to the forested lowlands.

The first hint of "Shire-making" is to be traced to the foundation of the Kingdom of Wessex, and the process marched side by side with every point in its expansion. About A.D. 500 the West Saxons had made good their hold on present-day Hampshire. Their rallying-centre, their great home or ham, was fixed where the Itchen enters the sea. When sufficient territory of land round this centre was conquered and occupied, it became the share (*i. e.*, shire) of convenient size to be administered from this ham (Hampshire), and it is noteworthy that Jutish Wight had been absorbed into this shire. About A.D. 552 the "tun" of Wilton became the chief place[1] of a part or shire of the steadily expanding kingdom of Wessex, henceforth to be known as "Wiltshire." In Dorset and Somerset there seem to have been at that time no particular "chief places" and shares or shires of land covered

---

[1] The French still use this term (chef-lieu) "chief place" to denote the capitals of their departments, which are similarly constructed "shares" of land arranged at the Revolution.

the territory successively occupied by the pioneers or settlers (A. S., settan) in these districts, while Berkshire (Boxshire) was apparently a unit of forest. East Somerset was early " Teutonized," but the British strain kept its place in the west. The Celtic tribe of the Damnonii gave a name to the shire in which they still maintained the continuity of British life (Devon), and for a long period the fortress on the Exe, that camp on the water (Exeter), guarded a stationary frontier of West Saxon rule. West Wales, or Cornwall, was a unit particularly fitted, by the strength of its British survivals, to be regarded as a shire of its own. The conquest of much of this land was probably only nominal. Ultimately " Wessex " extended eastwards to the Straits, the kingdoms of Sussex and Surrey—the latter originally a colony of the East Saxons—giving rise to shires of the same name as they fell in turn to the superior power, and the fact that the Bishop of Winchester ruled over the ecclesiastical diocese of Hampshire and Surrey proved how early must have been the West Saxon conquest of this " overseas " Essex. Finally the Jutes of East and West Kent became first a united kingdom of " Kentings " and later a " shire " of the great Wessex realm.

The shires of Wessex may be said to have occupied the open high ground adjacent to the forested lowlands, whose woodlands still harboured dangerous wild beasts, and were therefore capable of serving as frontiers. Thus the southern boundary of Surrey was an undefined tract of virgin forest of the vast Andreda's Weald and here, as elsewhere, the limits of the shire were ill-defined. It is also significant that Caint (Cantii, Kent) is the Celtic name for the " open ground" between the Weald and the Thames. In this connection it should be pointed out that North Woolwich, on the

TERRITORIAL DIVISIONS

Essex side of the river, belongs to Kent, this anomaly occurring from the fact that in King William I's time a great baron owned the estates on both sides of the river—to-day known as Woolwich and North Woolwich.

SHIRE-MAKING. GROUP II
Shires centring round towns on the waterways.

The Anglian Kingdom of Mercia seems also to have been portioned out into provinces or divisions for government comparable to the Wessex shires. Thus there was the Hwiccan province, comprising much of present-day Gloucester, Hereford, Worcester and south Shropshire, and the territory whose nucleus is now represented by Lincolnshire and Cheshire,[1] debatable ground, sometimes belonging to Mercia and sometimes to Northumbria. It was the work of unconquered Wessex, under her great King Alfred, and with the revived "burgh" of Winchester as capital to win a united "England" for the "English,"[2] and in the disorder following the repulse of the Danes, the old divisions disappeared. Hence as the great fortress towns successively surrendered to the victorious Saxons, shares of territory were apportioned to these different centres for purposes of administration. Thus Mercia furnished fifteen Midland shires—whose capitals were Oxford, Buckingham, Hertford, Bedford, Huntingdon, Cambridge, Northampton, Stafford, Warwick, Gloucester, Hereford, Worcester, Leicester, Derby, Nottingham. Each of these Midland shires is thus named from its county town, and consists primarily of the river valley of this town.

[1] Old Cheshire, for example, included Flintshire, and Lancashire as far north as the Ribble. It is significant that Flintshire now exists in two detached divisions. (Worcestershire has also detached fragments in Gloucestershire.)
[2] In actual practice Alfred and his successors endeavoured to conquer Angleland (Mercia and Northumberland) whether Danish or Angle, for Wessex, or the West Saxons.

These shires were of approximately equal extent, with boundaries roughly one day's journey from the county town, and placed, where possible, near to watersheds or along the less navigable streams at that time flowing in marshy valleys. Warwickshire was primarily the valley of the Stratford Avon, Gloucester of the lower, and Worcester of the middle Severn, Leicester the Valley of the Soar. The fact that the shires of Wessex are so much older than the Midland shires accounts for the navigable Thames forming part of five of the latter shires.

The palatine provinces of Lincoln and Cheshire, owing to the special quality already noticed, became Saxon shires from which portions were not "sheared," it being undesirable to break up the existing traditions of their inhabitants. Consequently they were extremely large during Saxon times, though they suffered the common lot at a later date.

About 907 Ethelred, King of Mercia, as it then existed, made the fortress of Chester the centre of a shire, which ultimately became a Norman county under the governance of Hugh of Avranches, or Hugh the Wolf, a nephew of King William I. Wherever there was a passage through its boundary marshes leading into the interior of Wales, castles were now constructed, Beeston, Halton, Hawarden, and smaller forts at places of less importance—Duddleston, Alford, Pulford, Holt, Shotwick, etc. Thus Cheshire (Flintshire, Cheshire, south Lancashire) became a "county palatine," a land of castles fortified against the foreigner as regarded its southern border, but within the shire much of the county was uncultivated marsh or woodland, the three great forests of the Wirral (from Chester to the sea), Delamere (from the Mersey to the Dee), and Macclesfield (separating Cheshire from

Derbyshire), forming an impenetrable barrier between the "county palatine" and the English land beyond.

Cambridge, Huntingdon, and Derby are among other Midland shires offering interesting features. Before the conquest of East Anglia by Mercia a dyke had been dug to mark the frontier between these two kingdoms. This dyke (the Devil's Ditch) ultimately became part of the southern boundary of Cambridgeshire.

Huntingdon probably means "Hunter's Down," and it is situated where hard ground (chalk) rose in an area of fen. The eastern border of the shire of Huntingdon was once almost a seaside, for the Ouse ran sluggishly into a huge tract of marsh which passed imperceptibly into the waters of the sea. The present Wash reached, with scattered islands here and there, to the "downs" upon which the "tun" was placed.

The word Derby has to do with deer, and Derby, Danish Deorby, was the old English village of Northweorthig, or place of the deer. Throughout the Middle Ages the county was scantily populated except in the south. The Peak was a well-stocked, Royal Deer Forest, and there were no less than fifty-four smaller forests in the shire.

A Midland shire not so far mentioned is Rutlandshire. In the Domesday survey this shire was represented by an ill-defined forested area shared between Nottinghamshire and Northamptonshire. It became a separate shire in the reign of Henry I.

The shires of Worcester and Hereford, Gloucester and Shropshire, received their present boundaries in the reign of Henry VIII (Act of 1535). At this time Bewdley, the capital of the Forest of Wyre, was added to Worcestershire, bringing to the county a considerable increase of trade in clothing for the British seamen. Hereford received thirteen additional townships and with Gloucester and Shropshire was extended at the expense of the Welsh marshlands.

The name "Shropshire" reveals that this county does not belong to the category of the more usual form of the Midland shires. About A.D. 583 the British town of Pentwyrn (Head of the Alder Wood) became the capital of the Land of Powys. In 780 it was captured by King Offa of Mercia who gave it the name of Scrobsbyrng, or Town in the Scrub, while Scrobshire became the shire of the bush or scrub region; Shrewsbury is therefore not responsible for the origin of the name of the shire.

Essex and Middlesex resemble Sussex and Kent in mode of origin. The former kingdom of the East Saxons became merged in the kingdom of Mercia, and after the Danish and Wessex conquests underwent the usual shearing process to give the shire of Hertford. However, the traditions of the East Saxons and the Middle Saxons (whom we have already seen did not represent a race or tribal distinction) were sufficiently strong to give rise to the "shire" of Essex, though Middlesex being very definitely right down to recent times the share of London ought to have been called "Londonshire."[1]

The sharing of the former East Anglian Kingdom is also of interest. East Anglia had become part of Mercia long before the Danish invasion but the Angle inhabitants were bound by blood and customs with the peculiar ties of an earlier autonomy. The two shares into which it was divided were separated mainly by the rivers Waveney and Little Ouse. One part became the

---

[1] The administrative "County" of London came into being in 1888.

shire of the North Folk (Norfolk) and the other of the South Folk (Suffolk).

Care of course was exercised in the boundaries of the shires, the essential need being some easily recognizable feature. A glance at any political map of England will show the many waterways which have (generally in those days unnavigable) become shire frontiers. Advantage was sometimes taken of other features where convenient, such as hill ranges; Warwickshire and Leicestershire have part of Watling Street as boundary.

SHIRE-MAKING. GROUP III

Shires carved out of the old Border Kingdoms.

The third class of shires comprises those carved out of the old border kingdoms of Northumbria and English Strathclyde (Cumbria), reduced to Earldoms before the Norman Conquest, but not marked out into shires at the time of the Domesday Survey. These " Counties " of which Northumberland and Cumberland are striking examples, have never been shires. Earldoms under the Saxon Kings, administered by Norman " Counts," these northern counties offer unique features which differentiate them very specially from the other " County " divisions of England.[1] However, it is convenient for us to *begin* with an undoubted SHIRE—Yorkshire—which offers certain analogies to the true border counties.

YORKSHIRE

Yorkshire is the largest of our shires and is divided into Ridings or Thirdings—Domesday " Tredings "—Westreding, Nortreding, and Estreding, of which the

[1] Through the Norman practice of making a Count governor of the various English Shires, arose the present generally accepted term of " County " in place of " Shire "; though this distinction is not rigid, and we still speak of the Shire of Leicester, or Leicestershire, and the County of Durham.

West Riding may be said to occupy territory greater than any other shire in England "except Yorkshire." These Ridings seem to have some relation to the position of three well-marked and distinctive settlements of the invading Angles. The East Riding occupies Holderness and the Derwent Valley; the North Riding occupies the Valley of the Ouse to York, and the Cleveland Hills to the Tees Valley; the West Riding, occupying the remainder of the shire was long held by .the fugitive Britons, whose dark-skinned descendants are said to be still found in the district formerly known as the Forest of Elmet, in the neighbourhood of Leeds. We have seen how the Danes founded a new Denmark, with York as centre, and then crushing back the Norse who were pressing eastward through the Aire gap, conquered their settlements right through to St. Bees Head. Domesday Yorkshire extended from the north to the Irish Sea, and the Danish character of the holding is marked by the number of "thwaites," "bys," "dales," distinguishing their settlements from the "hams" and "tons" of the English. The "Thirdings" received their definite boundaries during the Danish occupation, when York was made the centre of all the Ridings. In later times there seems to have been some unsuccessful attempt at "sharing" perhaps recorded in the areas known as Cleveland, Holderness, Hallamshire, Craven, Richmondshire.

LANCASHIRE

At the time of the Norman Conquest, what is now known as Lancashire was shared between York and Cheshire. The Cheshire portion, the territory between the Mersey and the Ribble, was known as "The Land between Repam and Mersham" (*Terra inter Repam et Mersham*), while Furness and North Lancashire,

TERRITORIAL DIVISIONS

together with part of present-day Cumberland and Westmorland appear in Domesday Yorkshire. This portion, known as Amounderness, became through the marriage of its heiress the property of a Norman knight, who, not finding it profitable, gave it to King Henry I in exchange for the Earldom of Chester. The King bestowed the southern portion and Furness on small barons. Henry II amalgamated these small baronies into the " County of Lancashire," with Lancaster as capital, at the same time conferring its earldom on his second son John (1177). This royal favour, however, proved a distinct disadvantage to the inhabitants of the county, for Lancaster was never the seat of a residential Earl, and the county therefore never united in a great baronial family. The lands of the county were also held by absentee noblemen, and were worked in consequence by small holders, and thus inefficiently. The monasteries, too, did little to help, for by the time Lancashire was ready to receive them, they had lost the pure fire of the initial institution and had become ambitious and worldly. The Lancashire " towns " were poorly populated, the chief being Preston (on the Ribble), Manchester (whose importance was originally due to its castle) and Liverpool, still little more than a fishing village at the close of the Middle Ages, though King John, who founded the last-named town, made it a port for Ireland. The shire, poorly cultivated, and little populous, came under the category of those Lands of Difficulty which generally upheld the conservative (Royal) and losing cause. Importance did not come till Tudor times when the smaller barons became country gentlemen, living at home and working their own lands. It is noteworthy that north Lancashire, in common with adjacent counties, has a population of mixed descendants of Britons, English, Picts, Scots, Norse, Danes and Saxons. The last-mentioned admixture of blood is due to William II, who in 1092 had New Forest exiles established in this scantily populated area.

NORTHUMBERLAND AND DURHAM

The northern part of the kingdom of Northumberland, from the Merse[1] of Berwick to the Forth, was quite beyond any attempt at conquest on the part of Wessex, and ultimately was incorporated in Scotland. The Earldom of Northumberland, the territory between the Tweed and Tees, at the Norman Conquest contained a population of mixed Danes and Angles, sometimes at enmity among themselves, and sometimes in close alliance with the Danes "across the water." From this Earldom the two counties were subsequently carved the counties of Northumberland (Tyne to Tweed) and Durham (Tyne to Tees). It should be kept in mind that the Humber at no time formed any part or boundary of the *County* of Northumberland.

[Berwick is now a legal part of Northumberland. It lost its prosperity when it ceased to be Scotch, because as a frontier town it had no country beyond with which to trade, and so became merely a military position.]

A speciality of this county is the Pele Tower (Pele = pale, or palisade). The earliest of these towers was erected in 1298. The Pele is a small, square, comfortless stone structure, with a basement in which the cattle were placed when raiders were abroad. It was sufficiently strong to delay a raiding band of "stark moss-troopers" without artillery.

Durham, the "home on the water" of the earlier Angles, had early become the centre of a great bishopric

---

[1] Or Mark, or border—compare Mercia, Marches.

TERRITORIAL DIVISIONS

—known as the Patrimony of St. Cuthbert—just as the territory about Rome was the Patrimony of St. Peter. This bishop exercised an ecclesiastical and territorial overlordship comparable to the great bishop-princes of Metz, Toul, and Verdun, in the Rhinelands. The diocese of Durham therefore clearly furnished a convenient unit for the share of Durham, and William I so defined it. Owing to the disturbed state of Northumberland, long raided by the Scots, and long raiding the Scots, William I made Durham into a county palatine, or fortified frontier county, ruled—not by an earl or count, but by its bishop, of whom it was said that "Whatever the King has outside the county, the Bishop has within." The inhabitants were known as "the men of the Bishopric."

[Until 1844 the possessions of the Ecclesiastical See of Lindisfarne—Norhamshire and Islandshire, or Holy Island—were collectively known as "North Durham." They were annexed to Northumberland in that year.]

CUMBERLAND

Whereas Northumberland represents the remains of an ancient Anglian, or "English" kingdom, that Royal territory now recognized as Cumberland was truly "British." Luguvallium (Caer Leul) or Carlisle was certainly on the Roman frontier, but the Celts inhabiting this region were in friendly relations with their kindred still further north. Later, in face of the Teutonic invasion these Britons organized themselves into the little kingdom of "Strathclyde," which extended from the Cumberland Derwent to Dumbarton. In 603 and again in 670 the Northumbrian Angles annexed first the plain of Cumberland and secondly the district between the Ribble and the Solway, and in consequence Cumberland received the ecclesiastical civilization of St. Cuthbert, Carlisle and the surrounding district becoming part of the diocese of Lindisfarne. The Britons, however, remained tributary to, and were not actual subjects of the Northumbrians, whose power was feeble, and in consequence they fell an easy prey to the Norse pirates, Norse place-names, gill, thwaite, haugh, fell, etc., occurring with such frequency that it is plain the Norse conquest was fairly complete. But in 875 Cumberland—that is Strathclyde—was threatened with a new period of warfare—by the arrival of the Danes "swarming" from their new Denmark in Yorkshire, across the Pennines through the Aire and other gaps, and who not only destroyed Carlisle, but carried their kingdom through to the Irish Sea. Later Cumberland was reconquered by the Britons of the West, who gave it the name of Cumbria, or "land of the Cymrie" (up to the Tay).

Cumberland shared with north Lancashire an attempt at repopulation by means of the New Forest exiles (1092), and here, as in the country between the Ribble and Solway, may be found a mixed descent of Britons, Picts, Scots, English, Norwegian, Danes, and Saxons.

In the reign of Henry I, Carlisle was made into an earldom—the "barony of Appleby" was separated from the earldom of Carlisle and became the County of Westmorland, which for a short period was rightly called "Applebyshire." This corner of the country belonged alternately to the English and Scottish kings, but Henry II decided that the English part should henceforward be known as "Cumberland," and that part of the West Riding of Yorkshire known as Amounderness was then distributed between Cumberland and Westmorland. Thus Cumberland, erected as a bulwark against the Scots, is another county of castles.

WESTMORLAND

As its name denotes, this county is the "Land of the Western Moors." We have seen that it consists of the moorland part of English Cumbria, together with an increment from the West Riding of Yorkshire, derived from the parcelling out of former Amounderness (1177).

THE SHIRES OF WALES

We have already seen that Wales was divisible by the nature of its relief and geographical features into the three "principalities" of Gwynedd, Powys, and Dinefawr.

The Principality of Gwynedd, the only part of Wales independent at the accession of Edward I, covers the modern counties of Anglesey, Carnarvon, Merioneth, and it was this principality together with the two districts now known as the shires of Cardigan and Carmarthen that after the conquest of Gwynedd became the Principality of Wales conferred on Edward's infant son. A new shire, the County Palatine of Flint, was there constituted to assist the County Palatine of Cheshire in its work of keeping the King's new realm in order.

William I may be regarded as being responsible for the conquest of Powys, which was nearly completed under his successors. Under them, too, Dinefawr, occupying mainly the southern plain, became a County Palatine. By the time of Edward III the "Principality of Wales" had increased and now included the two Marches of Pembroke and Morganweg (Glamorgan).

At the close of the mediæval period, Wales was finally incorporated in England (1535-6), and the division of the land into shires completed. For this purpose the larger of the two Marches was divided into six shires—Glamorgan consisting of Morganweg together with the Gower Peninsular, Monmouthshire, constituted from the former Gwent district of Dinefawr, Brecknockshire, occupying the Welsh Valley of the Usk, Radnorshire, the Welsh Valley district of the Wye, Montgomeryshire, in the Welsh Valley of the Severn, and Denbigh. Of these shires Monmouth was for certain purposes annexed to England. Not till the reign of Charles II was it made to form part of the Oxford Circuit for judicial purposes. In all other matters Monmouth is Welsh rather than English, and in legal affairs pertaining to Wales the words " and Monmouthshire " are generally added.

All the Welsh shires received the ordinary organization of English counties. (1543.)

CHAPTER XI

THE EVOLUTION OF COMMUNITY DIVISIONS: HUNDRED, VILLAGE, BOROUGH, PARISH

THE officer in supreme charge of the Shire was the "Shire-Reeve" (Sheriff), whose official head-quarters was the capital of his shire.

THE HUNDRED

Smaller divisions of the shires were the "hundreds" possibly constituted for military duties and purposes of taxation. The division into hundreds is far older than the divisions into shires, and some historians consider the system as being in working order previous to the Teutonic settlement in Britain. In its origin the hundred seems to have consisted of a hundred families or households, and hence the hundreds, regarded as territorial units, differed considerably in size according to the possibilities offered by the land to support sparse or denser populations. In course of time the hundred became a fixed unit of territory, and as such we find it to-day. The "Hundred of Manhood," for example, extends inland from the coast well towards Chichester.

THE WAPENTAKE

In the shires of Lincoln, Nottingham and Yorkshire the Hundred-moot or meeting became replaced by the moot or meeting of the Wapentake. This new name for the local subdivisions was due to the Danish influence and arose from the fact that the members attending it *took their weapons* with them.

THE HIDE

The households composing the hundreds were called "Hides," and it is significant of the ideals of equity underlying the original sharing of the land that the hide was also the amount of territory granted to and assumed capable of supporting one household. Here also in a district of very poor soil a hide would be larger than one in a more fertile region, so that at first the extent of a hide-land differed considerably. Later, in legal phraseology, a hide was 120 acres, or land which could be efficiently worked with one plough-team of eight oxen.

The Mediæval Manor, or Village

During the long Anglo-Saxon period (450-1066) the conditions of social life underwent profound changes. The self-governing "hams" or old village communities, with their populations of villagers or "free men," managing their own affairs as independent groups under their hundreds, gradually became subject to rule from a central spot. Small chiefs became small kings, and small kings greater ones. The military emergencies of the Danish invasions developed a military and ruling caste. A lord became owner of large areas of territory which, of course, increased with his greater importance, and the former free villagers became his villeins or feudal tenants, giving him tribute in kind and working his estate or demesne[1] by rendering him agricultural service in various degrees. At first the villagers merely "commended themselves" to a more powerful neighbour for protection in lawless times, but the relation ultimately developed into a more or less complete subjection. This system of land tenure, known as the Mediæval Manor, was already far advanced before the Norman Conquest, and the subsequent change was in nomenclature

[1] Origin of the word demesne: Latin, dominum, a lord. The demesne was that part of the estate held for the lord's own personal use.

COMMUNITY DIVISIONS

rather than character. The dispossessed Thegn or Saxon Earl was replaced by a Norman noble, styled the "Lord of the Manor"[1] a term not used in England before the reign of Edward the Confessor. At the period of the Conquest the Manor system was most greatly developed in the South and middle of England. In the Danish districts of East Anglia, however, the old system of independent groups still lingered, albeit in a weakened form. These "free men" were frequently Danish soldiers who had settled in the land, and who existed side by side with groups of freemen of pure Anglian descent. These freemen of both species cultivated their own lands and preserved much of the old liberty, but they, too, found it advantageous to be "under commendation" to a lord, to whom they rendered some military, jurisdictional or other personal service, but not as villeins, and therefore not the agricultural corvée.

The Manor-Village system, in its stricter application lasted up to the 13th century, when it became the practice for certain of the richer villages to purchase their freedom from manorial control and become "towns." But down to the close of the 18th century the Manor-Village was still in existence in a somewhat modified form in much of rural England.

The disposition of the manor-land varied with circumstances, but the following description of a Mediæval Manor may be regarded as fairly typical. The Demesne land round the Manor House or Hall was cultivated by the lord or his bailiff, all other land on the estate being held by the tenants as "land in

---

[1] Origin of the word Manor: Disputed—(1) from the French *manoir*, the residence of the owner on his land ; (2) from the Latin *manus* (a hand), a manor being that portion of an estate worked by the hand labour of those dwelling upon it. Note the restricted use of the word "Manor" at the present day.

villeinage." The arable land of the Manor-Village was rented by the tenants in *common fields*, open, that is unfenced, at the price of 6d. per acre. These fields were divided into acre or half-acre strips and allotted in such a way as to provide against the possibility of an undue proportion of good or poor land falling to any one holder, which was further guarded against by an annual redistribution of strips, so that no one held the same ground for two consecutive years. Generally every third strip in the common fields belonged to the lord, others to the parson (glebeland). Crop rotation was worked in a cycle of three fields, rye or barley, wheat, fallow, so that one-third of the arable land was always fallow. Each tenant held two strips (separated by a band of grass or balk, or a furrow) until the crops were harvested, when the cattle were sent into feed upon the stubble. Beyond the common fields lay an acre of common pasture for all tenants (including the lord), who generally, but not always, could only pasture a restricted number of cattle. From this common pasture or waste (which in some manors was apart from the common pasture) the tenants could cut peat, turf, or bracken for fuel. Beyond the common pasture and waste was forest or woodland belonging to the lord of the Manor, who owned all the timber. The tenants had the right of " lopping and topping " certain trees, and collecting fallen branches for fuel. They also possessed rights known as " pannage," and, under certain conditions, " swanage," in the one case the right to send their swine into the woodland to feed on the acorns and beechnuts, and in the other, where the estate possessed small lakes, to keep a certain number of water-fowl upon it. The " hog-ward," an important official in the Mediæval Manor village,

COMMUNITY DIVISIONS 121

had to see that the use made of the waste and woodland for the villagers' swine was fair and equitable. Meadow land, bordering the streams, belonged to the lord of the Manor, and might be rented out at 8d. per acre. The cluses or closes were irregular strips of particularly fertile river land, which were rented by the lord to his richer tenants.

In the centre of the village, especially when it was the meeting place of two or more routes, was the village green, upon which fêtes and festivities, incidental to village-life, might take place.

THE VILLAGE OF A MANOR BECOMES A TOWN

All kinds of factors might contribute to the wealth of certain villages, and clearly, as the tenants became rich, subjection to the Manor would be felt as vexatious and oppressive. In the 13th century it became the practice for certain villages to compound with the lord of the Manor for the various services they owed him and to buy their freedom to manage their own concerns. An interesting example of the process may be taken from the Manor-village of Wyk, or Wike, of which the Abbot of Meaux was lord. Towards the close of the 13th century this village had become large and prosperous, owing to the many advantages for home and continental trade (chiefly with Flanders) that Wyk on Hull possessed. Edward I visited the place in 1298, and was so much struck by its importance that he granted it a fair. Its villeins, wealthy traders, had long since been in the habit of paying tribute rather than corvée to the lord of their manor, but clearly the power of interference in their affairs which their lord might legally exercise was exceedingly galling. Edward I accordingly purchased Wyk from the Abbot of Meaux and made it into a " free borough " (modern " town "), the village name of Wyk being exchanged for that of " Kingstown on Hull " (Kingston-on-Hull), the "Hull" of a later democratic age.[1] The story of Wyk may be taken to serve as an example of the method by which Manor-Villages became towns. The Manor system in its stricter form, was obviously doomed when England passed from an agricultural to a pastoral country, the wealth gained in the wool trade being one of the contributing factors necessitating a change in the social life.

THE BOROUGH

It has already been noted how "strong" or "strategic" places became boroughs or burghs, that is military centres. At a later date the erection of a Norman castle fixed and often greatly added to their importance. Out of the Danish Boroughs and Anglo-Saxon Burghs (Burgs) grew the "English" Boroughs, in due course sending members to Parliament for the purpose, it is to be feared, of granting taxes to the king! The inhabitants of the English boroughs were called "burgesses" (note the connection with the word "bourgeois)", essentially not noble, but of the richer classes of town life. These burgesses enjoyed a variety of privileges, and a measure of self-government, for both of which they paid somewhat heavily. The mediæval boroughs originating previous to the Norman Conquest were Bridgport, Buckingham, Cambridge, Canterbury, Colchester, Derby, Dorchester, Dover, Droitwich, Dunwich, Grantham, Hereford, Hertford, Huntingdon, Ipswich, Lewes, Leicester, Lincoln, Louth, Maldon, Middlewich, Nantwich, North-

[1] Note the number of Kingstowns or Kingstons scattered up and down the country, many of them recording thus the metamorphosis from a Manor-Village to a "borough" or "town." Villages obtaining royal charters and privileges, and so becoming "boroughs," (and towns) often merely assumed the Royal title in addition to their ancient name, such as King's Langley, etc., not to mention the classic example of Queen's Crawley.

ampton, Northwich, Norwich, Nottingham, Oxford, Pershore, Pevensey, Romney, Shaftesbury, Shrewsbury, Stafford, Stamford, Taunton, Thetford, Torksey, Wallingford, Wareham, Warwick, Worcester, Yaremouth, York. Of these, no less than twenty-three are capitals of their counties. This list was greatly increased by Edward I and Charles II.

A few examples of the privileges enjoyed by these boroughs and of the payments exacted for these privileges will be instructive. At Dover the burgesses supplied the King (if required) with twenty-one ships for a fortnight each year, and undertook to pay 3d. in the winter and 2d. in the summer for the expense of transporting the King's messenger's horse. In return for these services they were allowed to adjudge causes and disputes (the right of sac) within a certain local area (or soc). Further, a constant resident in the town who paid rent to the King and was also a Dover burgess, was exempted from paying toll elsewhere in the Kingdom. At Lewes the burgesses also contributed to support the naval force when the King sent out a fleet to guard the seas. They also had to pay a toll for the privilege of selling saleable property. At Oxford twenty burgesses were obliged to accompany the King when he went out on expeditions, or pay a fine of £20. The tenants of the twenty mural houses had to keep the walls in repair. At Warwick, the centre of the honey-making district, ten burgesses had to accompany the King when he went in person on any land expedition, and Norwich, as well as Warwick, paid the King's dues in honey.

THE FREEMAN OF THE CITY

After the period of King Alfred of Wessex (871-901) the freemen of the cities and boroughs (or towns, as we should call them), citizens and burgesses as they came to be called, preserved the freedom which the villeins had lost. One current phrase "the freedom of the city," is a reminder of this inheritance.

BOOKLANDS

Not only did the King assign lands for the upkeep of the governing classes, but also for the Abbeys and Monasteries, which were sometimes granted on the manor-system so that the lord of a manor might also be the head of a monastery. These and other lands which were given to the Church by the Royal Charter or "Boc," were indicated both as regards position and extent in a *book*, so that the Church's claim to them might be clear and permanent. They were therefore known as "boclands" or "booklands" and it is interesting to note that "bookland" or "buckland" has now become a place name.

THE PARISH

We have seen that tradition ascribes the formation of the Parish to Theodore of Tarsus, Archbishop of Canterbury 669, and that it later became the custom for the thegns of two or three adjacent manors to unite in building a church and supporting a priest to officiate therein. In A.D. 800 these local clergy were under the control of the bishop, and "tithes" of corn, fruit, wood, animal produce, were now payable to the incumbent by the parishioners, who still, however, remained in possession of his glebe. After the establishment of the monastic orders part of the Abbey Church might also be the Parish Church, and thus at the Dissolution of the Monasteries (*c*. 1536) which may be taken as ending mediæval ecclesiasticism, some of the naves of the Monastic Churches were spared, as being also Parish Churches, and some of the Abbeys were purchased outright from the *King* by the people, to be also used for this purpose. It should be kept

COMMUNITY DIVISIONS

in mind that not every "ham" had a parish church and that a parish might consist of several "hams," as in the cases of Ripon and Ronaldkirk already mentioned. In broad terms a Parish may be regarded as occupying a certain area of land giving tithes to and supporting the Parish Church[1], a matter of some importance when the extent and productive resources of the Parish came to be considered.

Parish, in common with other boundaries, naturally require to be easily detected. A steep-sided valley can be taken as obviously terminating the parish area in a certain direction. The nature of the soil may also be pressed into service. In the case of Banstead Downs, the relief is suitable, but the soil is unsuitable for this region to rank as a simple homogeneous parish. The sandy soil is varied by a chalk area over the 500 foot contour. The grass of the chalk makes good sheep pasture, but wells for water supply must be deep and are difficult to dig. The area is therefore unsuitable for agriculture, and so surrounding parishes have "shorn off" portions, leaving unsymmetrical Banstead in the centre.

At first the parish boundaries were the outer limit of the group of Manors forming the parish, with boundaries coincident with such natural and local features as the Manors had utilized. Roads sometimes form Parish boundaries, but not often; the Dover Road partly divides the parishes of Greenwich and Charlton, Woolwich and Eltham, Plumstead and Eltham. Roads as boundaries are useful in chalk areas where there do not happen to be rivers. Rivers

[1] To-day the Parish is the unit area of Local Government, but as a "civil" parish is differentiated from the ancient ecclesiastical parish described above. These two kinds of parish have now separate and distinct administrations, and rarely occupy coincident areas.

make more useful boundaries, but in the case of the Thames, Woolwich stretches across the river to North Woolwich; elsewhere this river is both Parish and County boundary. In the case of Surrey, noted for the infrequency of streams, the River Mole forms a good boundary for several parishes, being at once a source of water supply and a visible line of separation. The parishes, of which Fetcham and Leatherhead are typical examples, extend for five or six miles north and south of the east-west line of the river, but are only about a half a mile wide.

In chalk areas dry valleys make good parish boundaries, but also the crest of the ranges of hills. The parishes of Cudham, Knockholt, and Shoreham are divided from the parishes of the Upper Darenth by the crest of the North Downs.

Geological structure may determine the "lie" of a Parish, according as there are or are not water-bearing rocks in the area. A simple example occurs where a chalk ridge separates two portions of a clay plain. The junction of the clay and chalk furnishes a line of water springs, and the parishes will extend across the ridge rather than parallel to it, so that as many as possible may share the water. The choice is:

```
| 1 | 2 | 3 | 4 |        rather   _ _ _ _ _ _ _ _ _ _ _
|   |   |   |   |        than    1                    1
|      Clay    |                 _ _ _ _ _ _ _ _ _ _ _
                                        Clay
|   |   |   |   |
                                 2 ─────────────── 2
|   C  h  a  l  k   |
|   |   |   |   |                  _C_ _h_ _a_ _l_ _k_
|   |   |   |   |
                                 3 ─────────────── 3
|     Clay      |                       Clay
|   |   |   |   |                _ _ _ _ _ _ _ _ _ _
| 1 | 2 | 3 | 4 |                4                   4
```

COMMUNITY DIVISIONS

This idea of sharing the water supply is similar to that mentioned above in the case of rivers in a generally streamless district. Here in addition the arrangement tends to give each Parish variety of soil and hence variety of vegetation.

The same arrangement occurs in the parishes near Devizes. This region consists of downland to the north of which lie alternate, irregular strips of sandy water-bearing land, and clay land. Here the parishes stretch across down, sand and clay strips. The *Churches* are all placed on the sandy, water-bearing soil, and the largest parish is that which contains the most down.

DIVISION OF LAND IN ENGLAND

It has now been shown that all the "soil of England" fell into one or other of four categories when the classification is made with regard to the actual owners.

The King's lands were Crown lands, belonging to himself, and entailed upon successive wearers of his crown. "Royal Eltham," the New Forest, the Royal Deer Forest of the Peak, are examples of these Crown Lands.

Next come the Monastic and Religious holdings, granted by the King or bequeathed by private owners. Before the coming of the Normans there were 240 religious establishments in England, and the Conquest added greatly to their number. Thus in one way and another the land held by the Church represented a very large proportion of the realm.

After the Church comes the Nobility, with their demesnes and manors for which they paid the King or their overlord in terms of military service,[1] the

---

[1] Commuted by the astute King Henry II to a fine known as "scutage" or "shield" money.

feudal system having been well developed in England before the accession of William I.

Lastly, there remains the Folk's Lands, or "People's Common Lands." This was frequently the poorer land on non-water-bearing strata; the heaths and commons from which turf and bracken could be obtained, and which afforded a rough pasturage. In counties where much of the soil is infertile these "commons" are still in existence.

CHAPTER XII

THE INFLUENCE OF GEOGRAPHY UPON MEDIÆVAL WARFARE

WHEN considering the influence of British Topography upon warfare the twofold division of the country into uplands and lowlands—the Upper and Lower Britain of the Romans—should be kept clearly in mind. Of the Mediæval warfare in the Saxon period the wars of invasion were confined to the lowlands, the uplands furnishing a refuge for the defeated tribes who were little molested even in later times. It was after England had been brought definitely under one monarchy that the character of the uplands began to influence the fortunes of those who warred in the plains. These lands of difficulty bred a conservative, chivalrous race, which generally sided with the lost or losing cause—while the lowlands, fertile, prosperous, commercial, bred a race which may be designated as progressive and was entirely *self*-seeking. The mediæval king, hungering after his rights *as* king, found little favour with these peoples, unless he adopted a commercial attitude as did Richard III and Edward IV, under which conditions their crimes, or reputed crimes, were generally forgiven.

The wars of mediæval England may be classified under three heads—wars undertaken to uphold or defeat a royal cause; wars undertaken for personal aggrandizement only; wars of invasion.

WARS UNDERTAKEN TO UPHOLD OR DEFEAT A ROYAL CAUSE

In these wars the value of the Lowlands versus

the Highlands, and even the more potent influence of commercial London are the decisive factors. Of the Thames castles, placed by the great William at the river crossings, all had a tradition of loyalty to the reigning monarch. Beginning with the Barons' Wars against King John it is noteworthy that in spite of the fact that all these castles—Windsor, Reading, Wallingford, The Tower, supported the Royal Cause, it was the barons who with the powerful, progressive, mercantile metropolis behind them, forced upon John the signing of the Great Charter (1215). It is also noteworthy that the influence of a great town could outweigh the value of a great castle, for though the Tower garrison was both large and loyal to its king, it refused to come out, and perhaps wisely, in the face of so powerful and hostile a people.

Owing to the folly of the barons in calling the French King to their aid, and thereby offending a large section of the English, John's position gradually improved, and he was able to garrison for his own side all the castles of the north and south, but these were too remote to weigh very materially against the defection of London.

In the Barons' War against Henry III the Cinque Ports and their Castles, and all the southern counties to England, together with London were on the side of Simon de Montfort. Again the dominating factor was trade, which the King's government did not encourage. The Royal troops held Rochester and the Thames strongholds, again including the Tower, but as before commercial London was too wide and too strong an area to be taken.

WARS UNDERTAKEN FOR PERSONAL AGGRANDIZEMENT

In this category must be placed the Wars of Stephen and the Wars of the Roses. In both cases the actual

MEDIÆVAL WARFARE 131

combatants were followers of a lord rather than a cause. King Stephen's reign offered the spectacle of a weak monarch and a barony anxious to get what power it could mainly for its own selfish ends. The result of this was the erection of numerous castles—the so-called adulterine castles—probably shoddy affairs of wood and wattle, which disappeared with the disorders of his reign and had no influence upon subsequent history or geography.

The Wars of the Roses were likewise wars of personal ambition, but in them the part taken by London becomes again significant. The coronation of those two White Roses, Edward IV and Richard III, depended on the choice of London which forgave the one his callous cruelty and the other his reputed murders for the sake of the peaceful commerce these reigns inaugurated.

WARS OF INVASION

Of the Wars of Invasion, notably in Wales, it is not commercial prosperity but land relief which was the predominating factor. There are three points to be especially noted.

The topography of Wales was averse to a national amity. It is a high plateau dissected by rivers, and hence parcelled out into small areas, making for groups and tribes rather than for a nation. Further, Wales possesses no national rallying point; its rivers run out to the English Plain by courses generally West to East. Communication was therefore especially difficult from north to south, and hence though Bangor or Cardiff might have been quite suitable "capitals" for the north and south respectively, obviously neither would do as a military centre for the whole country. Lastly, in the East the land drops down fairly abruptly to a level, fertile plain, which was the mark or border of the old Mercian kingdom, the County Palatine of William I and his successors. Here was established a series of castles governed by the Lords Marcher, whose purpose was to overawe the Welsh, and, confining them to their own region, prevent them from raiding or devastating the Plain. It was little likely, however, that the Welsh should be entirely overawed. Even during the Roman occupation they had descended to the Plain and utterly wiped out the great military station of Viroconium, and now border warfare was very common.

We have seen that William I put strongholds wherever there was a passage through the marsh in Cheshire which led towards Wales, so that castles rose at Beeston, Halton, Hawarden, and smaller forts at places of less importance and shallow river crossings—Doddleston, Holt, Shotwick, Alford, Pulford, etc., and that consequently Cheshire became a base of military operations against Wales. In 1069 Roger of Montgomery was made governor of Shrewsbury Castle, and this lord subsequently built the fortress known as Montgomery Castle[1] further west. William II carried the plan a step further, carving Earldoms out of the ancient Marchland, and appointing non-hereditary Lords Marcher[2] as their governors, and presently a line of castles spanned it from north, to south, of which Chester, Shrewsbury, Ludlow, Hereford, Monmouth and Chepstow castles are among the more important. In the present county of Monmouthshire, for example, there are twenty-five ruins of Norman castles. In this way the Welsh were not only prevented from expanding down into the plain, but

[1] The town which ultimately grew up round this castle gave its name to the shire of Montgomery.
[2] Note this survival of the old Teutonic term Mercia. Merse = mark, a frontier.

MEDIÆVAL WARFARE 133

were pushed continuously backwards, further and further into their mountain fastnesses. For as the Border Warfare continued, defence easily gave place to defiance, and many a successful English raid was conducted westward, up to the line of the river valleys.

In the southern March the story was precisely similar. We have seen that its traditions were Teutonic rather than Celtic, and the renown of south Pembrokeshire as " Little England beyond Wales " is supported not only by the Danish and Norse place-names already considered, but by such purely English names as Ludchurch, Loverton, Williamstown, Upton, Rosemarket, Barton, etc., marking the position of truly " English " villages. Early in the 12th century, when the sea overflowed large tracts of the Low Countries, forming the present Zuyder Zee, many of the refugees from the drowned lands came, homeless and destitute, to England, and were settled in this corner of Pembroke with the idea of increasing its commercial prosperity, these refugees being weavers. From the accession of the House of Anjou (1154) this lowland Pembroke was sharply distinguished from the highland or Welsh part, and definitely known as the *Englishry*, which could always be counted upon to maintain a stubborn and implacable hostility to the " Welshry." To further this end, Henry II imported soldiers from the Low Countries to this region, and to the weaving settlement of Flemings originally established was afterwards added English and Norman traders.

Here also this prosperous Marchland became a base of operations against the upland Welsh, and when Edward I ascended the throne of England (1272) all Wales, except that portion of North Wales known as the " Principality of Gwynedd " was in English hands.

This great king set about the final conquest, conducting it with much efficiency on the usual lines. The attack was made on Gwynedd by the northern lowland plain. At each point of his conquest Edward established "strong places," fitting them out with garrisons and military supplies. Conway, Criccieth, Carnarvon, Beaumaris, Harlech, falling successively into his hands, were thus made into military forts and occupied, castles to be presently erected upon their sites. The last stand of the resistance was in the district known as Snowdonia, within whose oak woods the Welsh kept their cattle, with Anglesey across the Menai Straits to provide them with corn. Finally King Edward summoned the fleet from the Cinque Ports to intercept the Anglesey assistance and the surrender became complete (1284). The "Act of Union" of Wales and England did not take place till much later —in the reign of Henry VIII (1536).

CHAPTER XIII

THE BATTLE OF LAND AND SEA
DISAPPEARANCE OF FOREST AND FEN

1. THE BATTLE OF LAND AND SEA

This great battle of land and sea has been raging since the beginning of time. So long as water has power to dissolve, rivers to lodge their contribution of land waste into the receiving shore waters, currents to transport, tides to ebb and flow, winds to hurl waves and wave-carried missiles against crumbling cliff or rocky headland, and, finally, while the great cosmic processes of upheaval and depression of vast areas are in continual operation, just so long will the water in this place defeat and overwhelm the land, and the land elsewhere lift its victorious head above the greedy sea.

The weapons of the combatants, collectively designated as the agents of construction and destruction, have not infrequently been at work over contiguous and sometimes successively coincident districts. The wearing away of the softer portions of cliffs to give "islets" off our headlands is a sufficiently common feature of our coasts to require no particular mention. In Roman times the marshes of the Wash extended far beyond the present-day coast line, but the scour of the tide has swept away that land over which King John and his baggage-train once adventured so fatally, and popular legends of wave-rung church bells and more authenticated records of submerged villages testify to the great encroachments of the sea.

Especially along our east and south-east coast has this destruction taken place. Tynemouth Priory, now in a perilous position on a steadily crumbling cliff, was built a mile at least inland. The peninsula of Holderness, whose soil is mainly composed of ice-carried boulders, sands and clays, and therefore offering little resistance to the disintegrating forces of the waves, has suffered very considerably in quite historic times. The villages of Auburn, Hartburn, Hyde, Owthorne, etc., are now remembered only by their names; Hornsea Church, a mile from the coast, is reputed to have been at one time ten miles inland. The services of Kilnsea Parish Church had to cease in 1823, and at Withernsea, the site of the old church is now beneath the water. Each year the sea robs the coast of Holderness of two yards of land, the shore line having travelled westward approximately two miles since the days of the Roman occupation. This shore waste is carried southwards by tides and currents, the clay choking the estuaries of the Humber and Wash, the stones and sands piling up on Spurn Head whose growth can be traced by the successive lighthouses that have had to be erected in consequence. There was the same victory of the sea in the Humber Estuary, and Ravenser, which sent Members to Parliament in the reign of Edward I, and Ravenserodd which paid the same king £300 (a very large sum in those days) for a charter, are so completely engulfed that their very sites are now unknown.

On the coasts of Norfolk and Suffolk we have the same story. Mention has already been made of the Wash area (again, however, in process of reclamation), and the shores of these two counties are prolific in "drowned" settlements. Conspicuous among the latter is "old" Dunwich, once one of the chief ports of England. It was famous in Roman times, but even then troubled by inroads from the sea. It was

THE BATTLE OF LAND AND SEA 137

once a "Bishop's See," the metropolis of Eastern Anglia, containing both Royal and Episcopal palaces. Early in the 11th century the town was inundated, but was rebuilt by the Normans, and even succeeded in regaining much of its old importance, and until the 13th century the King relied for ships on Dunwich. But it suffered badly in the tempest of 1289, and was finally wrecked by a great storm in 1329. Four hundred houses and forty churches are said to have been swept away by the ocean. Now all that is left of " old " Dunwich is a church on the cliff with a ruined monastery behind.

A similar fate overtook "old" Winchelsea and other villages on the Sussex coast. Winchelsea was overwhelmed by the sea in the reign of Edward I (1288). To reclaim the coast the Romans, much earlier, had built a dyke between Dymchurch and Romney.

On the West the gain of the sea on the land has been slower, owing to the harder nature of the rock, which was sufficiently resistant to supply the coast with a protection of high and not easily weathered cliffs. Still, the Atlantic surges are very powerful and the rainfall high, so that, even here, some damage is being done. In the lowlands dividing Wales from the Cumbrian Mountains there has been much loss to the sea, probably through some coastal movement. North of Liverpool lies a submerged forest, visible at low tide as an area of peat in which tree trunks are still standing and which, dipping beneath the broad waters of the Mersey Estuary, reappears on the opposite shores of the Wirral Peninsula. Much of this submerged land was forest as late as Norman times. In this region the land is again gaining on the sea, as the uprising of the buried floor of the forest proves. At

Southport, in the present generation, the sea has receded to such an extent that in order to keep up the "holiday" reputation of this place, the authorities have constructed two great lakes upon the shore, as if to remind holiday-makers at low tide that the water is really not far away. The meeting of high tides from opposite directions has resulted in the piling up of sand in the former estuary of the Dee, so that there are large extents of reed-grown flats where waves once rolled, and in consequence Chester has quite lost its value as a seaport.

Further south there is a tradition that Cardigan Bay was a stretch of low-lying land extending westward to the 20-fathom line, and that its loss occurred in the 5th century; remains of Neolithic man and contemporaneous tree trunks are frequently dredged up from what was apparently a belt of woodland now submerged, but once extending round Carmarthen Bay. At certain states of wind and tide the sea still overflows inland along portions of these low coasts.

On the other hand, the tides have contributed to the building up of land along our southern shores. Those which sweep *up* the English Channel are very much stronger than those which pass into it from the North Sea. Hence there is a steady drive of the shingle eastward which the westward-flowing tide cannot counteract.[1] This has resulted in the building up of shingle bars and promontories in certain localities where natural barriers have arrested the eastward progress. Among the numerous gains accruing to the land in historic times there are a few of pre-eminent

---

[1] The tides entering the English Channel from the West may be said to " originate " in the open ocean, whereas those entering it from the North originated in this same open ocean about twenty-four hours earlier, and have lost much of their strength during the passage through the shallow North Sea.

THE BATTLE OF LAND AND SEA 139

interest. The ridge known to-day as " Chesil" (that is " Stony ") Beach has thus been built up, whereby Portland Island has been converted into a peninsula. The two islands now united and known as Selsey Bill[1] stood some little distance off Porchester (Portsmouth), Beachy Head did not then possess its present sharp outline, and the shingle promontories off Langley Point (off Pevensey Level) and Dungeness had not accumulated, the Romney " marsh " area existing as a sheet of water with an island barrier affording safe anchorage. But even then the lagoon was already doomed, continuous collection of shingle round the islands and the steady deposition of silt where the Rother entered the protected waters being causes simultaneous and related. The inlet was perceptibly reduced at the time of the Norman Conquest, and the draining of the marsh went on steadily. The seaward extension of Dungeness had reached one and a half miles early in the 18th century, but since then there has been a cutting back reducing it to half-a-mile. Parts of this area have now to be protected from inundation by artificial dyking, e.g., from Appledore to Romney.

The former greatness of the ports of Rye, Dover, Sandwich, etc., illustrates further the gain of the land on the sea. The early 13th century was a period of violent atmospheric disturbances resulting in tremendous storms and gales ; river mouths were choked, harbours silted and shingle bars rapidly accumulated. By the 15th century many of the smaller ports were practically abandoned, and by the 17th century some of the larger ones had become mere fishing villages

---

[1] But the varying fortunes of the battle can be better appreciated when it is remembered that Selsey was once the seat of a cathedral, now " drowned."

or were now definitely inland. Among these latter may be mentioned Sandwich, once the most famous port in the Kingdom, now rising into new fame on account of its golf-links—a factor which tells its own tale. Other vanished ports are Hythe and Romney, which had replaced Portus Lemanis, at or near modern Lympne, and Hastings, which had replaced Pevensey, which in its turn had replaced Roman Anderida as a natural harbour. In this category also belong the "ancient" towns of Rye and Winchelsea, which grew up on islands in the west of the Romney inlet, and which together with Romney and Hythe, are now lying inland at distances varying from half to two miles. "Old" Winchelsea, indeed, was overwhelmed by the sea in 1288, and "New" Winchelsea, which continued its traditions, was at the time of the catastrophe on the top of a flat cliff above the sea, and this is the town which is now two miles inland.

The history of the rise and decline of Hastings is no less interesting. Originally two valleys, approaching at the mouth, gave a tidal haven of a mile and a half of sheltered water. The first site of the settlement was at the mouth of the now submerged west valley. As the sea washed back the headlands silt was thrown across the harbour entrance rendering the situation impossible. The population migrated to the east arm, but owing to constant silting the use of Hastings as a natural harbour was completely gone by the reign of Elizabeth. The town then existed as a mere fishing village until its modern development as a seaside resort.

Dover was a well-known Roman and Teutonic port, but there was very early silting of the Dour estuary and its importance to-day is merely artificial and strategic. In the 13th century a harbour was

THE BATTLE OF LAND AND SEA 141

constructed; in the 15th a sea-wall, but there were constant periods when the harbour was in disrepair—there is always a great amount of cliff erosion coupled with the tendency of the shingle to pile up in piers. When the sea-wall was broken it was the custom for the Mayor to summon every householder by drum to come with his spade to the repair. Further north the headlands which once made Herne Bay a real bay have been completely washed away. The Goodwin Sands, which once formed part of Earl Godwin's mainland estate, were overwhelmed by the sea in 1099.

When the Romans came to Britain Wantsum Strait separated the Isle of Thanet from the mainland and at its north and south issues stood the Roman ports of Regulbium (Reculver) and Rutupiae (Richborough) which latter had an outpost at Ramsgate. The River Stour, then tidal to Canterbury, contributed its quota to the in-falling of the channel. Several small ports sprang up on this reclaimed area, of which Sandwich, which developed on the south bank of the Stour, is perhaps the most noted. It originally had an excellent harbour, and controlled the London trade. Deposits of sand, not shingle, forced the Stour further and further north. The port declined after the 13th century and, as we have seen, the sand makes famous golf-links to-day.

At the present day attempts are made to arrest the eastward travelling of the shingle by the practice of " groyning " the shore. Thus from Sandgate to Folkestone the groynes divide the beach into a series of parallel strips which are nearly level with the top of the barrier on its western, but considerably below it on the eastern side. The local authorities can then deal with any section of the shore as occasion requires.

The tide that sweeps up the English Channel,

after leaving the Straits of Dover, advances along the Continental coasts leaving our eastern shores to be influenced mainly by the southward-flowing tide. The history of the north-eastern corner of Norfolk is a repetition of that of Romney Marsh. Here, when Caesar came to Britain, stretched a great bay fringed seaward by islands upon which the tide and currents could heap up large quantities of water-borne detritus, while the Yare and other rivers poured their load of silt into the ever shallowing lagoon.

Spurn Head, at the southern extremity of the coast of Yorkshire, resembles Chesil Beach in being a ridge built up by the sea from the débris of the coast of Holderness. The growth of this natural dyke affords protection to the mouth of the Humber, and has been very beneficial in the rise to greatness of the port of Hull. Part of this débris, however, is driven into the Humber, where it forms shifting banks, while the rivers entering the estuary also contribute their quota of sediment, and the Humber would probably be choked with sand and mud were not a channel kept clear by constant dredging. The old *port* of Hedon is now two miles from the estuary waters, and cattle graze over tracts that once were busy dockyards. "Sunk Island," part of the south-west projection of Holderness, a fertile tract of more than 6,000 acres, was once but a sand-bank, as its name seems to testify.

2. THE DISAPPEARANCE OF FOREST AND WOODLAND

In the earliest days of our history about three-fourths of the surface of England was covered with morass, wood, thicket and scrub, harbouring wolves and other wild beasts dangerous to a people deficient in the possession and knowledge of the use of implements. It should be kept in mind, however, that our use of the word "forest" is incorrect, for the British

THE BATTLE OF LAND AND SEA 143

woodlands were at no time dense forests in the Continental meaning of the term.

During the Roman occupation the British woodlands were roughly defined in eight or nine great areas which, using modern nomenclature for purposes of identification, may be detailed as follows :

1. The thickly forested areas beyond the Thames marshes, harbouring the bear, wild boar, wild ox. These forests enclosed the vast marshes extending from Fulham to Greenwich, nine to ten miles long and two to two and a half broad. The marshes and forest made a very adequate protection for the original site of London on firm upland rising from the morass. (Ludgate and Tower Hills.)

2. Down to the date of the Norman Conquest, Essex was almost entirely forest, Epping Forest is a very diminished survival, and Hainault Forest, a little to the south-east of Epping, is now a great crop-growing area.'

3. Most of present Sussex, and a considerable portion of Kent and Hampshire was occupied by the Anderida Silva of the Romans—the Andrea's Weald of the Saxons—the "Weald" (Teutonic wald = woodland) of our own day. This woodland, though it later afforded a protection for King Alfred in the times of the Danes, and appeared to have formed an impassable barrier by the earlier Saxon and Jute invaders was nevertheless crossed in its day by a Roman road, and contained much waste and heathland upon its outcrops of sandy soil. The Venerable Bede (673 to 735) left it on record that the Weald was "thick and inaccessible—the abode of deer, swine and wolves." This weald was originally a hundred and twenty miles by thirty; this woodland was exhausted for fuel purposes in connection with the iron-smelting industry between the 13th and mid-eighteenth centuries.

4. Wiltshire, Dorsetshire, and other southern counties contained extensive woodlands. The New Forest, a very small remnant of the original Wiltshire and Hampshire "Forests," contains, and always must have contained a large proportion of heath and waste land.

5. The shires of Warwick, Northampton and Leicester might almost have been described as an extensive and continuous stretch of woodland.

6. Nearly all Nottinghamshire was forested (Sherwood Forest) and this woodland passed well into Yorkshire, e.g., Elmet Forest round Leeds.

7. Derbyshire was a very extensively wooded county. Besides the Forest of the Peak it contained fifty-four other tracts of forest-land.

8. Lancashire forest was really wilderness, and "forest" and woodland occupied one quarter of its million acres. Between the Mersey and the Ribble the land was covered with a network of separate and dense woods.

9. The scrublands of the Shropshire area were very little investigated by the Romans, being debatable frontier ground in which the British (Celtic) power was still strong. They were acquainted with the forests in the lower plains of the Dee, and with the Forest of Dean in Gloucestershire.

During the Middle Ages these broad areas of woodland became more accurately differentiated, and a classification involving these mediæval and modern names will perhaps be instructive. It would not be possible, however, to enumerate all the forest lands of Britain, and consequently a few examples must suffice to indicate their one-time wide extent.

THE FORESTS AND WOODLANDS OF NORTHERN ENGLAND

Inglewood Forest in Cumberland; Pendle Forest

THE BATTLE OF LAND AND SEA 145

in Lancashire; Sherwood Forest, in which wolves lurked as late as the days of Robin Hood, and of which remains are to be found to-day in the "Dukeries"; the Forest of Knaresborough, between the rivers Wharfe and Nidd, 160 square miles in extent, during the Middle Ages; the Forest of East Yorkshire, between the Ouse and Derwent, of which fragments remain in Escrick Bank; the Forest of Galtres north of York between Aldbrough and Crayke; Elmet Forest in the neighbourhood of Leeds; the Forests of Wensley Dale, Pickering, Skipton, Bolland, etc., also in Yorkshire.

THE FORESTS AND WOODLANDS OF CENTRAL ENGLAND

Wirral Forest, extending from Chester to the sea; Delamere Forest, from the Mersey to the Dee; Clee Forest; Macclesfield Forest between Cheshire and Derbyshire, and contiguous to the Peak Forest; Needwood Forest, from the Peak to the Trent Valley; Charnwood Forest in Leicester; Cannock Chase; Forest of Arden in Warwickshire; Forests of Holdenby and Rockingham, the latter of which lay between the Nen and Welland; Yardley Chase between Watling and Erming Streets; Forest of Wyre, in Worcester; the Forests of Feckenham, Ombersley, Horewell and Malvern in the Middle Ages more or less made up the County of Worcestershire; Derby (Danish) signified "Place of the Deer." The Peak Forest was Royal hunting ground, and, as we have seen, the wooded county contained fifty-four other small forests.

THE FORESTS AND WOODLANDS OF SOUTHERN ENGLAND

Essex was largely woodland, Epping and Hainault being its chief forests. Regarding the latter the original name was Hainhault, but may have been connected with Hainault in the Low Countries. Edward III, whose Queen was Philippa of Hainault,

K

established Flemings in the neighbourhood of London in connection with the weaving industry. This forest, three miles from Romford, was south-east of Epping Forest and separated from it by the Roding Valley. It harbours the famous Fairlop Oak, under which a fair was held for centuries. The trees were cut down about the middle of the nineteenth century, when this ancient forest became arable land.

Other forests of southern England were—the Forest of Dean in Gloucester, the Forest of the Weald, mainly in Kent and Sussex, the New Forest, and a great northern extension in the Hampshire Basin, including the Royal Forests of Bere, Savernake, and Windsor; Selwood Forest, separating Somerset and Wilts, with the outlying Royal Forests of Kingswood (Bath) and the Mendips, and Exmoor, still further west.

So much of this ancient woodland has been cleared that it is no longer easy to estimate either its nature or its extent. However, the Anglo-Saxons, in the later stages of their "colonization," frequently chose names for their villages having reference to the nature of its site, and in this way something of the former conditions can be learnt. Taking Yorkshire, then heavily wooded, as an example, such names are found as Oakworth, Ackworth, Ackton, in districts where the prepondering woodland was probably oak. Escrick, Esholt, Eshton recall ash trees; Allerton, Allerston, Ellesburn, perhaps Ellerby (Danish) were settlements near alder groves. Beeches, birches, poplars, hazels, lime or linden trees are represented by such place-names as Buckrose, Bugthorpe (Danish), Poppleton, Hazelwood, Lindley; Appleton, Appletreewick, recall a useful fruit, and thickets of thorn and brambles no doubt made good defences for little communities

THE BATTLE OF LAND AND SEA 147

living at Thorn, Thorner, Thornton, Bramham, Bramhope. No doubt ferns grew in great profusion at Farnley; Harewood, Cawood, Meanwood, Fulwood, Woodhouse tell their own tale. Ley (Angle) thwaite (Danish and Norse) means a clearing in a wood, and finds adequate representation in Barnsley, Batley, Headingley, Shipley, Braithwaite, Hampsthwaite, Synningthwaite, etc. Royd, a place *rid* of trees. -cup, -holt (Esholt, Holtby) -hurst, signify a coppice; -shaw, a shady place; -den (Rippenden, Denby, Howden), a wooded valley.

In Kent it is the same story. From the Ordnance Survey Map of the Croydon district the following may be selected: Oakley, Oxted, Elmstead, Ash, Kingswood, Woodcote, Woodside, Norwood, Swanley, Hartley, Farley, Henley, Farningham, Farnborough, Farnham, Hockenden, Mussenden, Timberden, Ramsden, Cockerhurst, Chislehurst, Pickhurst, Selhurst, Hurst, Knockholt, Holtwood—a very few examples of the total list in this small area of Kent alone.

Sometimes the tradition of woodland is lost by the gradual, and probably quite unintentional alteration of the place-name. Thus the " Hundred of Manhood," near Selsey, is really " Mainwood," the formerly forested area of the Selsey Plain.

In the Middle Ages a forest usually belonged to the Crown and a chase to a private individual, and it is quite possible that the latter may have contained by far the greater (relative) number of trees.

Deforestation began with the Roman occupation though their work in this respect was slight with the area of the country and the woodland remaining. The rise of the iron-smelting industry in the 13th century gave the death-blow to our forests, as their trees were needed for fuel (charcoal) in the smelting operations. In course of time much timber was also required for shipbuilding, and steps were taken to protect the forest, with this end in view, at least as far as the central woodlands were concerned. In the reign of Elizabeth (1568) an Act of Parliament was passed forbidding iron-smelting within fourteen miles of the coast, but by the 18th century England was very generally deforested, a few " samples " only remaining. In this respect both our climate and soil may have materially suffered, for the presence of woodland is known to make for a more even distribution of rainfall, and for a protection to the underlying soil against being washed away by fierce rains and their gathering rills ; indirectly river navigation has also been adversely affected, owing to the silting of streams through this cause.

3. THE DISAPPEARANCE OF MARSH AND FEN

Before the days of systematic draining and embanking many of our rivers were bordered by swamps and marshes. The Thames Estuary may be quoted as a good example, the marshes of Greenwich, Plumstead, Erith, Dartford, Stone and Swanscombe on the right bank, and those of Aveley, West and Little Thurrock, Chadwell and Tilbury on the left bank still testifying in more than name to the incompleteness of the riverine reclamation. The marshes of the River Severn once extended far towards the foot of the Welsh mountains, forming a very effective barrier between the wild British tribes and the spreading Roman civilization. This marsh land, the river's flood-plain, has now through silting and drainage become the "fruit garden" of England.

The River Parret in Somerset once flowed sluggishly through a wide sedge-grown marsh, now reclaimed and known as "Sedgemoor." Athelney "island"

THE BATTLE OF LAND AND SEA 149

represented firm ground in the formerly wide-extending morass between the rivers Tone and Parret and which was, in fact, on occasion invaded by the sea. Sedgemoor to-day would be a dreary fen were it not protected by dams, and when the rivers are in flood Athelney again becomes the "island" in whose security King Alfred once found refuge.

The Mersey marshes, between the Cheshire woodlands and that river formerly occupied a width of forty miles between the Pennines and the sea. In this wilderness of quaking mosses and wooded swamp, a feature repeated in much of the Lancashire lowlands further north, the Roman military station of Mancunium was fittingly situated on an outcrop of hard rock rising conspicuously above the treacherous surface.

Romney Marsh, in Kent, to the east of the Rother, had a limited existence as true fenland. In A.D. 893 the Danish fleet sailed up the "marsh" to Appledore, over an area to-day supporting more sheep for its size than any other district of Kent—in itself our sheep-rearing county *par excellence*.

From Norwich to Liverpool, from Lynn at the mouth of the Great Ouse formerly extended a great uncultivated belt of marsh and morass separating the northern counties from the midland districts and making an effective frontier to the old kingdom of Mercia. Beyond the eastern extremity of this belt lay a wide region of swamps, quagmires, small lakes and "broads," nearly two and a half thousand square miles, and covering much of the present counties of Cambridge, Huntingdon, Northampton, Lincoln, Norfolk and Suffolk, of which the three words "fog," "fish" and "fen" epitomized the chief characteristics. The prevailing marsh was broken here and there by outcrops of harder, higher and drier ground, or by "islands" of gravel upon which, in remote ages, primitive man found a home.[1] The Romans seem to have made some endeavour to reclaim, or at least control the Lincolnshire fens, and tradition ascribes to them the construction of the Foss Dyke between Lincoln on the Witham and Torksey on the Trent to intercept water from the heights which otherwise would have frequently inundated the level. This dyke fell into disrepair during the Anglo-Saxon period, but Henry I (1121) had it restored and perhaps improved for both navigation and drainage. Another drainage dyke, the Car Dyke, also of reputed Roman construction, began near Peterborough and ran to within a few miles of Lincoln.

While the rivers in this region have to be prevented from flooding by an elaborate system of drainage, the area has also to be protected from the invasion of the sea. The Romans attempted this by means of sea dykes, one of which, 150 miles long and still 10 feet high, ran from Gedsey Marsh near the Norfolk border to the Welland and then to Swineshead. Others were erected along the east coast from the mouth of the Witham to Mablethorpe,[2] and were known as "The Old Sea Dyke," "Sand Hills," etc. Roman roads are often to be found upon them.

From the departure of the Romans to the establishment of the monasteries probably nothing was done in connection with the draining of the Fen district, and the next step in the reclamation must be put down to those ecclesiastical institutions. Monastic buildings came to be erected on high, dry ground. Cambridge, Peterborough, Bury St. Edmunds, Crowland are

[1] Ey, Ea, Teutonic affix for "island" in sea, river or marsh.
[2] Mablethorpe—Magh-bulg (Great Bend ?)

THE BATTLE OF LAND AND SEA

examples, and the monks taught the people how to drain and cultivate the marsh land—a process sometimes good for the peasant, but even more advantageous for the monastery which owned so much of this otherwise waste land. Monastic buildings also sprang up on the gravel "islands," Ely (= Eley), Thorney, Whittlesea, Eastrea, Ramsey, and in due time towns—Ely, March, Spalding, etc.—followed in their wake, but it was not until the modern period that the drainage of the area as a whole was systematically and seriously taken in hand.

[In 1629 Parliament appointed a Commission of Sewers to investigate the flood dangers in the Fen district and the Commission invited a certain Dutch engineer, Cornelius Vermuyden by name, to suggest some adequate draining scheme. The Commission came to nothing through lack of funds and the matter was then taken up by private enterprise. The lands of the Thorney Monastery were owned by the Earl of Bedford, who persuaded other landlords of the district to subscribe the money for the purpose of carrying out Vermuyden's plans. The Dutch engineer brought workmen from Holland—a very natural proceeding inasmuch as that heroic nation had already mastered this identical problem. The "Bedford River" was then cut to relieve the Ouse, but as it did not reach the sea, the results fell very far below their anticipation. There were other difficulties. The Fenmen objected to this introduction of foreign labour, the more so as it was likely to destroy their fowling and fishing grounds; they broke the dykes and attacked Vermuyden's men. Their opposition found a support in a certain squire of Huntingdon, known as Oliver Cromwell, and the work was completely stopped. After the opening of the Civil War the Earl of Bedford resumed his enterprise, with Vermuyden still in charge of the operations. The danger in the political situation, which carried Cromwell to so high a destiny, perhaps assisted to revise his opinion, and he was now in active favour of the scheme which accordingly was brought to a prosperous issue. More than forty thousand acres of territory were reclaimed thus and became fertile corn and pasture lands. The drainage was not completed, however, till 1831, when Rennie and Telford succeeded in obtaining a new outlet to the Wash for the river Nen.[1] Whittlesea mere was not drained until 1854].

The Norfolk Broads, perhaps to be regarded as a type of lake, belong to this category. They may be regarded as marshes in the making. They are formed by the silting up of the main channels of rivers once reaching the sea as estuaries. They are of no great antiquity. Even as late as the time of the Saxons, Norwich was on an estuary. The silting of the mouth of the Yare furnished a sand-bank upon which Yarmouth now stands, but which did not become sufficiently firm to support human dwellings till 1008. The channel called " Grubbs Haven " at that time separated Yarmouth "island" from Caistor but the haven was silted up in the reign of Edward III. The rivers flowing into this area swell out into the shallow freshwater lakes (the Broads), sometimes in the direct course of the streams, frequently alongside, but separated by banks of reeds and rushes, sedges and watergrass. The rapid growth of marsh plants is contributing very largely to the refilling of these broads by peat formation, which in some future age will afford, by draining or removal, tracts of good, fertile ground.

[1] Note, the river known as the " Old Nen."

THE BATTLE OF LAND AND SEA

The rate of this infilling is said to be one foot in twenty years.

Somewhat separated from this low country are the marshes along the coast of Lincoln extending from Louth to Great Grimsby, and in former times the fen-land ringing the Humber head in both counties of Lincoln and York, lying between the Trent and the lower windings of the Ouse and hugging the shore to Hull, offered an interior area of hard ground midway between the Humber and Gainsborough, known as the "Island of Axholme." Like Ely, Axholme (holme = wooded island) has also served its turn as an unassailable refuge against the pursuit of a conqueror. The region between the Ouse and Humber, and known as the Louth (or Low Ground) was marsh until the 18th century. Hatfield Chase, some seventy thousand acres between the rivers Idle, Don, and Torne was fen until the reign of Charles II (1660-1685). The fen south-east of Goole is still called "Marshland." The road from Beverley to Hull was marked by willows—a tree of the marshes—while such names as Hubberholme, Hipperholme, Sandholme, Saltmarsh, Broomfleet (or flood), Willerby, Marishes Road (in the Vale of Pickering), Fenton, Mars(h)ton, Marton, etc., prove the former extent of the swamps in the East Riding. Sledmere, Sand-le-Mere, and similar names testify to other localities formerly marsh in this country, in which the Hornsea Mere is alone left unconquered to-day.

SECTION III

THE MIDDLE AGES—II
(5TH TO 15TH CENTURY)

THE DEVELOPMENT OF TRADE AND INDUSTRY

CHAPTER XIV

THE INDUSTRIES OF THE MIDDLE AGES

I

THE HISTORY OF MINING AND SMELTING

[FROM very early times iron, tin, copper, lead, and silver ores were mined and quarried in South Britain. Julius Caesar recorded that iron ore was found on the coast in small quantities, and that the metal was used for currency (the "bar" money of the Ancient Britons). The Romans put the metal to a more effective use, and ironworks speedily sprang up in all parts of the country. The reduction of the ore was effected by charcoal, so that smelting operations were carried on in the vicinity of woodland. Rhyddlan (Flintshire), the Forest of Dean, and other parts of Gloucestershire, Yorkshire, South-West Britain, Sussex, contain extensive traces in enormous deposits of cinder and slag, in which Roman coins and relics are found embedded, pointing to the ironworking activities of this period.]

From the 5th century until the reign of Edward the Confessor (1042-1066) there are no traces of iron workings. The Domesday Book records that at the time of the Conquest horseshoes and ships' bolts were made at Gloucester, that Hereford contained six smiths, each of whom made annually one hundred and twenty horseshoes for the King, and that "iron-mines" existed on the border of Cheshire and in Sussex.

During the 12th century the industry greatly expanded, and this largely through the work of the monasteries. Iron mines were granted to the monks of St. Bees, and various ecclesiastical "houses" were given not only smithies, but the right to cut fuel to feed their forges. The iron of Hallamshire began to be worked in the reign of Henry II (1154-1189), the confluence of the Rivers Sheaf and Don providing a site calculated eventually to make Hallamshire iron goods world-famous through the water power available to operate the tilt hammers.

But in this country the greatest development of the industry was in the Forest of Dean (a Plantagenet Birmingham), where iron bars, nails, picks, hammers, etc., were made to be sent from the port of Gloucester to wherever the monarch's extensive building operations were in progress. Here, in addition, horseshoes were made for the army, and arrow-heads for our " expeditionary forces " in France. At the close of the 12th century there were sixty itinerant forges in blast in this region, which as far as the southern counties were concerned, retained its practical monopoly of the English iron trade.

But a rival, and a successful one, was growing up in the Weald of Sussex and Kent. In 1254 the Sheriff of the former county was called upon to provide thirty thousand horseshoes and sixty thousand nails for the Government requirements. The Wealden works had the advantage of a short water-passage to London, for the heavy iron goods, and it soon obtained a footing in the London markets—its output being effectively increased after 1256 by the additional use of imported Spanish ore.

In the 14th century Furness and Cleveland became quite important centres of the iron-smelting industries. The forty forges working for the Abbey of Furness (built *c.* 1271-1300) made weapons for the Border warfare, but in 1316 all the northern iron was utilized for local needs only; small amounts of iron were

INDUSTRIES OF THE MIDDLE AGES 159

obtained from Northamptonshire, Rutlandshire and Derbyshire (Duffield). The iron mills of Sussex were not established until the 16th century on account of the badness of the roads over the Weald clay. In Sussex were cast the first cannon and mortar made in England. From 1540 the manufacture of heavy ordnance so increased that our export trade became possible. Church bells, fire-backs and tombstones are other examples of the Sussex iron trade.

Until 1720 charcoal was in use for the smelting and consequently the possession of workable iron ore in any district meant the deforestation of its neighbouring woodland. The Government was long in realizing the danger of this reckless destruction of timber, especially needed for shipbuilding, but in 1568 an Act was passed permitting no iron-smelting within fourteen miles of the coast. This naturally brought a decline to the Sussex iron industry, which finally ceased in the 17th century. Moreover, the discovery of the superior advantages of " pit-coal " in smelting operations (1720) resulted in the emigration of the industry to the coal-fields, South Wales and the Black Country becoming its new and greatest centres.

The iron industry has died out in Kent and Sussex, but the various phases of its former existence are recorded in many a place-name of the Wealden district. Thus "Cold Harbour" recalls the cold water required for washing the ore. Cooling Street may have reference to the tempering process and not to the tribal name of any Teutonic invader. A " bloom " was an ingot of iron, a " bloomer," the local name for a smith, and the village of " Bloomfield " tells us where at least one forge was set up. These " iron " villages are typical among the " hursts " of Kent and Sussex, Kilndown near Lamberthurst being but one example, while "Hammer Stream" flows through Sissinghurst, showing how intimately the iron industry was formerly bound up with a well-watered, wooded country. In Sussex, within ten miles of East Grinstead, are to be found such significant names as "Furnace Pond," "Forge Pond," "Wirewell Pond," "Hammer Pond," "Caseiron," "Shovel-Strode," "Horseshoe Farm," etc.

COAL

[The possibilities of coal as a domestic fuel were early recognized. The shafts of Roman coal mines are found in various parts of the country and notably along the Northumbrian coast from Warkworth to Coquet Isle.] Its utility, however, was very limited, and not until 1228 did London receive any import of this most useful fuel.

London coal probably came from Blythe (Northumberland), and since it was brought by sea it was known as "sea-coal," to distinguish it from charcoal. It seems to have been warehoused in "Sea-Coal Lane," pending its use for the lime burning required for cement making in connection with the building of the Tower. Sea-Coal Lane (London) had accordingly the alternative name of "Lime-Burners Lane."

About this time Commissioners were appointed to enquire into the value of the coal that could be obtained from the Forest of Dean (1244), Forest of Clee (1260), and certain parts of Derbyshire and Nottinghamshire (Duffield Frith, 1257). This coal, wherever obtained, kept the distinguishing name of sea-coal. It was mainly used by smiths and lime-burners, but in the construction of feudal castles and ecclesiastical buildings at the time of and subsequent to the Norman Period sea-coal was used for work which could not be efficiently done with wood and charcoal firing.

INDUSTRIES OF THE MIDDLE AGES 161

The smoke arising from using coal as a domestic fuel in those days of open hearths and no chimneys drove Queen Eleanor from Nottingham Castle, and in the 16th century brewers and dyers in London were forbidden to use coal in their trades on account of the smoke nuisance.

By the end of the 13th century practically all the English coal-fields were worked to a small extent, but it was not until the reign of Queen Elizabeth, when the difficulty of obtaining wood for household fuel was becoming very great, that the use of coal crept from the forge to the kitchen and the hall. The Queen herself, however, objected to its use in this respect, but her successor, accustomed to the coal fires of " Auld Reekie " (Edinburgh) caused coal to be brought for fires in his own rooms at Westminster Palace.

The mineral rights of coal mining were exceedingly various. At Bolsover, for example, the tenants of the manor might dig for " sea-coal " for their own use in waste and forest land; at Wakefield a fine was exacted for this right. In copyhold lands the lord of the manor or his farmer could dig for this mineral without the necessity of compensating tenants who lived on the surface of the suspected coal-fields!

TIN MINING.

[Tin Mining is generally regarded, but perhaps on somewhat slight authority, as the most ancient of all our industries. The Cassiterides or Tin Islands visited by the Phoenicians about 500 B.C. may have been parts of Britain (Cornwall and Devon or the Scilly Islands or the Outer Hebrides, as the latest geographers assert), or on the other hand, they may not.]

Certainly the tin mines of Cornwall were neglected by the Romans, who did not waste time in exploiting the difficult lands of " Upper Britain," nor is tin mentioned in the Domesday Book. From the 12th century onwards, however, much is heard about the tin-mining in our West Country.

Tin occurs in veins or lodes, and at times rises to the surface. Weathering with the enveloping rock the particles may drop into a stream. The high specific gravity (or great heaviness) of tin in its ores causes it to sink speedily to the bed of the stream, whereas the lighter particles of clay are carried along much further. This "stream tin" is also known as "alluvial tin," and the deposit may be as much as twenty feet thick. Alluvial tin was "mined" in prehistoric and later mediæval times.

The tinner's value as a miner was fully recognized, so that he came under special protective laws. He could not be subjected to villeinage (that is, required to give forced labour) and was a "free" man. Except in churchyards, gardens, and on highways, he could prospect for the coveted ore anywhere in Cornwall and Devon. He merely staked out his claim by cutting shallow holes and piling turf at its four corners, which then became his own property so long as he paid his lord a certain tribute of ore. He might divert streams for ore-washing, dig in their beds, and compel landowners to sell him fuel for his furnace. The Black Death (1348) put an end to his prosperity owing to the new labour laws entailed by the resulting dearth of labourers. The tinning industry did not recover until the close of the mediæval period.

[Cornish copper was not worked until late in the 16th century.]

LEAD AND SILVER MINING

The beginnings of lead mining in England were probably coeval with iron mining, but the ore was not worked for silver till the Middle Ages.

INDUSTRIES OF THE MIDDLE AGES 163

[Roman workings have been identified in the Mendips, where pigs of lead, bearing the stamp of Britannicus (A.D. 44-48) and Claudius (A.D. 49) have been found. Roman hearths for smelting lead have also been discovered at Minsterley (Shropshire) and Matlock (Derbyshire).]

As usual during the main part of the Anglo-Saxon period there are no traces of lead mining, but as late as 835 the lead mines of Wirksworth in Derbyshire were leased by the *Abbess* of Ripton, while lead was worked in Gloucester in 882. The Domesday Book alludes to Edward the Confessor's mines at Bakewell, Ashford, Hope, Wirksworth, Mettesford and Crich—all in Derbyshire.

In the 12th century the lead-mining industry was becoming quite vigorous, the mining of Carlisle (Alston Moor on the borders of Cumberland, Northumberland and Yorkshire) was greatly flourishing, while the lead of Derbyshire, carried to Boston and thence shipped to London and the Continent, has had a continuous prosperity unapproached by the lead-mining of any other part of the country. The silver-lead mines of Shropshire were granted by King Stephen to the Bishop of Durham.

II

THE HISTORY OF QUARRYING

Quarrying operations first came into prominence in the late Norman and early Plantagenet period. The Roman walls, whether of frontier, town, castle, or villa, were generally of bricks, in the making of which these people were adepts, but the chalk for their exceedingly effective cement was probably obtained by excavations in such areas as to-day are said, somewhat mysteriously, to possess "caves." The natives used wood or mud and wattle in their domestic architecture, a practice followed by the Teutons. The earliest attempts at stone-quarrying on any large scale seem to be due to the enthusiasm of the monastic orders who desired to erect permanent buildings at least as far as their churches were concerned.

FREESTONE

The founders of the monasteries frequently made grants, either of existing quarries or of the right to dig stone in them. The quarries in Barnack—situated between the Welland and the Nen—were granted in this way to the Abbeys in the Fen district, Peterborough, Ramsey, Crowland, Bury St. Edmunds, and Sawtry, with results that violent quarrels took place over their respective rights. The material for Westminster Abbey and the Tower of London came from the quarries of Surrey.

CHALK

Kent, Surrey and Sussex furnished the chalk for the "lime-burning" in connection with the cement-making for the works in London and its neighbourhood. The so-called "caves" of Chislehurst and Guildford, and the Deneholes or Daneholes of Bostall Wood and elsewhere were probably excavations made for this purpose in earlier or Roman times, a purpose which would not prevent the hard-pressed Saxons at a later date from using these refuges against their dreaded foes.[1]

SLATES

Slates for roofing purposes were quarried as early as 1296 in Devon, Cornwall, Northampton (Collyweston) and Sussex (Horsham), while—

---

[1] Denehole would mean a hole found in a den or wooded valley—a description fitting these "caves" even at the present day.

INDUSTRIES OF THE MIDDLE AGES 165

BATH STONE

Bath Stone (notably from Wiltshire) was in great demand for ornamental tracery and image work.

PURBECK MARBLES

The Purbeck marbles, which take a high polish, were used extensively from the 13th to the 15th century. The stone was used in the cathedrals of Chichester, Dublin, and Durham (1205-1235). Corfe was the centre of this industry. The columns were generally constructed in the quarry works so that the effigies carved upon them are hardly likely to be actual portraits. The Eleanor Crosses[1] of Waltham, Northampton and Lincoln, were made of this material.

ALABASTER OR GYPSUM

Alabaster had a great, if temporary, renown for church mouldings and image making. Tutbury, whose Norman church contains mouldings in this material, was the cradle of the English industry, but by 1360 Nottingham had become the centre. Alabaster was quarried at Chellaston, in Derbyshire. The industry died out at the Reformation, which put an end to the demand for images and carved tables. When not suitable for carving, the gypsum was converted by burning into Plaster of Paris, or ordinary builders' plaster according to the fineness of the material.

FULLER'S EARTH

Our supply of Fuller's Earth is somewhat limited. Nutfield and Reigate are the main sources in the South-Eastern counties. In the West Country it lies between the Inferior and Great Oolite, the most extensive and

---

[1] Queen of Edward I. She died at Lincoln, and her body was brought to London for burial. Wherever the coffin rested a night on the journey, a monumental cross was afterwards built. Buried at Westminster Abbey, Charing Cross records the last stage of her journey.

valuable area being in the neighbourhood of Bath. Other less valuable beds occur near Cirencester and Stroud. In Wiltshire good supplies of this material were obtained from the green sands in the neighbourhood of Haddington. Its use in the woollen industry and for bleaching calico made it valuable, and owing to its scarcity its exportation was forbidden—without, however, much effect. In the Middle Ages the Cloth Industry of the West Country was hardly in existence, so that Nutfield and Reigate were then the chief sources of the supplies of Fuller's Earth.

SALT

" Rock Salt " was not worked in England until 1670, and so does not come into the category of mediæval industries, but salt obtained from sea-water and brine springs held a recognized place in mediæval commerce. The first record of this " commodity of prime necessity " appears late in the Anglo-Saxon period when King Archibald of Mercia (716-717) granted the monks of Worcester Cathedral a piece of land on the right bank of the Severn for salt works, and King Cynewulf (774-778) granted the Bishop and Monks of Sherborne a " salt pan " situated on the west bank of the River Lyme. Worcester and Cheshire are the two chief areas mentioned in the Domesday Book. Along the coast the precious mineral was obtained by evaporating sea water, inland by boiling the water of the brine springs. The old English word for salt was wych or wick (probably akin to the Danish wich, a creek, whether on coast or river), and in the Domesday Book it is recorded that the right to use the salt springs of Nantwich, Middlewich or Northwich had to be paid for by dues to the King and the Mercian Earl. Droitwich was the centre of the salt industry in the Middle Ages, during which period, the town of Worcester excepted, salt extraction was the only extensive industry of the shire.

III

THE HISTORY OF CERTAIN ARTS AND CRAFTS

METAL-WORKING

As is usual in the Middle Ages, it was the Church that "mothered" the industry of which we first hear in connection with bell-making. There are some vague references to bells in the closing years of the Anglo-Saxon period, but the industry did not become prominent until the latter part of the 11th century. Bell founders were called "Bellyters," and the London centre became located in Billiter Street. Another great centre for bell-making was Norwich, with its seventy churches and Cathedral Priory. Early cannon were made of a bronze similar to bell-metal. *Chimes* were introduced into Kent in the 16th century. Metal working also entered into domestic economy, pewter ware, or "fine tin" and silver plate being in great demand—by the wealthy—for such household utensils as salt-cellars, drinking cups, basins, plates. A Venetian merchant, writing in 1500, records his impressions of the London metal-ware thus : " In one street named the Strand are 52 goldsmiths' shops, so rich and full of silver vessels great and small that in all the shops of Milan, Rome, Venice, Florence put together, I do not think there would be found so many of the magnificence that are to be seen in London."

POTTERY AND GLASS-WARE.

The making of earthenware vessels is almost as widespread and as ancient as the primitive civilizations of man. The simple device of baking clay to form pots must have been discovered quite early, and pots of the Stone Age have been found in plenty. The Romans introduced improved methods of manufacture, which were especially carried on in two or three pre-eminently suitable areas. For example, the clay of the Nen Valley served them for the production of a blue and grey earthenware. Kent, especially in the Valley of the Medway, gave clay suitable for the black and grey wares of domestic use. The New Forest Potteries produced Samian Ware, often tastefully decorated. But Castor, in Northamptonshire, was the " Staffordshire " of the Romans.

The name of " Pottersfield," in Sussex is a survival of one of the few authentic references to early mediæval pottery ; " Kingston-on-Thames " certainly owned extensive pottery works (extensive for that date), as in 1260 the town bailiffs were ordered to send a thousand pitchers to the King's butler at Westminster.

Clay was also used to make tiles, in the manufacture of which the Romans were adepts, but after their departure no more is heard of tile-making for many centuries. From the 13th century, however, tiles increasingly took the place of grass or reed thatching for roofs, owing to the very great danger of fire in summer-time—indeed in London and Norwich, 1212 and 1507 respectively, tiles in place of thatching became compulsory for roofing purposes. These tiles were known as " thakkityles " or " thatching-tiles," but from the middle of the 14th century " Wat-tyles " or bricks are increasingly mentioned. They were introduced, perhaps, from Flanders.

There were great tile works at the Manor of Wye, in Kent, and it is not uninteresting to recall that a certain " Walter " of Kent who enjoyed his day of fame also followed the honourable profession of tile-making.

The sand of Surrey and Sussex began to be used for

INDUSTRIES OF THE MIDDLE AGES 169

glass making in the 13th century. The glass was, of course, for church windows, the table glass ware—only used in the houses of the wealthy—coming from Italy.

BREWING : ALE, BEER, CIDER

Brewing must be regarded as one of the more domestic arts. The making of mead from honey goes back to prehistoric times, and malt liquors in various forms have always been the natural drink of England. By the middle of the 12th century English ale was already famous, and especially Canterbury Ale, so that in 1157 Thomas of Canterbury took ale as an acceptable present to the French Court. Each village brewed its own ale, but it was subjected to all kinds of dues and taxations. In the 13th century the brewers of Shoreham, where ale was sold to foreigners, paid $2\frac{1}{2}$ marks yearly to escape the vexations of the manorial court, and the Hundred of Shoyswell (Sussex) paid a yearly fine in order that the " ale-wives " might be excused attendance at the law courts. (From this last episode it may be inferred that the trade was largely in the hands of women.)

In 1400 beer was imported from Flanders to Winchelsea, but its use was mainly and its manufacture entirely confined to foreigners—as the names of the 15th century brewers clearly show. These alien brewers amassed great riches, a practice that began to be followed by English brewers a century later, when the taste for beer was rapidly spreading.

Cider (or pomage) and perry (or perrie) became very common in Sussex, Kent, Worcester about 1577. The industry was probably introduced from Normandy.

LEATHER WORKING

In the Middle Ages the difficulties and kinds of transport in vogue necessitated the preparation of much leather, so that the dressing of skins for this purpose was one of the most widely diffused industries of that time. Ox, cow, calf hides were tanned by immersion in a decoction of oak-bark, the skins of sheep, deer, horses were tawed with alum and oil. The tanning and tawing trades were kept quite distinct, tanners and tawers being forbidden to use skins belonging to each other's trade.

In 1184 a law forbade tanners and tawers to practise their trade within the bounds of a great forest except in a borough or market town. This was to prevent deer poaching. Butchers in the market towns had to bring the hides with the meat to market when, and when only, tanners and tawers could buy them.

Steps were early taken to regulate the sale of the finished article. In 1271, in London, shoes could only be hawked in the districts between " Corveiser-strete and Soperes Lane " (Conduit Street and Soper's Lane) —in the morning on ordinary days, morning and afternoon on the eve of feasts. Leather could not be sold at the " eve-chepings " (compare Cheapside), when bad light might assist the vendor to palm off inferior material, though this law at the same time prevented competition between the pedlar-hawkers and the shopkeepers.

At this period Oxford was at the head of the shoe-making industry. [Northampton did not acquire its fame for the English Boot Trade until the 17th century, when its central position for route, and for supply of raw material became the dominating factor—" Northampton stood on other men's legs."]

The reign of Queen Elizabeth witnessed the rise of commercial capitalists, and in consequence the control of the industry passed in practice if not in theory from the Leathersellers' Company to that of a few wealthy members of the Company. The result was the inflation of prices, and fraudulent selling of inferior material and short measure, so that in 1593 it became necessary to issue a Royal Grant of "searching and sealing."

IV

THE HISTORY OF THE CLOTH-MAKING INDUSTRY

(Staple Industries)

So far the industries of England have been for use in the home country. We now come to other industries which lent themselves to an overseas trade.

The change from agricultural to pastoral industry made rapid strides during the long Plantagenet Dynasty, hence wool became a most important article of export. This wool went chiefly to Flanders, whence cloth was imported to England.

Another factor now becomes prominent—the desire of the King to reap a profit, to levy a tax or duty for the purpose of increasing his revenue for expenses (technically) of Government. The duty on the wool export was one of the chief sources of the Crown revenue, and the importance in which it was held may be estimated from the fact that the Lord Chancellor still presides in the House of Lords seated upon a Woolsack.

To facilitate the collection of taxes derived from the various branches of the cloth-making industry, they were forced, by Edward I, with fixed channels—that is, merchants were obliged to go to certain towns to conduct their trade, and the industries were accordingly known as fixed or "staple" industries. Sheep-rearing, owing to its intimate relationship to cloth-making, likewise became a "staple" industry. Edward III made the "Merchants of the Staple" a highly organized body : wherever there was a staple town, that is, a town containing a body of staple merchants, there was also a port which served the town—and through which the goods supplied to the merchant must pass. Thus Yarmouth was the port for Norwich and Sandwich for Canterbury.

In its beginning the making of cloth was a pure " domestic " (as opposed to factory) industry, and its production was limited to no particular part of the country. Wherever the material could be either produced or easily bought, there the industry might be carried on. The numerous " cloth halls " found all over the country show how widely cloth-making was distributed. In the 12th century—the earliest period when documentary evidence concerning cloth-making begins to appear—weaving was frequently carried on in the towns ; by 1150 the weavers of Winchester, London, Lincoln, Oxford and Huntingdon and the fullers of Winchester had formed themselves into guilds sufficiently wealthy to buy from the King the monopoly of the cloth-making in their respective districts, but here as in the leather trade, the curious mediæval specialization still persisted, no weaver or fuller being allowed to traffic in cloth or sell it to anyone except the merchants of the town. From this time we begin to hear of specialization in processes of producing—the dyers of Worcester (1173) and Darlington (1183), the scarlet cloth of Lincoln and Stamford (1182) coming into prominence. A Venetian customs list (1265) refers to English Stamfords, Dyed Stamfords, Milanese Stamfords of Monza (a copy of good English cloth), showing how the reputation for English cloth was growing abroad. Winchester, then buying coarse " burel " for the soldiers in Ireland (1172), was in the next century a centre for the manufacture of chalons

INDUSTRIES OF THE MIDDLE AGES 173

(Châlons-sur-Marne) or Shalloons, which were rugs for coverlets or counterpanes. By 1300 London was making all kinds of material " audley, porreye, menuet, lumbard," etc., but the English clothworkers were losing in competition with Continental rivals. And the cloth trade of Northampton, which employed three hundred men in the reign of Henry III, had almost died out by 1334.

Simon de Montford (killed at Evesham, 1265) and Edward I did much to encourage the native production of wool and to urge men to weave it. Flemish weavers, introduced by Edward III, whose wife Queen Philippa, came from the cloth country of Hainault, gave a new impetus to the cloth trade. Some of these Flemings settled in the Fen District, that " Little Holland," and others went to reinforce the descendants of Henry II's colony of weavers in " Little England beyond Wales." Others apparently settled round London in the district known as the Forest of Hainault. Some went to Leeds, but Yorkshire was not yet adapted for a great manufacturing centre. These Flemings were under contract to teach their trade to the natives, but not to make the English workmen the poorer by a greater competition.

Considerable strength was required to weave cloth textures, and at Norwich women were forbidden to weave worsteds (originally manufactured at Worstead) because they had not sufficient power to work them properly, and in 1389 the Fullers' Guild at Lincoln forbade a man to work at the perch with a woman unless she were the master's wife or her handmaid, lest men skilled in the craft and returning from the wars might find themselves ousted from their posts by cheap, female labour !

Like every other trade of Mediæval England (and

perhaps the adjective may be omitted) the Cloth Trade was subjected to fraudulent practices. Thus cloth was stretched immediately before sale and therefore sold "short"; or poor material was substituted for good when a formerly high reputation might be expected to avert suspicion, and by these and similar ingenuities the English cloth trade fell into such disrepute that the King resolved to remedy it. Accordingly an officer called an Ulnager (Ulnage or Aulnage, from aulne, an ell) was appointed to investigate cloth before sale, and to certify by means of a seal that it did really contain the stated number of (permanent) lengths and breadths, and was of the specified quality. In 1390 a Cloth Assize, very necessary in the cloth areas of Somerset, Gloucester and Dorset, ordered all cloth to be sold *open*, and not tacked or folded. The Statute of 1473 ordered that cloth should be measured precisely and exactly by the yard (the origin of the cloth yard) and the inch, to avoid the trickery arising out of hand measurements owing to the thickness of the thumb!

In East Anglia the Norwich district was for many centuries the metropolis of the Worsted (from long wool) industry. Here were manufactured damasks, says, serges, etc., fabrics not requiring water-power in their production and therefore eminently suited to a flat region where, moreover, the extensive sheep pastures gave wool of sufficient length. The chief centres for these "Worsted" cloths were Norwich (Norfolk), Sudbury and Lavenham (Suffolk), Alton (Hampshire). In Essex, a mixture of woollen and worsted (short and long wool) was worked up into baize (Colchester); here a little water-power is required, but for scouring the cloth, not for milling.

Norfolk was already famous for its cloth trade by

INDUSTRIES OF THE MIDDLE AGES 175

the end of the 13th century, and Norwich, the earliest manufacturing centre in England, was during the Middle Ages considered the second city in the kingdom. Its wool had brought it sufficient wealth to pay for the carriage of stone for its Cathedral Priory, though its parish churches were of flint.

Another East Anglian fabric was known as Kersey, a woollen cloth made of short wool from chalk areas. Kersey (Suffolk) was an early centre of cloth-making, and gave its name to this kind of material. The Kerseys of John of Winchcombe were very extensively known. " Hampshire Kerseys " were made in Hampshire, Surrey and Sussex.

"Blankets" (short wool—woollens) were named after Thomas Blanket, a cloth weaver of Bristol (1340). They were chiefly manufactured at Maldon and Hereford.

The serges of Devonshire (Worsteds) were made at Exeter, Crediton, Honiton, Tiverton and in North Devon; they were exported to Holland.

The Leicestershire wool industry developed mainly after the Reformation, and began to acquire a fame for stockings. The rich grasslands of this county were especially favourable for the rearing of sheep with fine, long hair. The wool was woven into cloth, and stockings were generally stitched cloth, woollen stockings as they are known to-day being a luxury for the few. Hand-knitting was laborious, but the invention of the stocking-frame, by the Rev. William Lee, gave a great impetus to the manufacture of hosiery.[1] The frames were worked by hand, and at home—still a domestic industry.

---

[1] There are various accounts given concerning the mode of origin of Lee's invention. The following version appears to be as well authenticated as any: " Lee found his courtship hindered by the constant knitting of his lady-love, and the annoyance he experienced due to this cause resulted in his invention."

The importance of Worcester, through which flowed that highway of commerce, the River Severn, was greatly increased in the reign of Henry VIII, when Bewdley, the capital of the Forest of Wyre, was incorporated in the country, thereby adding to its industries a considerable trade in clothing for the seamen of Bristol (Welsh friezes, a noted Welsh cloth).

We have seen that certain of the " East Anglian " fabrics were manufactured in the West Country, but the true West Country Cloth Industry is concerned with a material of an altogether different type—the manufacture of various broadcloths and cloth serges, of which the first were made from fine short wool, the second from both long and short wool, while both required to undergo a process of " milling." The power to drive the mills resulted from the heavy rainfall in this region due to the hills (800-1,000 feet), thereby giving rise to numerous and rapid streams, which were also permanent, and therefore excellently suited for turning water-wheels. This West Country Cloth Industry began in Gloucestershire (Stroud) about the middle of the 15th century, but the period of its zenith and glory was not until long after the close of the Middle Ages and will be dealt with more fully in a later chapter.

In the reign of Edward IV, the Cloth Industry spread to Kent, with Cranbrook as its first centre, but the importance afterwards acquired by Canterbury[1] was so great that the history of cloth-making in that town may be taken to epitomize the development of the industry in the region, and we shall carry on its story to the present day.

---

[1] The Canterbury cloth was made from the " short wool," characteristic of sheep of a chalk area ; it was therefore " Broadcloth," otherwise a typical West-Country cloth.

In the 15th century refugees from Lille, Waterloo, Turcoing and elsewhere in the Low Countries, settled in Kent and were allowed to continue their trade of weaving, in which they were very skilled, on the understanding that they wove none of the cloths produced by native workmen.

[A century later foreign weavers were still settling in Kent, and notably at Canterbury, where they obtained certain privileges. At the Revocation of the Edict of Nantes (1685) many Huguenot silk-weavers from southern France settled in Canterbury,[1] adding the manufacture of a new material to its ancient cloth-weaving, and thereby carrying the prosperity of the cathedral city to its zenith. Later, foreign importation injured the silk trade to such an extent that by 1786 there were only twenty looms left, which by the end of the century, were reduced to ten. Early in the 19th century the trade had practically ceased. However, from 1896 there has been a re-establishment of the weaving trade in Canterbury, under more modern conditions.]

The practice of forming "cloth guilds" naturally led to the establishment of a few definite "cloth" towns of the first importance, and as in the case of the Leather Industry, a few wealthy members of the several guilds tended to get the main control into their own hands. But in the latter part of the 16th century certain great "clothiers" come to the fore—*John Winchcombe*, or "Jack of Newbury," who once sent a hundred workmen to join the King's[2] army, and the *Springs* of Lavenham, employers of labour on a scale which soon ruined the independence of the small

---

[1] Note the comparatively low rainfall and good summer heat of Kent—factors necessary for silk-weaving.
[2] King Henry VIII.

cloth-maker. This brings us to the third step in the development of the weaving industry, which may be epitomized thus :

(1) The Family System. The family worked for the family.
(2) The Guild System. The small master employed apprentices and journeymen to make the cloth, and sold it when made.
(3) The Domestic System, as in (2), but the small master sold the finished cloth to the merchants.
[(4) To complete the epitome we may add the Factory System, as in operation at the present day.]

The mediæval period of the Woollen Industry closes with the introduction of new draperies, by foreign refugees, early in the reign of Queen Elizabeth.

v

The History of Miscellaneous Industries

The remaining industries of the Middle Ages are varied, but local.

SHIPBUILDING

Shipbuilding was carried on at certain suitable localities, and must have been in a fairly flourishing condition, for vessels were required not only for coastal commerce and the fishing fleets, but for transport of troops and army effects in our numerous wars with France and expeditions to Ireland. In the reign of Edward I, the Cinque Ports were ordered to furnish ships to convey troops to North Wales, where the final steps of the Conquest were in progress. Cargo boats also carried casks of "corrupt wine," kerseys and kettles to the troops in Ireland, but the ships were small, and throughout the whole of the Middle Ages

INDUSTRIES OF THE MIDDLE AGES 179

the overseas commerce of Western Europe was carried in Venetian vessels.

EXPORTS AND IMPORTS

The exports were mainly wool, cloth, hides, corn and beer. Newcastle, in the reign of King John, was importing to Flanders wool, hides, foxes' skins, "sables" and beavers. In the main, therefore, exports can be designated as "dull," but this cannot be said of the imports, which, naturally, had a somewhat devotional character. An import list of 1399 mentions images of painted wood or tin, Oriental "kerchiefs," and "pins with which to fasten them." A century later another import list includes "ivory combs and apes" ("4 dozen baboons")—which latter, however, were grotesque figures, charms, or mediæval mascots, perhaps, but certainly not the living creature. Bears were imported for the noble sport of bear-baiting, and at Norwich, the records state, a custom duty of 42d. (£2 7s. 6d. of our present money) was paid on each animal imported.

But whereas most of the English cloth had ceased to find favour in foreign markets, foreign cloth forms a heavy item in the imports of this period. The 1490 import list quoted above makes mention of damask, satin, pipes of wine, razors, needles, mantles of leopard's skin, playing cards, and plaques brought into Winchelsea by the ships from Dieppe. As regards wine, the close connection with Gascony resulting from the marriage of Henry II to Eleanor of Aquitaine brought an increasing carrying trade to Bristol.

Other imports were iron and wool, both from Spain.

It has been mentioned that during the Middle Ages the commerce of Western Europe was conducted in Venetian vessels. During the 13th, 14th, 15th centuries a great rival to the Venice trade reigned in

North Europe. As early as the year 1300 seventy towns of North Europe, with Lübeck at their head, were united for trade purposes in a union called the Hanseatic (or Hansa) League. Newcastle, Lynn, and Boston in England had relations with this league during this period, hence the closeness of their trade with Flanders, whose Hanseatic port was Bruges, then on the sea-coast. This league was virtually broken by the Treaty of Westphalia, 1648.

CHAPTER XV

GUILDS, FAIRS AND MARKETS

GUILDS AND COMPANIES

The period of internal peace and order which resulted from the Norman Conquest, and which not even subsequent civil wars could greatly shake, led to the rise of the Merchant Guilds, an entirely new feature in English life. Even at the time of the Conquest the "villages" were administered by the Thegn (later lord of the manor) or his representative, and village life was continually hampered in its development by taxes and dues that had to be paid in money, kind, or labour. Now, in the security of the Norman rule, such localities as possessed special advantages as depôts or distributing centres, or proximity to raw materials, or other causes for commercial prosperity, became centres of commercial enterprises regulated by "Guilds." These Guilds may be regarded as Committees of merchants, which presently became sufficiently wealthy, and especially in the 12th and 13th centuries, when the influence of the Merchant Guilds was at its zenith, to buy from the King or overlord those charters of privileges which so powerfully stimulated the growth of the great towns. In fact, it may be said that town life in the Middle Ages *was* guild life.

The guilds were so called because each member had to make a payment to the common fund,[1] and inasmuch as they were designated to protect their trade from people in their town who had not entered into their corporation, they may be regarded as "trades'

[1] Note the connection between Guild and Geld, e.g., the Danegeld, or money paid to the Danes by the Anglo-Saxons.

unions" of the Mediæval Period. The Guilds, however, went even a step beyond their modern representatives in this matter, claiming monopoly of their trade against traders in other towns whom, equally with Flemish weavers, they regarded as "foreign." To the Guild Merchants matters of commercial etiquette might be referred. At first the trading was "collective," the Guild as a body buying mixed cargo, which was then repurchased by its different members, who might be of very different trades. This method was found to be cumbersome and was given up in favour of separate Guilds, each one being concerned with its own trade. Thus there was a Weavers' Guild, a Bakers' Guild, and so on, the members still being merchants engaged in these different businesses.

By the end of the 13th century, a new kind of Guild, the Craft Guild, had become common. These were corporations, not of merchants, but a trade. The merchants were craftsmen as well as salesmen. At Coventry there is still a Bakers' Guild of this nature.

About the time of Edward III a new commercial organization came into being—the Dealers' Company. Its purpose was to make selling more easy. The Companies were composed of the richer burgesses; in 1364 the Vintners' Company, with the exclusive right of selling retail wine, was formed. The Drapers' Company (1366), the Grocers' Company (1343), with its later offshoots of the Apothecaries' and Turkey Companies, the Mercers' Company (1347), which later gave rise to the Haberdashers' and Merchant Adventurers' Companies, are a few examples.

Both Guilds and Companies possessed Halls, often in good preservation to-day, wherein the custom of a Guild or Company Banquet is still frequently kept up.

GUILDS, FAIRS, MARKETS

FAIRS

Down to the end of the 14th century England was little more than a collection of isolated communities owing to the badness of the roads, and the general trade of the country was mainly conducted by means of a system of fairs and markets. Foreign merchants would attend them, and English traders from different parts of the country with different commodities for sale or exchange. The business done was mostly wholesale, of the kind to-day effected in the modern public exchanges, or in the enormous private warehouses of London, Liverpool, Manchester and Birmingham. To these fairs also came the villagers of the district, who were forced by the lack of shops to lay in winter stores of dried meat, salt, spices, and other " luxuries " that could not be supplied by the local markets.

Fairs were usually associated with saints' days. They took place on days of dedication, festival of monastery, church or cathedral, all of which, together with visitation of shrines by pilgrims, brought together crowds of people who were thereby afforded opportunity to purchase or trade in commodities which otherwise they might find it difficult to procure.

In return for this opportunity given, the Church as well as the King obtained a substantial revenue. At one time, indeed, fairs were held in churchyards, but Edward I put an end to this practice, and henceforward they took place on open spaces a little outside the town, and on ground surrounded with a palisade. Within the fair-ground covered booths were erected for the goods and amusements provided for the people. The dates of the most important fairs were so arranged that foreign merchants could visit them all in turn. The favourite fair-time was autumn, when winter stores could be laid in, and spring, when the depleted stock could be replenished before the summer.

All fairs were subjected to regulations governing their conduct. Royal grants of fairs were sometimes made to needy or benevolent institutions, whose head —whether Bishop, Abbot, Abbess or Prior—became the titular " ruler " or " governor " of the fair. This ruler received the dues and was technically responsible for the good conduct of the people during fair-time, both on the fair-ground and in the neighbouring town, and for the honesty of the weights and measures employed, etc. During the fair trading was prohibited in the neighbouring town, but buying and selling had to be effected between definite hours.

Choice of site had much to do with the importance of the fair, hence fairs often took place at route centres, or in the meadows bounding navigable streams. It was the position of Winchester on the great route, London-Guildford-Basingstoke-Winchester-Southampton-Normandy, that gave its great fair such importance. The fair-ground was placed at the most convenient centre behind the port, and where valleys and lines of down converge. The Stourbridge (or Sturbridge) Fair was held in the fields bordering the Stur, a tributary of the Cam, in its turn a tributary of the Ouse. Of all the fairs in England these two, the Winchester and the Stourbridge Fairs, were the most important.

The Winchester Fair took place on a common outside the city walls and while it was being held all other trade within a seven-leagued circle was prohibited. It was established by William II. In the succeeding reign it lasted for sixteen days, from

August 31st to September 15th. It was ruled over by the Bishop of Winchester. This fair decayed during the 13th century, when intercourse with the Continent passed more definitely to the South-East quadrant. It is interesting to remember that the Pilgrim's Way, leading to the shrine of Thomas, Archbishop of Canterbury, has one terminus here.

The Cambridge or Stourbridge Fair.—The importance of this great fair was bound up in the neighbouring town of Cambridge, which had risen to greatness as a Danish and Saxon borough in early English times. Possessing a Roman road and bridge, lying in the neck of land between Fen and Forest, with the Ichnield Way not far distant, Cambridge was clearly marked out as a collecting and distributing centre for commerce. Stourbridge, the scene of the Cambridge Fair, lies to the south-east of the town, the Stour bordering the fair-ground. This fair was one of the most ancient, and certainly the most important, of all the English Fairs. From the middle of the 12th to the middle of the 13th century the export of our wool, leather, tin, and other English commodities was entirely in the hands of foreign merchants, and at Stourbridge they were able to purchase the raw material and sell or exchange the products of their own or other countries. Thus Stourbridge, by virtue of its inland communications, was a commercial trading centre for both foreign and English traders.

Foreign goods came to Lynn Port, on the Ouse (Bishop's Lynn, later King's Lynn), and from there were taken by barges along this river, and then up the Cam and Stour and so to the fair ground. Heavy goods from London, and hops from Kent, travelled by the same river-route. Goods from the Midlands were similarly carried from Stourbridge to Lynn

Port, to be shipped to Hull and Newcastle for the Humber and Tyne hinterlands.[1]

Stourbridge Fair was the meeting place of people from the great towns and representatives from many nations. There were gathered together the money-exchanger from Lombardy, the merchant from Venice and Genoa with Eastern spices and cloths, and silk, velvet and glass from Italy. From the Low Countries the Flemish trader brought linen from Liege and Ghent; iron ore arrived from Spain, and tar and pitch from Norway.

The Gascon merchant was there with his famous wines, and the towns of the Hansa League sent furs and amber.

To the fair came also the " Woolpacks " of England, Cornish tin, Worcester salt, Derbyshire lead, Sussex iron, and many other products of the home country. The harbours of Blakeney, Colchester, Lynn, and Norwich were filled with foreign vessels, " and under the influence of this great and various trade the countries of eastern England grew rich and prosperous."

The Stourbridge Fair was held four times a year: at Midsummer, when the fair lasted four days from the Feast of St. John the Baptist, with the Prior of Banwell as governor; at the Feast of the Assumption, the fair lasting two days, and ruled over by the Prioress of St. Rhadegund—this latter fair was known as the Garlic Fair, and still lingers; during Rogation days, when the Burgesses' Fair was held.

The fourth fair was the great Stourbridge Fair. At Stourbridge stood a Leper Hospital, to which, about 1211, King John made the grant of a fair. It was this

---

[1] The Scottish student came to the University by the same river-route. It should be noted that " Cambridge University " came to the trade centre.

GUILDS, FAIRS, MARKETS 187

fair which became the most notable in England. The Master of the Leper Hospital was the governor, and the fair began on the Feast of the Holy Cross (September 14th). In the 18th century this fair was still vigorous, but to-day it is represented by a few mean stalls.

The Stamford and Boston Fairs.—On the other side of the Fens were the Stamford and Boston Fairs. The first of these had its day of considerable renown. The Boston Fair, known as St. Botolph's Fair, was situated at a spot where transport could easily be effected inland up the rivers Welland and Witham. It had reached its prime about 1327, and finally disappeared in the opening years of the 15th century.

The London Fairs.—London boasted of two quite distinct fairs—one held in May on grounds whose name still recalls this mediæval custom, known indeed as Mayfair, and the other, St. Bartholomew's Fair (August 24th). This latter fair dealt chiefly with the cloth of Bruges, Ghent, Ypres, and therefore decayed as soon as English manufacturers could produce cloth of similar nature and equal value to the Flemish article. In the 17th century both these fairs were much restricted owing to the disorders in the shape of mob oratory and political disturbances to which they gave rise.

The Chester Fair dates from the reign of Henry II. *Yaremouth* grew up on the site of the Herring Fair, emulating Amsterdam, which may be said to have "risen on herrings"! Edward the Confessor granted three fairs annually to *Beverley*, Henry I a fair to *Whitby* to take place on St. Hilda's Day, King John a horse fair to *Howden*, and Henry III to *Scarborough*, to be held on the sands from mid-August to Michaelmas, and to "his borough of *Retford*," a fair lasting eight days, beginning on the Eve of Holy Trinity. These are but a few examples of the many small fairs that took place in different parts of the country.

The great days of the English Fairs were prior to the 15th century. At the end of the 14th complaints were made that the fairs were declining, sometimes because the badness of the roads prohibited transport of the necessary goods, and sometimes because of the increasing strictness of the regulations governing them, due to the fact that the King began to look with suspicion on these great gatherings and their opportunities for sedition. After the 15th century improved conditions of transport and home manufactures brought about a more general expansion of the retail trade, and the great fairs accordingly decayed. In their place a large number of small fairs were created for local products, so that the fairs survived exclusively as " cattle fairs," " sheep fairs," " horse fairs," or " cheese fairs," etc., or as " pleasure fairs " with ginger-bread stalls and roundabouts as their chief attractions, as at the fairs of the present day. These small fairs, unattended by foreign merchants, possessed an importance purely local, and no town grew immediately in their neighbourhood as they declined.

MARKETS

Markets differ from fairs in being of a bi-weekly, weekly, or fortnightly occurrence, and also in being less ambitious and more local in design. Their purpose was a *retail* disposal of the surplus products of the surrounding districts. The Domesday Book mentions fifty-three markets, including those of Faversham (Kent), Basingstoke, Wallingford, Cookham, Bradford (Wilts), Frome, Ilchester, Taunton, Ilminster, Launceston, Bodmin, Liscard, Berkeley, Tewkesbury, Luton, Tutbury, Louth, Spalding and Beccles.

GUILDS, FAIRS, MARKETS 189

During the 13th century markets were often held on Sundays, but most of them were later shifted to weekdays, whereas fairs were usually associated with Saints' days.

Markets held on a highway, or at places where routes converged (places of nodality), frequently resulted in the growth of towns, owing their origin to this possibility as a centre for trade and commerce in the local produce. The names of certain towns record such an origin, as in the cases of Downham Market, Market Deeping, Market Drayton, Market Harborough, Market Lavington, Market Basen, Market Weighton, Rosemarket, etc.

As in the case of a fair, the possession of a market was duly sought after—and duly paid for. Henry II " granted a market to Scarborough," Edward I to Hull, and to Retford " any Saturday."

Many mediæval towns had a double market, a " civic " market under the protection of the castle, and an " ecclesiastical " market under the protection of the Church, symbolized frequently by that " Market Cross," round which gathered the Stout Old Sheriff and his Yeomen in Macaulay's famous ballad.

Examples of towns with double markets are Norwich and St. Albans. " Cheapside," the great London market in the Middle Ages, is well placed in the shadow of St. Paul's.

CHAPTER XVI

TOWNS OF THE MIDDLE AGES

WE have already considered the manner in which certain settlements record their mode of origin in their place-names—the -hams, -ings, -tons, etc., of the Anglo-Saxon period. The *growth of towns* in the Middle Ages is due to many and interesting causes, but no less interesting is the investigation as to the reasons why some formerly famous centres of trade and population have now become of little or no account.

All the more important of our mediæval towns possessed a certain degree of "natural nodality," that is to say, were situated in good positions with reference to such inland communication and trade as existed at that time. Such advantageous sites might be on a natural inlet from the sea, so that the coming and going of trade followed, as in the case of Bristol (Bridgstow), or upon a well-placed bridge-place at the head of navigation for small sea-craft, as indeed was also the case for Lincoln, Norwich, Canterbury, while London, Rochester, Southampton, Exeter, Gloucester, Chester and York could receive much larger craft.

The same natural nodality applied to the smaller inland towns, all of which were seated upon navigable rivers, of which no better examples can perhaps be found than the five Danish boroughs of Nottingham, Derby, Leicester, Stamford and Lincoln.

To this river navigation must be added the possibility of fording or bridging the stream for land communications or routes, determining the choice of

TOWNS OF THE MIDDLE AGES 191

site of a town at this place on a river rather than at some other.

In addition to the bridge or ford, a castle, cathedral, or abbey might make a centre of population, whereby trade was attracted.

The position of some towns was originally chosen for reasons of defence, as in the case of Durham and Shrewsbury, built in river loops dominated by castles. Both of these places possessed cathedrals, and always where original settlements came to have more than one advantage of this kind or of site, the town that grew up would generally be a large one as towns went in those days.

Our towns will accordingly be classified as sea and river ports, borough and castle towns (formerly strong places), county towns, cities and towns originating through the influence or under the patronage of the Church, and trading towns. Clearly some of the English towns must be placed in more than one of the foregoing differentiations.

At the opening of the Middle Ages the motive underlying the choice of site for settlement was the satisfaction of the fundamental needs of food, water to drink and shelter. Round these settlements agricultural villages grew up, each producing its own food, often with results inducing considerable hardships and poverty where the soil was infertile or non-suitable, or the climate adverse.

Under the Normans and their successors the modes of life of the inhabitants became more settled and better organized, and the advent of the Plantagenet Dynasty saw much of the former agricultural industry exchanged for sheep-rearing for wool production, geographical conditions permitting. Henceforward certain communities, formerly self-supporting, were reduced to obtaining even their prime necessities from other localities, with a concomitant improvement in trade and transport especially benefiting those places as either had surplus goods to exchange, or some specially favourable site-position upon commercial routes. In this way certain villages (e.g., Wyk) acquired sufficient wealth and importance to purchase certain charters or privileges from overlord or King, causing them to rank as towns, often sending Members to Parliament, and taking a prominent place in the commercial life of the country.

The causes later operating to reduce the importance of certain towns will be dealt with in the course of the classification under the appropriate headings.

I.—Marine and River Ports

(a) Sea Ports for Commerce

The ports of England in the Middle Ages are not in general the present-day ports. This is partly because of the changed burden of the ships, making for fewer ports, but increasing the commodity of those left, and partly because of the newer industries, which demand a coastal outlet to a hinterland of little value during the Mediæval period, and partly to changes in the coast line whereby harbours have not only been silted up, but also washed away. A list of important " sea-ports " given in the 13th century is as follows: London, Boston, Southampton, Lincoln, Lynn, Hull, York, Dunwich, Grimsby, Yarmouth, Ipswich, Colchester, Sandwich, Dover, Rye, Winchelsea, Seaford, Shoreham, Chichester, Exmouth, Dartmouth, Esse, Fowey, Pevensey, Coton, Whitby, Scarborough, Selby, Barton, Hedon, Norwich, Orford.

It is interesting to note that some of these " sea-ports " are up rivers to-day no less than then—York,

TOWNS OF THE MIDDLE AGES

for example, which as a "sea-port" claimed a share in the salvaged wrecks of the Humber, or Holderness coast! Hedon, in the East Riding, was an important centre of trade and commerce, and sent two Members to Parliament in the reign of Edward I. Its harbour became choked with sand and is now a meadow.

The mediæval ports fall into three divisions: the Cinque Ports, the East Coast and particularly the East Anglian Ports, the Ports of the South-West.

1. *The Cinque Ports (The Five Ports).*

This federation of the seaports of Kent and Sussex probably began before the Conquest. However, the *Norman* kings granted privileges to the five ports of Dover, Sandwich, Hythe, Romney, and Hastings, demanding in return for the right of a certain measure of self-government the annual unpaid service of fifty-seven ships for fifteen days.

Dover and Sandwich had to provide 21 ships each, Hythe, Romney and Hastings each five. Before long the ports of Winchelsea and Rye were hereafter affected by all writs and warrants dealing with the Cinque Ports. Later twenty more "daughter" ports were added to the five "mother" ports—Tenterden, for example, was once a member of the Cinque Port of Rye; it also has the distinction of being among the earliest places in which Edward III established the woollen manufacture.

At the time of Edward I these twenty-seven ports had to provide a number of ships for the King's war on the Welsh coast, and they fulfilled this obligation as a whole, by friendly arrangement among themselves. Subsequently the assessment for war service was made separately on the different ports.

2. *The East Coast Ports.*

Those of East Anglia were neither of great importance

nor well-recognized position until the end of the 12th century, but from that time until their decay they were very serious rivals of the Cinque Ports, with which they were continually in dispute. Until the 13th century the King relied chiefly for ships on Dunwich, once one of the first-class ports of England. The causes of its subsequent decline have already been related.[1] By 1570 Aldeburgh and Southwold in the same county had risen to considerable greatness.

Ipswich was another formerly famous Suffolk port. At the beginning of the 13th century it was ordered to prepare two ships for the Royal use, but three centuries later it was making vessels above 300 tons for London merchants and shipowners.

Bishop's Lynn, now King's Lynn, had its day of prosperity, owing to the wool trade. Lynn is still of considerable value, but Yarmouth ultimately outclassed the other Norfolk ports. Its coastal fisheries, its position as an outport for Norwich—the first provincial " inland " town to rise to greatness, and for long second only to London in commercial prosperity—contributed to the greatness of Yarmouth. Colchester was another of the East Anglian famous mediæval ports.

In the 13th century Boston was classed as a " seaport." It was the outport for Lincoln, later becoming the staple town where wool could be collected and stored as well as shipped. With Lynn, Boston had commercial relations with the German ports of the Hanseatic League.

3. *Ports of the South-West.*

Norwich and Yarmouth, Lincoln and Boston, were pairs of ports with an intimate association. In the South-West this pairing was even more common.

[1] See page 136.

Exeter and Exmouth, Newton Abbot and Teignmouth, Totnes and Dartmouth, Lostwithiel and Fowey, Truro and Falmouth, are some examples. The "inland" port was probably served by the tide, whereas the outport was on the natural harbour at the sea. These " up-river " towns were parliamentary boroughs, with a population of merchants exporting wool, and importing Gascony wine. Their wealth rendered them eminently suitable for payment of the King's taxes, but it was first necessary that they should send Members to Parliament for the purpose of assessing and offering these same taxes ! The mouth-town had a population of fishermen or seamen ; they " carried " wool, and wine, as coastal commerce, and troops to the opposite shores of France. They were not regarded as of sufficient importance to be represented in Parliament, though Edward I made Dartmouth, the chief port of the Cornwall-Devon peninsula, a parliamentary borough.

Southampton, the commercial outlet of the South ever since the Anglo-Saxon period, was a great port in the Middle Ages, dealing with most of the French and Venice trade that came to England.

(b) THE RIVER PORTS FOR COMMERCE

The river ports (or inland ports) were places on navigable rivers which were otherwise suitable to receive or distribute goods. Often placed at the head of navigation, inland merchandise could be brought to them by pack-horse, or other methods common to the time. Frequently the navigation was of the " barge " type, but where the river was sufficiently wide and deep a certain proportion of foreign shipping could come up it and effect an exchange with local products.

Boston, Lincoln, and York, though counting themselves as true "sea-ports" must also be placed in the list of river ports.

The Severn ports of Gloucester, Tewkesbury, Bridgnorth and Shrewsbury are all mentioned in the Anglo-Saxon chronicle. Bewdley is another formerly famous Severn port. Other river ports of the Middle Ages were London and Oxford (Thames), Ware (Lea), Rochester (Medway), Canterbury (Stour), Lewes (Sussex Ouse), Winchester (Itchen), Salisbury (Wiltshire Avon), Exeter (Exe), Bristol (Bristol Avon), Hereford (Wye), Caerleon (Usk), Ludlow (Terne), Chester (Dee), York (Ouse), Doncaster (Don), Lincoln and Boston (Witham), Spalding (Welland), Peterborough (Nen), Norwich (Yare), Colchester (Colne), Cambridge (Cam).

(c) THE STAPLE PORTS

So far the mediæval ports have been classified with regard to position, but they can also be classified with regard to kind. During the Middle Ages the Crown exercised considerable jurisdiction over commercial enterprise, setting aside certain towns in which certain trades must be carried on, and certain ports to which goods of certain kinds must be taken for import or export. Edward I forced the wool trade into fixed channels, so that the taxes he obtained from it might be the more easy to collect, and Edward III instituted the "Merchants of the Staple," who alone could buy and sell wholesale the particular article which was the staple of that place. (Note, in this connection Barnstaple, which received the Irish wool.) These staple towns were so chosen that there was a port to serve the town (whether from home or abroad), through which the imports supplied to the staple merchant

TOWNS OF THE MIDDLE AGES 197

had to pass.[1] Yaremouth served Norwich as its staple port, and Sandwich served Canterbury.

The decline of many of these old ports was partly natural and partly due to human agency.

Many old *sea-ports* declined :

(i) Owing to the eastward drift of the shingle, due to the superiority of the up-Channel tide, causing the shingle on our coast, and the sand across at Ambleteuse to accumulate in these natural inlets which had formerly favoured port sites. In this way were the harbours of Chichester, Winchelsea, Romney, Hythe and Sandwich destroyed. Winchelsea—the continuation of that " old " Winchelsea destroyed in 1289— owed its long renown to the large perimeter of its walls, themselves encircled by a non-productive " scrub-" land, upon which no agriculturist cast a too envious eye, so that expansion of the town was rendered possible when new methods of trade demanded such expansion. Though the Tudor period saw its glories on the wane, it was still sufficiently flourishing for Queen Elizabeth to bestow upon it the title of " Little London." The case of Rye, on the Rother, was quite otherwise, its cramped position forbidding expansion, so that it became too small for the growing commercial needs apart from the fact that ultimately its harbour suffered the silting operations common to this neighbourhood.

As the facilities of its harbour declined Sandwich made efforts to retain its importance, but on other lines. A colony of Flemish weavers settled there in Elizabeth's reign, and the inhabitants engaged in the manufacture of baize and in market gardening. Its present revival as a golfing centre is significant of the cause of its decline.

[1] Sea and river transport took very generally the place of the road and rail transport of the present age.

In certain places the drift of sand and shingle was in other directions; thus the tides and currents conspired to silt up the once famous port of Hedon, in the East Riding of Yorkshire, so that cattle graze luxuriantly where once ships were moored.

(ii) In certain places inroads of the sea have destroyed the ancient harbour and port. The storms of the 13th and 14th centuries seem to have been particularly vigorous in this respect. To the cases of Dunwick and "Old" Winchelsea must be added Ravenser, in Holderness, which sent Members to Parliament in the reign of Edward I and when Henry IV[1] landed in 1399, has been swallowed up by the sea, so that its very site is to-day unknown.

(iii) The artificial preservation of some ports resulted in commerce being confined to a few large harbours, and many small ones, in consequence, were quite neglected. The reign of Henry VIII may be taken as the starting point leading to the decay of certain mediæval ports. In 1545 an Act was passed resulting in the repair or building of good harbours; the cost of these repairs was so great that funds were lacking to repair the smaller ones. In Devon and Cornwall, many harbours, notably Plymouth, Dartmouth, Falmouth, Fowey, had suffered much injury by silting due to mining refuse. Steps were now taken to clear them (1545). A year earlier Winchelsea and Rye Harbours were rebuilt.

(iv) The old ports also decayed on account of the passing of the old natural anchorages and birth of harbours almost entirely artificial. This change accompanied the increased size of shipping, which required a depth of water greater than the natural anchorages could supply.

[1] Ravenspur, that is, Ravenser Spurn. See p. 136.

TOWNS OF THE MIDDLE AGES

One advantage of this practice of artificial construction was that a harbour could be placed to serve a large and populous hinterland.

The artificial harbours naturally attracted the larger trade—thus assisting to destroy the smaller ones, only accessible to a very restricted commerce.

Piers were now built at Dover and Scarborough to give a safer anchorage, not otherwise natural.

[It is noticeable that Bideford, Barnstaple, and most of the Devon ports that equipped ships for the Spanish Main, to-day do little but harbour coasting vessels, their natural anchorage being altogether too small for modern shipping. Trade has therefore left them. On the other hand, some ports, which are good for trade, have no natural shelter for anchorage. Thus Cardiff, to-day a great port, has a splendid harbour entirely artificial. The harbour of Fishguard was "created" by the Great Western Railway Company, to suit the requirements of its passengers for a shorter sea route to America. Plymouth owes her present prosperity to the breakwater, the inner harbour and the Callewater being too shallow for modern needs.]

The decline of our *River ports* is due to two quite distinct causes—the larger build of vessels in later years and the formation of shallows in the river bed.

The former "sea ports" of York and Boston are now quite out of the reach of sea-going vessels, and Bristol nearly so. In many cases the shallowing of a river bed (and also its estuary, prohibiting the entrance of craft which the *river* might support), and the formation of shoals and sand-banks, impeding navigation, is due to the great denudation of the land surface owing to the excessive deforestation to which our country has been subjected. The silting of the Dee is partly through this cause, and partly through the up-stream wash of tide-carried sand, so that by the 17th century Chester had quite declined as a port—when Liverpool took its place.

In some cases, however, it is the river that had dwindled, possibly through diminution of its catchment basin. This appears to be the case with Lewes, on the Sussex Ouse, Deeping on the Welland, Cambridge on the Cam, Ely on the Ouse, West Dean on Cuckmere, Bawtry on the Idle.

The decline of the *staple ports*, and in large measure of their associated staple towns, naturally followed the introduction of more freedom in trade. With the passing of the monopoly which had given them their importance, they found themselves greatly handicapped in the competition with other ports of greater natural advantages.

II.—RIVER TOWNS

FORD AND BRIDGE TOWNS

From the earliest days of our history navigable rivers have exercised a most important influence on the settlements of tribes, adoption of town sites, and trade development.

They were the natural " highways " through a land still three parts forest and fen, and even in later times, when the one was largely cleared and the other partly drained, they offered an obvious means of transport for commodities too heavy for pack-horses.

It has already been noted how a ford across a river furnished a suitable site for a house or a village, not only for personal reasons, but as a vantage point where a river might be guarded, and also conveniently crossed by horses and cattle. These " ford " villages, or towns, are sufficiently numerous and have already

TOWNS OF THE MIDDLE AGES

been mentioned in detail. Later a ford was frequently replaced by a bridge, with its advantages of a " dry " crossing, though once at least the reverse process was effected when the ruins of the Roman bridge at Stamford, fallen into the water, gave it sufficient shallowness to be forded.

The " bridge towns " often proclaim their manner of origin by their name, as in the case of Cambridge, Bridgnorth, Woodbridge, etc., but not always. Thus Staines (= A.S. stones, and Roman pontes or " bridges ") rose round the bridges which the Romans joined to the gravel islands in the Thames. Other bridge-places on the Thames are Wallingford, which the Saxons regarded of such importance and which they made the famous " burgh " of Berkshire ; Dorchester, which had its brief spell of importance ; Windsor, the favourite town of the Plantagenets ; Reading, at the junction of the Kennet and Thames. This latter town, in the mediæval period, outstripped all the others in importance owing to its possession of an abbey, founded by Henry I, but its position helped it greatly. Other bridge places are Boston, on the Witham, and Gloucester, whose importance as a port was checked by the Severn bore, so that it was outclassed by Bristol ; but Gloucester was always the lowest point at which the river could be bridged, and therefore was always important as an inland road to South Wales.

III.—BOROUGH (BURGH) AND CASTLE TOWNS
(STRONG PLACES)

(1) BOROUGHS

The Borough and Castle towns owe their origin to the military necessities of the time, but it should be kept in mind that the " growth " of these towns was naturally due to periods—sometimes very lengthy ones—of peace, though the cause of these towns was as naturally due to the use to which they might be put in time of war. In general, the boroughs were the older of the two. They arose out of the needs of the Danish and Anglo-Saxon warfare. The great confederacy of the five boroughs of Nottingham, Leicester, Derby, Stamford and Lincoln, held the Danelaw, and the Saxons, following their enemy's example, established a number of "strong places," or Burghs, as rallying centres or military capitals of the various districts of their territory. Thus Wallingford, the great Saxon burgh of Berkshire, was at once a ford and a strong place, and the interdependence of these two qualities is obvious. Hastings, Chichester, Wareham, Exeter, Winchester, Wilton, Bath, Chester, Tamworth, Colchester, etc., are other examples.

These "boroughs," as both varieties came to be called, often maintained and increased their military importance as "Royal Boroughs" under the Normans and their successors, who furnished them with a castle, "loyally" garrisoned, with a view to that prevention which is ever better than cure. The security afforded by the presence of a castle sometimes attracted the Bishop of the Diocese there to fix his seat, and this added importance made it a suitable centre for the King's judges when they were on circuit. In this way Norwich displaced Thetford as a Bishop's See, and Exeter displaced Crediton, while Exeter, Winchester, York, show many reasons for becoming provincial capitals—*provincial*, in contrast to London, whose peculiarity of site and position, whose transcendent qualities of natural nodality, had already caused it to become "national" by the time of Edward the Confessor, whereas Winchester was never greater than

TOWNS OF THE MIDDLE AGES 203

as a centre of Old Wessex, or York as the capital of Northumberland.

Oxford was at first a ford and then a bridge-place. Later it became an important burgh, and then a military centre round whose *castle* much fighting took place right down to the 17th century.

As the mediæval period drew on, the word " borough " came to have a new meaning. Such of the old important boroughs and burghs as contained " boroughs " had the right (for which they paid in some form or other) to send " burgesses " or " representatives " to Parliament. Edward I, the Tudors, and Charles II added greatly to the list of " Parliamentary Boroughs," which is now a recognized term quite alienated from the Anglo-Saxon or Danish " strong-place " from which it drew its origin.

(II) CASTLE TOWNS

There were many castle towns which were not " boroughs "during the pre-Norman period. They had no other importance than that originating in the castle of the district, and in places where the military importance early vanished, these castle towns enjoyed but little fame. Regarding the site of these new Norman and Plantagenet castles, it must be borne in mind that some advantage of route was necessary, as the castles were bound to be in a position to communicate with each other, to receive troops and transports, and generally to command and overawe the district in which they were placed. Hence they were erected to watch a ford, or guard a bridge, or were placed on a natural eminence, to command a route gap through hilly country. Typical " Defence " towns, growing round their castle hill, are found in Durham and Shrewsbury, which were built in river loops protected by castles.

Until the reign of Henry I or Henry II, castles were built of wood. In the Domesday Book ditched and walled towns are not numerous, though Canterbury, Nottingham and York were surrounded by a deep trench or foss, and Oxford, Hereford, Leicester, Stratford, Chester, Lincoln, and Colchester had walls. The Domesday castles numbered forty-nine. To-day all over England and Wales there are little towns which have grown up round castles, either of the early Norman days, such as Ludlow, Hereford, Barnstaple, Preston, with a population descended from Norman and French retainers of the earliest Norman settlements, or of the castles erected by Edward I, such as Conway, Carnarvon, Beaumaris, Criccieth, Harlech, etc., which the King garrisoned with English colonies; in these latter places there are populations of "English" blood in regions geographically Welsh.

A third type of castle towns arises from baronial castles such as those of Clare, Tunbridge, Arundel, Launceston, Castle Rising, Tamworth, Richmond (Yorks), Pomfret, Appleby, Kendal, etc., causing the growth of "towns" in localities formerly of much less importance.

Castleton[1] (Castletown) in Derbyshire grew entirely out of the influence shed upon the region by the castle which "Peveril of the Peak" built at this spot. Newcastle originated with the castle built by William I near the site of a Roman camp (castra). Castleton has no great present importance, but Newcastle, once but a fortified place in a disturbed territory, then, later, possessing a harbour at the mouth of the Tyne, a centre of export trade to Flanders, exporting as early as King John's reign wool, hides, and the skins of foxes, "sables," beavers, has become

---

[1] Note also Castleton in the Isle of Man.

TOWNS OF THE MIDDLE AGES 205

one of the leading commercial cities of the present day.

Another strictly " Castletown " is Montgomery, of whose origin and growth mention has already been made.[1]

IV.—COUNTY TOWNS

" County Towns " rose out of certain of those Norman Royal Boroughs which had formerly been military centres (boroughs or burghs) of the Danes and Kings of Alfred's time, and in which were placed royal castles for the purposes of dominating them. As we have seen, previous to the Conquest, they were the capitals of the different shires.

Some of these county towns were not fitted to grow in importance, so that it is not uncommon to find in a county several towns of status, wealth, and enterprise far superior to the historic capital. Thus of Dunstable and Bedford in Bedfordshire, the former has long been of the greater importance, though the latter is the capital of the county. But Bedford was not on a Roman road, and as trade developed was found to possess little advantage as a route centre. Dunstable, on the contrary, at the junction of Watling Street and Ichnield Way, was a well-known meeting place of people before it was a town. Here a priory was founded by Henry I, and on account of its advantages of position the Royal Judges held their assizes at Dunstable in preference to Bedford. On the other hand Huntingdon, at the junction of various Roman roads, among which was Erming Street, was otherwise rather out of the way for trade development, and so is of no more importance than Bedford. Other county towns which were quite insignificant were Hertford and Buckingham ; the latter has now been replaced

[1] See page 132.

by Aylesbury as county town. In the north-west we have the case of Lancaster, on the Lune, made capital of a county at a time when southern Lancashire was still little better than a wilderness of swamp and woodland, and the future importance of Liverpool and Manchester quite undreamt of. Newcastle, Durham, Carlisle, Chester and Shrewsbury are fortresses which have become county towns, and which, with the exception of Chester, were at no time Danish boroughs or Saxon burghs.

V.—Church Cities and Towns

(I) Cathedrals

The possession of a cathedral in any locality raises the community growing up round that locality to the dignity of a "city." Most of our cathedrals go back to the time of the Saxon Heptarchy.[1] Our oldest cathedrals and therefore our oldest cities are as follows: Canterbury, Rochester, London, Norwich, Chichester, Winchester, Salisbury, Bath and Wells, Exeter, Hereford, Worcester, Lichfield, Lincoln, Durham, York and Carlisle. York and Carlisle were erected Bishops' Sees after the Norman Conquest; certain of these places to-day possess little but their ecclesiastical importance.

(II) Abbeys, Minsters, Priories

The possession of an Abbey or large ecclesiastical institution other than a cathedral in any locality raised the little settlement that grew round it to the dignity of a town. Benedictine abbeys have given rise to the towns of Glastonbury, Peterborough (Meadhampstead), Bury St. Edmunds, Reading, etc. The

---

[1] Some exceptions are Newcastle, Liverpool, Manchester, Sheffield, Chester, Westminster, etc. In 1889 Southwell Minster (Notts.) was raised to the dignity of a Cathedral; in 1918 the old Parish Church at Bradford was elevated to Cathedral status.

TOWNS OF THE MIDDLE AGES 207

only abbey of the Cluniac congregation was at Bermondsey. The Cistercian Abbeys of Fountains, Waveney, Tintern, Melrose, Walden, Kirkstall, Woburn, Furness, etc., were placed intentionally in isolated localities offering no inducement for men to congregate. The towns that have grown up round some of these Cistercian Abbeys are generally small and of little importance. Ely, for example, was only for monks, and no city grew up here in the Fen district until well on in the mediæval period. Peterborough grew up round its abbey, but its position was a noteworthy asset to its growth. Stoke Abbot, Newton Abbot, Hemingford Abbot, are examples of smaller " Abbey " towns.

Among the minster towns are Axminster, Beaminster, Ilminster, Kidderminster, Leominster, Minsterley, Porthminster, Southminster, Sturminster Newton, Warminster. Prior's Marston should come into the same category.

The wealthy bishops were great builders of churches, and the barons followed their pious example. Bodies of canons were established in connection with these churches and in course of time prosperous " towns " sprang up around them, of which Abbots, Priors and Bishops were the great landowners. Examples are : Bishop's Auckland, Bishop Barton, Bishopbourne, Bishop's Castle, Bishop's Caundle, Bishopstone, Cropwell Bishop, Bishop's Wilton, etc., Alvechurch, Chapel Allerton, Chapleton, Church Oakley, Hawkchurch, Northchurch; while the Norse influence is still felt in such names as Felixkirk, Ormskirk, Oswaldkirk, Ronaldkirk, Kirby, Kirkburn, Kirkby, Kirkdale, Kirkham, etc.

Conventual buildings for women also gave rise to towns, as the following names will illustrate : Nunburnholme, Nuneaton, Nunkeeling, Nunney. Some additional "monkish" houses gave rise to Monk Bretton, Monkseaton, Monkswearmouth, etc.

VI.—Trading Towns

The staple towns were already important centres of population before the staple was taken to them, and hence must belong to the previous classifications. Thus York, an industrial town of the Middle Ages, was a staple town. Similarly fairs and markets were naturally held where conditions of population guaranteed a good sale, though perhaps such towns as Market Drayton, Downham Market, etc., may have owed their growth as towns specifically to their markets.

CHAPTER XVII

Means of Communication and Transport

THE prehistoric "highways" and the ancient Roman roads did not afford the only means of communication and transport before the Anglo-Saxon period. The Romans understood the convenience of river transit, and by embanking had endeavoured to improve certain of the navigable streams. In the case of the Trent and Witham, they even cut a ten-mile dyke, now known as the Foss Dyke, to secure water communication from one river to the other, and between Lincoln on the Witham and Torksey on the Trent. This dyke intercepted the water from the heathy uplands, and in the reign of Henry I was so improved for purposes of river navigation and drainage that it is often regarded as having been cut during the reign of that great monarch. However, after the departure of the Romans road-making and river improvement was a lost art for close upon a thousand years, and in consequence during this time rivers naturally navigable constituted the most important means of inland transport. Most of our older towns and cities not on Roman roads were near or within easy reach of a tidal or navigable stream whereby full advantage could be taken of the transport facilities these waterways offered. Monasteries, castles, baronial halls, for similar reasons, were generally established near rivers, and it is significant that the site of our two oldest university towns—Oxford and Cambridge—were chosen because of their river ways, rendering them accessible by sea and river passage to students from Scotland and elsewhere, travelling along inland roadways being difficult if not altogether out of the question.

ROAD TRANSPORT

During the Middle Ages the State appears to have held a very loose control over the Roadway Systems of South Britain, certainly in the period immediately succeeding the Norman Conquest. As we have already seen,[1] the Monastic Orders took upon themselves much of the responsibility for the work of preservation and repair of such roads as there were, though the hermit, whose solitary mode of life was not seldom assumed by the sinner in the throes of remorse, also took no small part in "the pious and meritorious" labour of road tending and toll collecting.

In course of time this ecclesiastical control became open to abuses, the hermits collecting the tolls without preserving the roads, the monasteries drawing into other channels the legacies left them for this purpose, and in the latter Middle Ages road repairing declined. It was during this period that the building of wayside oratories and chapels-of-ease became common, in which the households of the rural nobility could hear Mass, thus avoiding the often long and dangerous journey along the ill-kept roads to the distant parish church.

Nevertheless there was a considerable "packhorse" or "pack-mule" trade along the better roads, carrying salt, woolpacks and other commodities to markets and fairs, though heavy or bulky goods necessarily travelled by water.

It should be kept in mind that in spite of the disrepair the Roman roads long did good service. Thus the speed of Harold's journey from the north to London to meet Duke William's invasion was such, Mr. Belloc

[1] See page 99.

COMMUNICATION AND TRANSPORT

tells us,[1] that he must have travelled by the Great North Road, and that in a fairly good condition.

The first recorded Act concerning road legislation was passed in the reign of Edward I (1285). This Act provided that on the highways leading from one market town to another there should be neither dyke, tree, nor bush within 200 feet on either side of the way "whereby a man may lurk to do hurt." This Act therefore involved the protection of travellers against robbers, and while having nothing to do with road repair, at least gives us an insight into the existing travelling conditions where it was necessary for traders to combine to send wool, etc., about the country with an armed escort as protection against robbers.

Edward III (1346) imposed tolls for the repair of three roads in London—the King's Highway between the Hospital of St. Giles and the old Temple Bar (Toll Bar) in Holborn, what is now Gray's Inn Road, and St. Martin's Lane.

RIVER TRANSPORT

The main natural waterways north of the Thames were three in number, the rivers of the Severn, Wash, and the Humber groups.

The Severn Group includes the Severn, Warwickshire Avon and Bristol Avon, with Bristol the head-quarters of navigation of the whole system. It was once the great highway for the trade and traffic of Western England and much of Wales, and this accounts for the early development of the Severn counties while others were struggling with the bad roads of the time. The Severn is naturally navigable from Welshpool, 155 miles from the Bristol Channel by the winding stream, a stretch of river navigation unsurpassed—indeed unapproached—without artificial means by any other

[1] "Warfare in England," by Belloc.

river in England. The early Britons came down it in their coracles, and as trade developed towns and cities, each a distributing centre or depôt for large areas, began to rise on its banks, while Bristol, its southern terminus, became a great national port when Liverpool was only an insignificant fishing village.

This river-way was protected as a " King's highway " and made a free river (1430-1), though, of course, landing dues were charged at certain places.

The early commercial prosperity of the Severn towns partly arose out of the important trade in Welsh flannels taken to the fortnightly market at Welshpool, a centre very convenient to the drapers from Shrewsbury. At this latter town the wares brought down the Severn from Wales were bought chiefly by London merchants for their London and Continental trade. Bewdley in the Forest of Wyre developed an extensive export trade in Welsh flannels, timber, wool, leather, sailors' caps, etc., which were sent down the river to Bristol, the exchange of up-river cargo being imported groceries and other commodities for distribution throughout Wales and Lancashire. Bridgnorth also became important through its Bristol trade, via the Severn, in goods brought by road from Cheshire and even Lancashire.

Stratford, Evesham, and Pershore were the chief towns concerned in the Warwickshire Avon trade; the Wye was not navigable till 1661.

The Wash Group includes the Bedford Ouse and its tributaries, of which Lynn is the main outlet; the Welland, with Spalding for its inland port; the Witham with Boston for its " sea-port."

The Ouse-river system supplied six counties wholly and three in part with commodities from Newcastle, Sweden, Norway (firs, timber), Lisbon, Oporto (wines),

COMMUNICATION AND TRANSPORT 213

etc. At Lynn sea cargoes were transferred to river barges and so taken up the Ouse, and the Cam, to the great Fair at Stourbridge, returning thence with Midland and other produce for shipment to Hull and Newcastle, as distributing centres for the Humber and Tyne hinterlands.

Prior to the Conquest the Witham afforded a tideway navigation as far as Lincoln. Its importance is shown by the fact that Henry I caused the Foss Dyke Canal to be scoured out and repaired that Lincoln might reap the benefit of both Trent and Witham trades (1121).

The Humber Group consists of the basins of the Yorkshire Ouse and the Trent. The Ouse and Trent are both naturally navigable rivers. The former is formed by the confluence of the Ure and Swale, and after passing through York, Selby and Goole joins the Trent to form the Humber Estuary. In 1462, Edward IV, the "commercial king," appointed the Lord Mayor and Aldermen of York "overseers and conservators" of the Ouse and its tributaries, the Aire, Wharfe, Derwent, and Don, and the Humber, for the proper navigation of which they thus became responsible.

For many centuries the Trent was the chief means of communication between south and north Nottinghamshire, the dangers of travelling through Sherwood Forest with its robber bands being thus avoided. Nottingham hence became a place of great importance. The Trent-way was at one time the alternative route for conveyance of Cheshire cheeses to London, the order of transit being as follows: by pack-horse or waggon to Burton-on-Trent, from Burton to Hull by barge, from Hull to the Thames by sailing vessel; whereas the second route was by the Mersey in barge, and then sailing vessel to London, via Land's End, the English

Channel, and the Thames Estuary. A direct route across the English lowlands was impossible, owing to the badness of the roads.

The Trent navigation was sufficiently good for ships of large burden to reach Gainsborough, 40 miles up, and barges could go without locks or stops as far as Nottingham, and indeed as far as Burton in Staffordshire " by the help of art." " Art " was also responsible for the navigation of the Derwent up to Derby.

A tributary of the Trent, to-day little known, was once a famous waterway. This was the River Idle, which joins the Trent at Stockwith, twenty-one miles from the junction of the Trent and Humber. Seven miles up the Idle is the once-famous port of Bawtry, eight miles south-east of Doncaster, on the Great North Road. Until the navigation of the Don was improved (Act of 1727), Doncaster, the distributing centre for foreign products[1] into Yorkshire, and for Yorkshire products for London and abroad, received goods via the Humber-Trent-Idle and Bawtry route, at which latter river-port goods were received from and sent on to Doncaster and elsewhere in Yorkshire by pack-horse and waggon, rather than by the restricted Humber and Don route, or Humber, Ouse and Aire route. The fame of Bawtry is thus accounted for; its market dates from the 13th century. Down to the middle of the 18th century the Sheffield cutlery—a famous Middle Age industry—and the Hallamshire iron goods (the trade dating from the reign of Henry II) passed through Bawtry on their way to London, the Eastern counties or the Continent. The transit effected by pack-horse from Sheffield to Bawtry was twenty miles.

[1] That is foreign to the *Shire.* They might come from home or abroad.

The Thames Group includes the Rivers Thames, Lea, Wey and Medway.

The number of early settlements that have been discovered along the banks of the Thames, the cities and towns that border it, the number of monasteries, abbeys and kindred establishments in its valley, the presence of our oldest University town, show how early and completely the Thames was recognized as an important waterway. It was, in fact, the main and most useful " highway " for its riverine counties.

As early as 1424 the Lea was regarded as one of the great rivers, and it had a large carrying industry. The history of Ware goes back to the 9th century, when the Danes brought their long, light, sea-going vessels up to the place where they were stranded as a consequence of King Alfred's device of diverting the stream! Ware was a good up-river port, convenient for trade with several inland counties.

The Wey, navigable to Godalming, carried the London trade in timber from Sussex and Hampshire. The Medway supplied London and elsewhere with timber from Sussex and Kent.

Another famous waterway for trade was the Exe; from Exeter woollen goods were sent down the river for Holland, Portugal, Spain, and Italy. Exeter, Crediton, Honiton, Tiverton and the north of the county were famous for the manufacture of Devonshire serges, of which the Dutch bought large quantities.

CHAPTER XVIII
THE GREAT AWAKENING

IN these two sections we have followed in some detail the story of South Britain throughout those long centuries intermediate between the Roman Empire and the Discovery of the New World. Beyond the remoter limit of this mediæval period Britain stood alone, on the edge of the then known world, almost isolated from its great movements, almost untouched by its great ideals; a country half mythical, a land of "barbarians," some of whom might be and were tamed into subjects. Beyond the latter limit Britain truly becomes Great Britain in fact as well as name, takes, and for a time at least is keeping, the lead among the nations. At this point it will therefore be worth while to consider briefly what sequence of influences and events paved the way for this stupendous progress.

Situated on the edge of the world, Britain was for long ages the refuge of many races of people entering at the Continental angle at the south-east and successively forced north and west by the oncoming waves of emigrants, each ranking a little higher in the stages of civilization than its predecessor. But it was not until the English lowlands became part of the Roman Empire that Britain was brought into the civilized world.

After the departure of their Roman masters the native populace were without any central organization, and found themselves exposed on all sides to the successful attacks of "the heathen swarming o'er the Northern Sea." Saxons, Angles, Jutes, Danes, and

THE GREAT AWAKENING 217

Norsemen invaded the country on the south and east and south and west, setting up small states, introducing new ways of living, which are not without their influence even at the present day. Towards the close of this period the former Roman Province of Lower Britain became part of the Northern Empire of Canute (1014-1035), centred in Denmark and South Norway, a connection with Europe, certainly, but temporarily and not with the part that greatly counted. With the coming of the Normans and their oversea connection with France, the government of the country naturally focused in the south-east quadrant in which London possessed many advantages of geographical site. Near the limit of sea navigation, on the first outcrop of firm ground (lying between Tower Hill and Ludgate Hill), amid the marshes on the river's northern bank, it was at once the natural crossing place for converging roads from the Thames valley and a port for both river and sea. The only possible rival to London as a metropolis lay at Winchester, with its traditions of Wessex supremacy, and great Alfred's capital, somewhat similarly situated in the Hampshire Basin, on the Itchen, and with that "queen's chamber" known as Southampton Water and the Solent taking the place of the Thames Estuary. But when South Britain became "England" rather than "Wessex," clearly Winchester was somewhat remote, and its advantages (and traditions) too local for the capital, so that London had no difficulty in holding its own. Indeed, at one time, it seemed as if London might be the centre of rule for Western France, when the great Angevin Empire of our King Henry II extended to the Pyrenees, but beyond this temporary connection, even then England had few relations with the outer world.

The Crusades did something to link us to the distant East, and the wealthier inhabitants of our country at all events came to desire Eastern produce, among which spices formed an important part, as by their means our otherwise monotonous store of winter food was rendered more palatable. But the world's commerce was carried in Venetian, not English, ships, though our increasing number of fishing and coasting vessels were laying the foundation of a future and far different state of affairs.

On the other hand, coherence within our realm was growing steadily. The obvious advantages of London had made it a great city, easily ruling the very accessible districts of the English lowlands, a unit not too large to be homogeneous and hence welcoming one government for the area. Ultimately this government control extended to the English uplands, though the highlands of Wales long stood apart.

During all this period a climatic factor was making for industry and national wealth. The insular position of Britain, the currents setting round our coasts, the warm moisture of our prevailing westerly winds, made for a mild winter—bracing without numbing, and for a cool summer, warming without exhausting. Hence all the year round it was possible to do work, and all the year round cyclonic winds guaranteed sufficient rain for permanent *grass*. The result of this was extensive sheep-rearing and allied industries, which went their course under the protection of the girdle of the sea and a strong central authority, and therefore unhampered by fears of invasion from without or (save in a few cases, hardly, however, touching the commonalty of the people) of anarchy from within. The selling of wool to foreign merchants was naturally accompanied by a return trade in foreign commodities.

THE GREAT AWAKENING

but still, in spite of all its prosperity, Mediæval Britain remained " on the outer fringe of all the world that mattered."

In 1453 the south-eastern corner of Europe underwent a great calamity. With Constantinople as leading city of culture and enlightenment, it fell into the hands of the conquering Turk. For some time this catastrophe seemed overwhelming, especially as it closed the land way to the East and to those Spice Islands (the East Indies) whose productions had now become the necessities of Western Europe. This closing of the East by the Infidel had far-reaching effects, not the least of which was the shifting of the " carrying trade " from the Central Mediterranean to the Western Nations of Europe. The decline of Venice and Genoa as " the carriers of the world " was now assured, but England was to wait long before she profited to the full from their adversity. On the other hand men were determined *not* to forgo the luxuries to which they had become accustomed, and bold attempts were made to find the East by other routes. Meanwhile the Western Passage was suggested on the assumption that the world was " round," an assumption for which, not so long ago, men had been martyred at the stake.

The story of the epoch-making voyages of Christopher Columbus, Vasca da Gama, and that host of adventurers who followed them out upon the unknown seas, has been told in other places. Their outcome was the discovery of vast lands of great and diverse natural resources, and a new understanding of the ocean as a safe vehicle for transport and a bond of union rather than a division between the continents, portents worthy to herald the dawn of a new age. Britain's insular position, once cutting her off from the rest of the world, now linked her to its remotest bounds; and when, at a later date, traffic developed along the ocean ways to the Indies and to America, it became clear that she too, like the Venice of the Middle Ages, was an intermediate station along the great sea routes instead of a terminus that led no-whither.

And gradually the water-borne commerce of the world changed hands; after Venice, Portugal; after Portugal, Holland, came to the front as trading sea-powers, the supremacy ever passing westward till that day when the sailors of Britain, nursed amid the turbulent waters that wash her tide-swept coasts, wrested the prize from Holland and bequeathed it as their dearest legacy to her people.

SECTION IV

THE MODERN PERIOD

CHAPTER XIX

REVOLUTION IN TRANSPORT: ROAD WAYS

I

ROADS AND ROAD MAKING

THE AGE OF BAD ROADS

THE inadequacy of the highways, and still more of the by-ways of Mediæval England, kept in erratic repair by men (fortunately pious) in their vicinity, received no serious consideration until the 18th century was well upon its way.

The deep lanes which are to be found in many parts of England and especially in Devonshire, represent roads worn down by centuries of traffic. In winter most of them must have been quite useless until the modern practice of protecting their surface with stones came into vogue. The Great North Road, much of it the old Roman Way, between London and Berwick provides a good illustration of the badness of the roads down to the introduction of the Turnpike System. The greater part of this road was only an open track across commons, fens, marshes, heaths, or through woods, and the custom of the drivers of carts, waggons, or coaches to discard old paths when rutted, for new ones, probably accounts for the seemingly aimless twisting and turning of many old county roads whose " devious paths " are otherwise hard to explain.

At the beginning of the 18th century the badness of the roads was a serious drawback to internal trade owing to the difficulty of conveying goods from the place of their manufacture to the market, but the military needs of 1745 (the year of the Jacobite rising) caused the Government to consider the matter, and the outcome was the " Turnpike System."

THE TURNPIKE SYSTEM

In the Middle Ages the " ecclesiastical " supervision of road-repair was supplemented as regarded the main highways by State control, but at the Dissolution of the Monasteries (1536) the question as to the State's real responsibility became very pressing. The Parishes were perhaps regarded as the natural inheritors of the Monastic System, and upon them was placed the duty of keeping the roads in repair—a duty they had certainly come to share with the former clerical houses. In course of time the Parishes declared it unjust that they should have to pay for the upkeep of roads used by " outsiders " and accordingly the State took over the major portion of the main roads, while the Parishes were responsible for certain portions of them and all other roads. Toll-bars, or pikes, gates, etc., were placed across the roads and turned aside or opened on payment of a toll. In this way it was expected that the roads would be kept in repair by means of the charges taken from the people using them. By 1767 the System had become quite general, Parish labour or contributions being given to the " cross roads " which were regarded as Parish highways, no toll being exacted for their use.

The defects of the system were many and serious. The lack of uniformity in quality and quantity of the repairs carried out, the administration by means of " Turnpike Trusts " whose members frequently diverted the toll to their personal advantage, the costly systems of collecting the tolls, the passage of the money through the hands of dishonest lawyers and officials, mitigated much of the good to be expected of a system not in itself well-organized or conceived. Yet the improvement in road-travel was real and recognized, and the adverse criticism of Arthur Young, the Travelling Secretary for the Ministry of Agriculture, and others upon the newly " turn-piked roads " redound less to their inadequacy than to a dark hinting of an inconceivably worse state that preceded them. He writes : " From Newport Pagenel I took the road to Bedford, if I may venture to call such a cursed string of ruts and holes by the name of a road ; a causeway is here and there thrown up but so high and at the same time so very narrow that it was at the peril of our necks we passed a waggon with a civil and careful driver." " From Grimsthorpe to Coltsworth are 8 miles, called by the courtesy of the neighbourhood a turn-pike, but in which we were every moment either buried in quagmires of mud or racked to dislocation over pieces of rock which they call mending." (Tour through the North of England, 1770). " The roads," declared a still more passionate writer, " were sloughs almost impassable by simple carts, surmounted at the height of several feet by narrow horse tracks where travellers who encountered each other sometimes tried to wear out each other's patience rather than either risk a deviation."

However, it is noteworthy that the limitations in travelling facilities resulted in many a country town possessing a far greater degree of social distinction than it has to-day, when its neighbouring aristocracy regard London as the proper place in which to enjoy its winter amusements.

ROAD MAKING AND ROAD REPAIRING

The Turnpike System was still in its infancy when men began to conceive projects of a more scientific road-making and especially road-mending.

As far back as 1765, "Blind John Metcalf" of Knaresborough proposed a hitherto unique method of road-making for the new road in contemplation between Harrogate and Boroughbridge. This road, crossing bogs and marshland, was constructed in accordance with Metcalf's suggestions. A safe causeway was made through the bogs by digging two parallel ditches and piling the excavated material on the ground between them. Upon this embankment were placed lengthwise bundles of heather and ling, and the whole was covered with stones tipped from the front of a broad-wheeled waggon pushed along the causeway bit by bit as it was completed. A section of the road between Manchester and Huddersfield was used regularly for twelve years without requiring much repair.

The usual method of road-making consisted in laying down a course of large stones, then of smaller ones, and a final covering of dirt, giving the road a convex surface to allow rain to run off to the sides, where, as there were no ditches to drain away the water, in wet weather it accumulated considerably. The traffic was therefore kept as far as possible to the central ridge, which was soon crushed in and heavily rutted, occasional repair being effected by tumbling loose stones between the ruts.

Thomas Telford (b. 1757), a Scotchman, began his career as a stone-maker's apprentice, but became an eminent road-engineer. He was selected by certain Parliamentary Commissioners of Scotland to construct good roads in the Highlands. In 1815 the English Parliament voted money for a similar purpose, and Telford was appointed engineer-in-chief of the new works. His method of road-making was as follows: the track designed for the intended roadway was

TRANSPORT: ROADWAYS

covered with stones, 4-7 inches in size, the broadest ends being placed by hand face downwards. The spaces between were packed with small stones to get a level surface. Above this there was an inch of gravel binding, and finally an upper course of broken stones. Every hundred yards a drain was cut across the road, which was only moderately convex. The constructing of such a road was very expensive.

John Loudon Macadam (b. 1756), also a Scotchman, was less a road-maker than a road-repairer. In 1785 he began to devote his attention to road mending, " perhaps the most important branch of our domestic economy." His method was as follows : the roadway under repair received a course of 8 to 10 inches of artificially broken stones (road metal) about $1\frac{1}{2}$ inches long. Consolidation was effected by reason of the sharp angles of the broken stones, and under the pressure of traffic a firm, compact, impenetrable mass as regards action of rain and wheels was obtained. Broken stones dovetail together under a pressure which would cause pebbles and flints to roll apart.

In 1816, Macadam became surveyor of the roads in the neighbourhood of Bristol, and two years later his system began to be generally adopted. New roads were laid down straight away by this process of " Macadamizing." Between 1818 and 1829, the length of turnpike roads of England and Wales was increased by more than 1,000 miles.

Later, consolidation was effected at the first laying down of the roads, the pressure being supplied by steam-roller.

Since Macadam's time timber roading is not infrequent in towns, e.g., London, where it is essential to deaden the noise of the traffic. The timber is cut into blocks, or bricks, or setts, and covered with a coating of creosote to prevent fungi growth. Asphalt (bitumen) from Trinidad is extensively used for this purpose. In cities and large towns stone setts—granite " cubes " of size from one and a half to three inches are often used in place of the more roughly broken stones.

II

Traffic on the Roads

Previous to 1564 horse-litters, agricultural carts, saddle-horses and pack-horses were the only means of travelling and conveying goods upon the " roads." Private carriages as an alternative to horse-litters or horse-pack were but gorgeously decorated springless carts made fashionable by Queen Elizabeth.

The Wain or Long Waggon

In 1564 the wain or long waggon came into use. It developed into a roomy, covered vehicle capable of holding twenty passengers and some merchandise. The bad state of the road demanded broad wheels and the waggon was drawn by six, eight or even ten horses—at a walking pace! These waggons made regular journeys between London, Canterbury, Norwich, Ipswich, Gloucester, etc., the whole journey being undertaken by the same horses. The London-Dover Road, with its Continental connection, was the best-kept road in the country and the journey—at first by river to Gravesend, but after 1643 all the way by road—occupied 3-4 days! In the 18th century there was a regular service between London and Bristol, the waggons taking 6 days for the journey, including rest at night for both travellers and horses.

The Stage Coach

Stage coaches were introduced about 1659. Three

TRANSPORT: ROADWAYS

stage coaches ran between London and York, Chester and Exeter (1673), carrying six passengers each per journey. The service was only possible in the summer months, on account of the badness of the roads, and even so the passengers might have to walk several miles at a stretch while the coach and horses made slow and painful progress through the mire. The usual speed was from four to four and a half miles an hour. In 1700 York was a week distant from London, but on April 12th, 1706, a tri-weekly coach was started to perform the whole journey in four days " if God permits." By 1751 the London-Dover stage coach was doing the journey in two days, the passengers dining at Rochester, sleeping at Canterbury, and arriving at Dover " the next morning early." The stage coach was so called because the same horses did not perform the whole journey, fresh ones were put in at certain definite intervals or " stages," thus increasing the speed. A " conveniency " (or basket) was attached behind for luggage and outside passengers.

In 1754 the Newcastle " Flying Coach " promised a journey to London in nine days (the former time required was twelve) for which purpose " eight stout horses are stationed at proper distances." A " Flying Coach " was soon running between Manchester and London, to perform the journey in four and a half days " incredible as it may appear," in 1757 a " Flying Machine on Steel Springs " was advertised to run from Warrington to London in two days, the journey between Warrington and Liverpool being done on horseback, as coaches could not travel on the bad road. By 1782 the time of the whole journey between Liverpool and London had been reduced to forty-eight hours. In 1795 the " Flying Machine " pounding along the Dover Road, did the journey in one day.

The Mail Coach

The next step in coaching development arose out of the defective postal arrangements. So far the mails were carried upon short journeys by post-boys or " veterans " at the rate of five miles an hour, while parcels or urgent letters, or letters for longer distances went with the coaches. In 1784 the mail coach was definitely established. It is said that a certain John Palmer, Manager of the Bath Theatre, urged Pitt to this step. The journey from London to Bristol was now accomplished in sixteen hours, the rate being eight to twelve miles an hour according to the weather. The favour found by the mail coach stimulated the making of better roads and coaches; the basket " conveniency " for example being exchanged for seats on the roof.

The mail coach era ended with the first despatch of mail by railway in 1830.

The palmy days of the coaching era were from 1820 to 1836, a period contemporaneous with the new development in road making and repair. By 1836 the competition of the rail-roads heralded the end of the coaching days, and by 1849 the stage coaches were practically supplanted by the locomotives.

III

Decline of the Turnpike System

Meanwhile the Turnpike System of road charges was also in a state of decline. About 1843 a reduction in the number of Turnpike Trusts was an undoubted boon to the users of the roads, though it threw a heavy burden on the local rate-payers—a reversal of the object for which Turnpikes were first instituted. In

1864 a Parliamentary Committee condemned the whole system as "unequal in pressure, costly in collection, inconvenient to the public, and injurious as causing a serious impediment to intercourse and traffic." Nearly twenty years later Mr. Gladstone's Ministry passed a Bill by means of which one quarter of the cost of maintaining the "disturnpiked roads" was to be met by an annual Parliamentary grant, four years later the relief granted was increased to one half the cost. Between December, 1864, and January, 1890, the number of Trusts had fallen from 1048 to 5, and the mileage of Turnpike Roads from 20,589 to 77. By 1896 the system of Turnpikes on public roads had wholly disappeared.

CHAPTER XX

REVOLUTION IN TRANSPORT. WATER WAYS

1. RIVER IMPROVEMENT

THE importance of river navigation as a means of interior communication was paramount during the whole of the mediæval period. The development of modern trade required larger boats, newer or different centres, and these in addition to the natural differences due to time upon the régime of the rivers, necessitated improvements in many of the existing water-ways.

RIVERS WYE AND LUGG (WALES)

In 1661 Sir William Sandys obtained Parliamentary sanction to make the Wye and Lugg navigable, an operation successfully effected by deepening the embankment and cutting new channels to avoid exceptionally injurious windings; and similar improvements, together with lock construction to guarantee the side streams their water supply, were soon in progress upon several of our other rivers.

In 1679 the Aire-Calder was made navigable, an important event for the then rising manufacturing towns of Leeds, Wakefield, Halifax, Bradford and Huddersfield. The main textile industries, originally established in the Eastern Counties by refugees from the Netherlands and France, but with offshoots on the gentle slopes and in the vales of the West Country,[1] migrated to the north at a time when the woollen industries were paramount and the cotton still in a

---

[1] The true "West Country Cloth" is not referred to at this place. See page 245.

TRANSPORT : WATERWAYS 233

comparatively early and unimportant stage. This removal to the Pennines was due to the superior condition of water power for the working of the newly invented " power loom " and to the *Eastern* Pennines partly because of the proximity to the East Anglian Industry about to be supplanted, and partly because Lancashire was still too commercially backward to be suggested as a proper alternative to Yorkshire. The rise of the Eastern Pennine towns and the importance of those of the Aire-Calder navigation is thus easily understood.

THE MERSEY AND WEAVER RIVERS

Until 1694 when the improvement of the Mersey was seriously undertaken, Liverpool had no chance of emerging from a situation of almost complete isolation. Sand-banks, rapid currents, adverse tides in the estuary all combined to hamper navigation which indeed went no further than Runcorn. Equally useless as " Ways " were the Weaver and Irwell. The mountainous areas to the North and East and the Marshes to the South isolated both Liverpool and Lancashire from England's general trade. It seemed as if only a miracle could bring the quiet fishing village to the fore. And that miracle took place. Twenty-two miles up the estuary of the Dee lay Chester, with its Roman Road to London, its tradition of Saxon and Norman greatness, and its Irish trade, which might have been a serious rival to Liverpool once the disadvantages of its position surmounted. But by the close of the Middle Ages the silting of the Dee, and consequent shallowing of the estuary waters were working its ruin as a sea-port, and simultaneously with this decline the American trade was developing, especially that part of it concerned with the importation of large quantities of cotton, demanding at once a port on the south or west and a climate of exceptional humidity, both of which were realized in Liverpool and its damp hinterland. A Parliamentary Act in 1694 sanctioned the improvement of the Mersey from Runcorn to Warrington, and a later one, of the Upper Mersey and its tributary, the Irwell, from Warrington to Manchester, thus giving a water transport between Liverpool and Manchester as an alternative to the road. Twenty-six years later sanction was obtained for making the Weaver navigable from Winsford Bridge beyond Northwich to Frodsham Bridge at the Weaver and Mersey junction. The advantage to Liverpool as a port is obvious, and was the first step in the development of the salt *mines* of Cheshire.

2. CANALS

In spite of all improvements the river navigation as a means of transport had some very serious drawbacks, such as floods, droughts, shallows, shoals, and the necessity for the time-wasting lock. In addition, as trade and industry increased the rivers could not and did not serve every place requiring transport of this character. The practice already gained in river improvement naturally decided the nature of the next step in the evolution of water transport, the construction of those artificial waterways commonly designated canals.

The object thus to be served was fourfold: water transport for centres of population not on or near navigable streams; avoidance of waterfalls, shoals, and rapids by an artificial side-cut furnished with locks or water-gates; connection between navigable inland water-ways, and lastly, connection between ocean, sea and inland towns. The canal system was only slowly evolved, and after enjoying a short zenith of popularity accompanied by wild, national specula-

TRANSPORT : WATERWAYS

tion, passed into a long period of decline, not as yet entirely terminated.

THE DUKE OF BRIDGWATER'S CANAL (WORSLEY-MANCHESTER)

The first true canal in England was constructed at the instigation of Francis, Duke of Bridgwater—a name of good omen in this new undertaking. It was the outcome of his desire to convey coal from his Worsley collieries to the suburbs of Manchester. The seven miles of roadway between these two places were impassable for heavy coal waggons and the improved Mersey-Irwell route was too costly. To construct this canal the engineer James Brindley (b. 1711), was faced with the difficulty of getting the water across the high banks of the Irwell at Barton, a difficulty that could be met by a stairway of locks on either side of the stream, or by carrying the canal in a viaduct right across the valley. The second alternative was chosen and the Worsley-Manchester Canal was completed in 1761.

THE LIVERPOOL AND MANCHESTER (BRIDGWATER) CANAL

The Duke's next project was for a canal between Liverpool and Manchester, and now he had to face a very determined opposition on the part of the River Navigation Companies, which greatly delayed Parliamentary sanction for the undertaking. The Canal was opened for traffic in 1767. It started at Longford Bridge, Manchester, where it connected with the Worsley Canal, and ended at Runcorn, a distance of 24 miles. It passed through a bog with quicksand at the bottom ; it crossed two rivers, requiring numerous aqueducts, and dropped down to the Mersey in a flight of locks at Runcorn. The Duke subsequently established passenger boats on these two canals.

This canal diverted to Liverpool the stream of export trade which had hitherto gone from Manchester by way of Bridgnorth and the Severn Bristol route. It enabled the manufacturers of Manchester to obtain raw material from Liverpool and opened that port to a large hinterland to its own benefit and to that of industrial Lancashire.

THE SANKEY BROOK CANAL

Meanwhile the growth of Liverpool as a port was being stimulated elsewhere. In 1775, Parliament sanctioned the project of the Liverpool Corporation and merchants to deepen three streams flowing from the St. Helens coalfield and combining to form the Sankey Brook which drains into the marshes two miles below Warrington. It was found impossible to make the brook navigable owing to the floods of water draining it from the hill-sides in the wet season, and accordingly a canal was constructed parallel to its course, but higher up the valley side where the flood water would be considerably less. As this canal was owned by a public body it may be said to have inaugurated the Canal Era. It provided for a convenient coal supply for Liverpool, and as the Weaver had already been rendered navigable put the Cheshire salt industry into direct communication with the Lancashire coalfields, at once expanding this industry and increasing the export of salt from Liverpool.

THE TRENT AND MERSEY CANAL (Grand Trunk Canal) opened 1777

Brindley's success in the Bridgwater Canals led to his employment in an ambitious enterprise financed by Earl Gower, the Duke of Bridgwater, the Earl of Stamford and Josiah Wedgwood, the great pottery manufacturer. The project was to construct a linking canal between the Mersey and Trent, and to fling out

TRANSPORT: WATERWAYS

"lateral" canals along the combined waterway. This canal is the first suggestion since the Romans made their roads of a real system of inland communication for the country as a whole, the Turnpikes generally serving local needs and in any case offering no well planned system of unity.

The difficulty of construction arose from the necessity of "taking the water uphill." This was met by the use of locks, the difference of surface level from the Mersey to the summit at Harecastle, near the Staffordshire Potteries, being 395 feet, of which the final climb of 314 feet was accomplished by a flight of 35 locks. A tunnel 12 feet high, 9 feet 4 inches broad, $1\frac{1}{2}$ miles in length was driven through Harecastle Hill, and in this tunnel barges were propelled by the legs of the bargees against its roof and walls. South of the tunnel the descent to the Trent was effected by 40 locks, bringing the water down 288 feet (a wider, higher tunnel was subsequently constructed by Telford). During its course of 90 miles the canal had to pass through four other tunnels, cross the River Dove in an aqueduct of 23 arches, and be carried at four points over the windings of the Trent which it joined at Wilden Ferry. The canal—opened for traffic 1777, was "the first connecting link in our national history between the ports of Liverpool and Hull." It carried much of the Midland manufacturing trade, especially when later supplemented by the Wolverhampton (now Staffordshire and Worcestershire Canal), the Coventry (the Trent, via Lichfield and Oxford to the Thames) and other canals.

The advantages of quicker, cheaper and more widespread transport reaped by the Potteries from the Trent and Mersey Canal were enormous. Fourteen years earlier Josiah Wedgwood had perfected a series of experiments in the pottery industry which were later to develop the coarse pottery of North Staffordshire into wares of the highest excellence with not only an English, but a world-wide market.

Birmingham, requiring ores to mix with the Staffordshire ores now obtained raw material much more cheaply than before and at the same time secured better facilities for distributing its guns, nails, hardwares, etc., to Hull by water. The fine ale of Burton-on-Trent formerly sent via the Humber to London and the Continent now, by means of the Trent-Mersey canal, found new markets in Liverpool and on the west coast.

The towns with least cause for satisfaction were Bridgnorth, Bewdley and Bristol, which had lost the to-and-fro traffic in connection with the pottery trade now passing by the Grand Trunk Canal to Liverpool.

THE LEEDS AND LIVERPOOL CANAL (opened about 1810)

This most useful waterway provides another example of the difficulties attending canal construction in England. The Foulridge Hills had to be pierced by a tunnel 1640 yards long; and the Aire and the Shipley valley had to be bridged by an aqueduct of numerous arches. The total length of navigation was one hundred and twenty-seven miles, taking forty-one years of labour, and a cost of £1,200,000. But the end more than justified the means; the effects on Industrial Lancashire and Yorkshire were as great as that of the Grand Trunk Canal in the Midlands, Wigan, Blackburn, Nelson, Keighley, Bradford and Leeds all reaping therefrom commercial advantages of the first importance.

Between 1755 and 1825 three thousand miles of canal were opened for traffic in the United Kingdom.

TRANSPORT: WATERWAYS

During the years 1791-4, on account of the profits arising from this species of water-way the country may be said to have been suffering from "canal mania," the three years witnessing the passage of no less than eighty-one Canal and Navigation Acts, the shares in the different undertakings selling for greatly inflated prices.

There were, however, certain drawbacks to canal transport, drawbacks brought into greater prominence by the competition of the railways. To be entirely successful the country traversed by canals ought to be level, requiring the minimum number of locks, so wasteful in time, so expensive in construction, and therefore in toll. In England the initial enthusiasm, especially of private owners, deprived the system of that organization only arrived at by careful and far-sighted consideration in the beginnings and accordingly the canals tended to be personal and local in use, and so various in width that passage of goods from one to another, though otherwise possible, often involved "break of bulk." The same lack of uniformity was displayed in the dimensions of the canal tunnels, where desire for economy did not even permit a towing path. The charge for use was often unduly high, and in winter, through neglect to provide ice breakers, transport was often impossible.

The canal owners, whether private or public, naturally put forward a strong opposition to the various Railway Bills which in time came before Parliament, and sometimes by this means succeeded in forcing the Railway Companies to purchase a canal already in existence and far gone in decline. In this way the Oxford, Worcester and Wolverhampton Railway was made to purchase the Stratford-on-Avon Canal, and the Great Western Railway the Kennet and Avon

Canal, under threat of seeing a rival railway built for these distances by the Canal proprietors. This was also the case with the London and Birmingham Railway (which had by now become the L. & N.W.R.) Company, which reluctantly acquired the Birmingham Canal navigation. The shareholders thus received back their original capital, while the railways were bound by Act of Parliament to keep the waterways in good repair, though run at great losses ever since the purchase.

The competition of the railroads was not the only disqualifying factor. The canals originated through the necessity of providing some new means of carrying coals from the mines to population centres. The subsidence of the land through mining operations very heavily increased the expenditure in canal repair. Thus the Birmingham Canal through the Black Country was undermined for a total distance of 80 miles by colliery workings, and now runs on the top of embankments raised at different times to maintain the waterway above the level of the sinking ground. The fact that it belonged to the L. & N.W.R., bound by Act to keep it in good and effective working condition, is the only reason for its continued existence.

Moreover the canals also share some of the defects of the rivers. There are some places to which they may not go, whereas railways can go anywhere, even to the pit's mouth. Where canals are only a short distance from the works, haulage to them is often so expensive as to use up the difference between the transport charges for the rail and cheaper water passage.

Some canals are not sufficiently wide for the increasing modern business; the Birmingham canal has reached its capacity, and cannot take any more traffic

TRANSPORT: WATERWAYS

unless it is widened, an undertaking impossible in view of the high cost involved and the position of the railway which has grown up alongside.

Of course some canals are still useful, especially when they meet the sea and ships can unload on to barges, which take the cargo straight to works on canal banks, and vice versa. In 1910 the pottery district of North Staffordshire received 200,000 tons of flints, clay and other pottery material imported at Runcorn, Ellesmere Port or Western Port (all on the Mersey Estuary) and carried by canal to the pottery works located on or near the banks. In the case of the Aire and Calder Canal coal is taken from collieries immediately alongside the waterway to steamers or coaling ships in the port of Goole. The Manchester Ship Canal, opened in 1894, extends from Eastham on the Mersey estuary to Manchester, a distance of 40 miles. Passing through Runcorn and Latchford, it bridges the Weaver and Mersey by means of aqueducts. It has made Manchester the fourth seaport in the kingdom, thus fulfilling the desire of its constructors for the carrying of "Manchester goods to Manchester docks."

To-day there is some talk of reviving the old canals as an obligation of State, but though some traders would benefit from this revival there are many who would not, and also, in company with the general taxpayer, would have to contribute to the cost if the State did acquire these waterways and failed to make them pay.

CHAPTER XXI

MODERN INDUSTRIES

THE change from mediæval to modern industries was so gradual, and so dependent upon the nature of the industry that no real date can be assigned to it. Of the modern industries themselves practically there are none that were not in operation in some form or other during the previous period. All that can be said, perhaps, is that old methods became superseded, raw material was discovered in unexpected places and in larger quantities, and that popular necessities—it may be merely popular favour—furthered the expansion of one industry at the expense of another.

SPINNING

The spinning of woollen thread was mainly done by young women (spinsters) and in the Middle Ages Parliament was so anxious to extend the manufacture of woollen cloth that an Act was passed ordering all persons to be " buried in woollens."

Manchester *cotton* spinning, like cloth weaving, resulted from the immigration of foreign weavers. Early in the 17th century cotton spinning declined at Antwerp, and it is generally supposed that the spinners came to Manchester, which certainly took its rise as an industrial centre from this time. Gradually in the 18th century, a new fabric, calico, was introduced from Calicut, India, but until 1722 it was a penal offence in England to wear or sell calico (all cotton), and until 1774 the making or selling a fabric of more than one-half cotton thread was liable to prosecution, so fondly did the country cling to its old staple wool. Cotton thread in England was therefore limited in demand until 1738, when the invention of "Kay's Flying Shuttle" enabled the weavers to produce twice as much cloth as before, thus increasing the demand upon the spinners who could not, in fact, meet it. This flung the weavers out of work, but their turn came in 1767 when Hargreave's "Spinning Jenny" so increased the rate of spinning threads that the spinners were left unemployed. Two years later Arkwright's "Spinning Machine," worked by water-power, made the matter still worse for the spinners, and indeed every change in the evolution of the Spinning and Weaving Industry was accompanied by rioting of a more or less serious character on the part of one or other class of the employees affected. In 1779 Samuel Compton invented the spinning machine known as "The Mule," but in 1785 his new "Power Loom" Machine increased the rate of weaving, and thus equalized the difference between the amount of thread spun and cloth woven. Later James Watt showed the superior value of "Steam Power." The setting up of a steam engine at Popplewick (Nottinghamshire, 1785) for the operation of the various forms of machinery now in use for the cotton industry marked at once the decline of domestic or home manufactures and the advent of the factory system which was to bring about a complete transformation in the industrial conditions of the United Kingdom.

The Power Loom was long in affecting the worsted, and still longer in affecting the woollen industry.

TEXTILES, WORSTEDS; EAST ANGLIAN CLOTHS

It has already been noticed that East Anglia and other regions of similar climatic and geographical conditions rose early to fame in connection with the so-called "Woollen" Industry (really Worsted), for which long wool was required or a mixture of worsted and woollen thread (long and short wool). The making of the material itself was effected without the use or the necessity of using water-power, though in the case of the mixtures a little water was required for scouring the cloth.

The various cloths, damasks, says, serges (long wool or worsteds), blankets, kerseys (the shorter threads of the long fleeces), baizes, flannels, and linseys (a mixture of worsted and woollen threads—while linseys had linen in addition), continued to be made right into the modern period. Even in the middle of the 18th century, East Anglia was still the greatest worsted centre, though the West Riding—whose beginnings in this industry are vague and obscure—was making progress with Bradford as chief centre.

At first the worsted yarn of Yorkshire was sent to Norwich to be marketed, and to be dyed and woven into fine stuffs, but gradually the Yorkshire workman equalled and then surpassed his East Anglian teacher, and the additional fact that in Yorkshire labour was cheaper, the labourer living more frugally on porridge, oat-cake and milk, was more industrious, thrifty and reliable—assets which he preserved—made secure the position the industry had won. After the Industrial Revolution the processes in vogue for the worsted industry (the power loom, etc.) required rapidly falling water, in which the Eastern Counties were deficient, whereas it was far otherwise in the Pennine districts, and by 1840 the struggle between East Anglia and the West Riding was going strongly in favour of the latter. Then came the need for more power, supplied by machinery, for which coal was used, and with the opening up of the coal-field of the Eastern Pennines,

MODERN INDUSTRIES 245

Yorkshire became supreme in the worsted trade, in which, in fact, the greatness of her future was to be so largely bound up. The discovery that new and elegant fabrics could be cheaply manufactured by a combination of worsted with cotton, alpaca or mohair gave a reputation of its own to the Yorkshire Cloths eminently desirable in an industry passing to a new region.

TEXTILES, WOOLLENS. THE WEST COUNTRY CLOTHS

About the middle of the 15th century, England began to produce a new kind of cloth, differing from the true worsteds in that water-power for milling was required in its manufacture. The wool, too, differed from worsted wool, being short and fine, whereas the worsted wools were made from long fleeces. These new cloths were various kinds of "broadcloths." In addition a serge *cloth* appeared, differing from the Anglian serges in that short wool was mixed with the long wool, and that, like the "broadcloth," this also was a milled cloth, requiring water-power for this operation.

As this industry had reached its zenith of fame in the middle of the 18th century, it will be classed in this section, among the modern industries.

Neither East Anglia nor Kent[1] were suited for the manufacture of these milled cloths, the one on account of its sluggish rivers, and the other because of the intermittent character of its obsequent streams[2], which do not guarantee a regular power all the year round, though the right kind of sheep—short wool—was bred upon its chalk escarpments. But it was far otherwise in the West Country, with its damp climate and rapid hill torrents, and its wide extent of good arable and natural pasture land, which had produced a large

[1] Though Canterbury was once famous for broadcloth.
[2] Streams falling down steep chalk scarps.

population disposed to industrial development and with sufficient means to supply the needs of a population increasing as manufactures progressed. It is to be noted that at this time Yorkshire, for all its water-power possibilities, was not a county capable of feeding a large population.

To Bristol, the chief port in this region, and long the second port in the kingdom, came the Italian oil and short Spanish merino wool, which was the basis of the finest broadcloth manufactured in the West Country, and Barnstaple imported the "long staple" wool from Ireland, so desirable for the Devonshire serges. Other requisites supplied locally were fullers' earth, used for scouring the cloth before being fulled or milled, and teasles, or fullers' thistles, used to raise the nap on the cloth.

The wool of the Cotswold (oölitic limestone) sheep was long and coarse, a worsted wool, and though spun in the neighbourhood at various places on the gentler eastern slopes of the Cotswolds (with their rather deficient water supply), and notably at Tetbury, Cirencester and Witney, was sent to the worsted markets of Leicester, Kidderminster, Andover, etc., to be made into stockings and worsted stuffs. To these centres came also long wool from the shires of Leicester, Northampton and Lincoln, to be spun like the Cotswold wool into worsted thread, and sent subsequently to the various worsted centres, including Taunton.

At Witney not only was thread spun, but blankets were made of the shorter lengths of the Cotswold wool, an industry probably arising from the character of the water of its river, the Windrush, which possessed good bleaching properties.

The eastern slopes of these western scarplands do

MODERN INDUSTRIES 247

not therefore belong to the true West Country cloth industry, even the Taunton serges—made from Cotswold wool—being of the East Anglia unmilled species, and not the true milled serge-cloth.[1]

The short, Spanish merino wool required in the broadcloth manufacture was later superseded by Silesian wool, but though imported wools were required for the very best quality material, quite good cloths were made from the short-wool breeds of Hereford (known as Ryelanders, which perhaps originated the industry of the Frome valley), Wiltshire and Dorsetshire (giving the typical short wool of chalk areas), and the Mendips in Somerset, whose small sheep gave an excellent short clothing wool.

In Gloucester the manufacturing centres were along the western scarp of the Cotswolds (but not using Cotswold wool), being thickly clustered in the upper valley of the Gloucester Frome and its tributaries, with Stroud as leading centre. In Wiltshire, Trowbridge and Bradford were the chief manufacturing localities, but a line of cloth-making villages extended from Calne and Devizes along the chalk scarp to Bratton and Westbury, and then across to Warminster and Heytesbury. Two clothing towns on the Bristol Avon, Chippenham and Melksham, were route towns for market rather than manufacturing towns, for here the river does not give " power " and the cloth had to be sent elsewhere for milling. The same might be said of the Salisbury Avon, in the eastern part of the county, and at Wilton and Salisbury flannels and lindseys, requiring scouring, but not milling, were characteristic manufactures. The long wool needed for these woollen and worsted mixtures had to be brought

[1] Note.—Taunton, on the Tone, is in a vale. Here is water, certainly, but not " water-power."

from elsewhere. In 1838 Salisbury had lost all its factories and Wilton only possessed two.

The Dorsetshire wool was employed with the Wiltshire wool for the purely "woollen" parts of the Salisbury fabrics, and at Ilminster, where it was chiefly worked up into livery cloths. In Somerset the chief broadcloth centres were at Frome and the surrounding villages, on the south slope of the Mendips and on the higher ground of the eastern part of the county.

The West Country serge cloths (made throughout Devonshire, and part of Somerset, with Wellington as centre) required a long wool for the warp, and a short wool for the weft. The sheep of Devonshire and the vale of Taunton are long woolled, though additional raw material was obtained from Ireland. The shorter threads of long wool fleeces were generally used for the wefts, though better-class fabrics employed Exmoor wool.

The configuration of the country made for an even distribution of the industry; Buckfastleigh, Crediton, Tiverton, Tavistock, were some of the centres, situated where steep-sided gullies cut into the great Dartmoor block. Barnstaple was the depôt for the long Irish wool and the worsted yarn used in the serge, and Exeter the market and outlet for the cloth of the whole region.

Up to 1840 the characteristic industries of the West Country had not suffered any great decline because of the difficulty of applying the power-loom to the woollen trade. With the coming of coal the cheaper trade emigrated to Yorkshire, and the West Country was obliged to specialize in goods of the highest class. Yorkshire has added woollen to her worsted industry, but the West Country cloth (now using the Bristol

MODERN INDUSTRIES

coal-field) still has a reputation for smoothness and finish.

SILK WEAVING

Silk weaving was introduced into England by the Huguenot refugees from the South of France. The Revocation of the " Edict of Nantes " (which had promised liberty of conscience to these Protestants) in 1685 sent us more than eighty thousand of these exiles. The number of French names in English villages is often traceable to this cause. If the names be many the French industry probably survives. The Huguenots also taught us lace-making.[1]

PAPER-MAKING

The first Paper Mill in this country was established by Sir John Spielman (d. 1607), jeweller to Queen Elizabeth, at Dartford on the Darenth. The industry, now fairly widespread, still survives in its place of origin.

SHIPBUILDING

In the Mediæval Period, as we have seen, the Ocean Trade was carried in ships belonging to the merchants of Venice and Genoa, and the Hanseatic League. England possessed a considerable coasting trade for home products, but shipbuilding was only a small industry. Queen Elizabeth, hostile to the great Sea-Power of Spain, realized the necessity for a Royal Navy, and caused Parliament to set aside the good timber of the Weald for this purpose. The more recent developments of this industry will be referred to later.[2]

COAL-MINING

In the 16th century coal began to supplant the already failing timber as a fuel. After the Restoration

---
[1] See page 262.
[2] See page 257.

ENGLAND AND WALES

(1660) the consequent expansion of trade and industry resulted in more extensive coal-mining, coal even becoming an article of export. The main coal-fields were still on the Tyne, because of the ease of working and riverine position.[1]

POTTERY

Our *modern* pottery apparently came to us "from Germany." About 1690 two Germans, probably exiles, settled near Burslem because they found the red clay in the neighbourhood well adapted for the imitation of the red ware of Japan. They introduced salt glazing. The Pottery Industry did not, however, make much progress till Josiah Wedgwood, himself one of a family of Staffordshire potters, gave hitherto unattempted artistic touches to the English ware (1759). To be successful his invention required methods of obtaining raw material, to which must be added quicker and cheaper ways of disposal of the manufactured product. The success of the modern English Pottery Industry in its initial stages is intimately bound up with improvements in methods of transport.

Following on the improvement of the River Weaver (Act of 1720) there were three navigable river-ways leading into North Staffordshire: the Weaver, Trent, and Severn. On the Weaver the nearest available point was Winsford Bridge, reached by a twenty-mile road. Wellington, the nearest available point on the Trent (and about four miles east of Burton) was over thirty miles by road from the Potteries; Bridgnorth and Bewdley, the nearest of the Severn inland ports, were thirty-eight and fifty-four miles respectively by road from Newcastle (Staffs), and forty-two and a half and fifty-seven and a half from Burslem. Along the

[1] But see also p. 258.

MODERN INDUSTRIES

Winsford Bridge Road pack-horses or waggons brought supplies of West Country clay[1] which had travelled by the sea-route to Liverpool, and by barges down the Weaver. Along the Wellington Road the Potteries received flints from the chalk districts of South-East England, which had travelled by the sea route to Hull by barge along the Trent and pack-horse or waggon from Wellington. In the reverse order, but precisely the same means, manufactured pottery for London or the Continent and the West Coast counties travelled down the Trent and Humber for Hull, the Weaver to Liverpool, and the Severn to Bristol.

The success of Brindley's Canal between Manchester and Liverpool gave the suggestion for the system of artificial and connecting waterways to Staffordshire, which, though drawing the Pottery traffic from the Severn route, gave it a great impetus in that with Liverpool and Hull as easily reached seaports, with its local advantages of clay and inherited skill, it was in a position to expand to the requirements of the world-market in wait for it.

THE IRON INDUSTRY

We have seen that the Weald of Sussex, Kent and Surrey was the early seat of the Iron Industry on account of the presence of iron ore in the neighbourhood of forests (fuel, charcoal), at a time when Northumberland and Yorkshire were still regarded as " uncivilized." In the reign of Henry VIII a timber famine was feared,

---

[1] This clay is the famous Kaolin found at St. Austell and other places in the region. As a surface deposit it occurs through the action of rain water on the felspar constituent of granite. Of recent years the clay has also been discovered in joints and fissures in the rock, having apparently been produced by the action of subterranean vapours (notably fluorine) upon the surface of the cavity. This is the mineral " Kaolinite," and these two methods of formation of china clay have already led to interesting legal controversies as to the respective mining rights involved.

and still more so in the reign of Queen Elizabeth, threatened with a war with the great Sea-Power Spain. It then became almost patriotic to preserve the timber of the Weald for the Royal Navy—to the great disadvantage of the Iron Industry in this neighbourhood. A complaint of less magnitude was that the heavy traffic consequent upon the industry injured the roads—still some centuries distant from the scientific improvements of Telford and Macadam. But by the beginning of the 18th century the Iron Industry had practically passed from Sussex, though it was still flourishing in Gloucester, owing to the fuel and ironstone in the Forest of Dean and the navigation of the River Severn system. In 1735 Abraham Darby showed how coke and a powerful blast of air could smelt iron ore much more easily than wood (charcoal), but the turning point in the Iron Industry is 1760, when Dr. Roebuck (Carron Works) built a new type of blast-furnace to be fed with coke.

The history of the Iron Industry of South Wales is also interesting. Here iron was mined and smelted by the Romans, who left various refuse heaps in connection with these operations marking their participation in them, but after the departure of the Romans, the South Wales iron seems to have been neglected till the close of the 17th century. The industry now began to develop because of the immigration into South Wales of iron workers from other districts, especially the Weald, as South Wales, besides extensive forests, was found to possess considerable iron ore. The bloomeries, or smelting hearths, were built at any convenient place where fuel could be easily supplied. About 1750 the use of coal for smelting operations had become general, and South Wales, fortunately, was found to possess this mineral in abundance. From

MODERN INDUSTRIES 253

1750 to 1850 iron was the most important industry in South Wales, the coal being mined mainly for smelting, and not for export. Accompanying this development was a second, in communication and transport. In 1750 there were no roads even along the main valleys, and transport was effected by ponies, waggons, or even wheelbarrows, along rough tracts over the hills. Before 1800 roads had been constructed in the eastern valleys, and even canals, and the later institution of tramways and railways was solely on account of the iron industry.

On account of the good iron found here, which was easily mined, the industry developed largely on the fertile dip of the north-east corner of the coal-field, such centres as Merthyr Tydvil and Pontypool coming into being.

Since 1850 steel has largely superseded iron, and for steel the South Wales ore is not suitable. Hence began large importation of ore—chiefly hæmatite from Spain—and the ironstone nodules of South Wales are practically unworked at present. The growth of the Tin-plating Industry is due to the expansion of the iron trade.

WATT'S STEAM ENGINE

A few years after the invention of Roebuck's coal-fed blast furnace, the Steam Engine came to revolutionize many of the industries. A steam engine had been used as early as 1717 to pump water out of the collieries, but the engine required too much fuel, and was therefore too costly for general use. James Watt (1785) discovered a method by which, at one and the same time, the amount of fuel could be reduced and the engine made more serviceable. Boulton, a man of means, became his partner, and they erected works at Birmingham, in which the new steam engine furnished the power. As this engine was dependent upon coal, it followed that its general adoption caused the transference of population from the South to the North, where coal-fields existed, and hence where food for the engine could easily be obtained.

It was soon found that the steam engine could be applied to the Iron Industry. It enabled the new furnaces to be supplied with a still more powerful blast and reduced the amount of coal required by two-thirds. The ironmaster could now dispense with both wood and water-power, and so became independent of the forests and rivers of Southern England alike, a factor leading to the further expansion of the Iron Industry in such districts as Staffordshire, the North-East Coast (with sea-coal from Newcastle), Scotland and South Wales, where the now all-important coal could be obtained as well as the iron ore.

THE FISHING INDUSTRY

Our fishing industry is probably as old as the invasions of those vikings who in the 9th century came to our waters at first to fish and then—as more profitable—remained to plunder. In the Saxon period Yaremouth was already famous for herrings. Owing to the small size of the boats, fishing remained a " domestic " industry until the Reformation, when the demand for this species of food became comparatively small, and the industry declined considerably.

Queen Elizabeth, realizing the value of the seafaring life as preparation for naval emergencies, did all she could to encourage the industry, even requiring the people, by Act of Parliament, to eat so much fish per year. However, it was not until about 1850 that fish trawling became a settled industry in England, though still characterized by small boats and local

MODERN INDUSTRIES 255

markets. At first the industry was best developed in Cornwall and Devon, owing to their splendid facilities for anchorage, but the scanty population of their hinterlands made marketing difficult. The fishermen of the West Country therefore gradually migrated to Margate and Ramsgate, on account of the London market, and this migration necessitated an increase in the size of the fishing smack. Later the great fishing-grounds were changed to the Dogger Banks, where the Sole and Silver pits between the Banks were about this time discovered. Those pits formed a refuge from gales and winter cold for plaice and flat fish of various kinds, and as the industry increased, the smack-owners realized that Hull was a better centre, so that thither the catch was taken to be sent by rail to the Yorkshire industrial towns and to London, and the Dogger Banks became the centre of the trade.

About 1880 ice as a preservative was introduced, and the smacks were fitted with an engine and boiler to heave up the bag or net. Twenty years later steamships to tow the net superseded the old smack. These steamships go far afield to Iceland (cod) and Russia.

Grimsby is now the most important centre of the English Fishing Industry; indeed it is the premier fishing port in the world. Before the War (1914) the annual value of its fishing trade was about £3,000,000. The order of value for the other British fishing ports is Aberdeen and Hull, London, Lowestoft, Yarmouth, Milford, Fleetwood, the last five being approximately equal.

Except for herring (caught in surface or drifting nets) and shell-fish, the Fishing Industry is run by Joint Stock Companies. On landing, the fish is auctioned and generally purchased by a fish merchant.

In the case of the Herring Industry the boats are owned by private individuals—often the crew. The steam drifter takes a crew of ten; the nets are hauled up about midnight, and the ships, which carry no ice, steam away quickly for the fishing station.

NEW LIFE OF FORMER INDUSTRIAL CENTRES

The great increase in the output of iron made a considerable expanse in the engineering trade of the country in general. New centres of industry and activity were opened up, and workers aggregated in a manner hitherto unprecedented in centres already established. These last were often old towns with some special advantage of geographic position. Thus Leeds, the centre of the Yorkshire Woollen Industry, commands the Aire gap through which the produce of its district might pass, in the early days by canal, to the great hinterland of Liverpool; Manchester, now by virtue of its ship canal a veritable seaport, was a town of some importance in the time of Henry VIII as centre of the Lancashire Cloth Trade (not cotton), and earlier still a Roman military station guarding the gap between the Mersey marshes and the Pennines. The historic industries of Birmingham go back for at least a thousand years, owing to its neighbourhood to the Forest of Arden (iron ore and fuel), and its essential central position in the heart of England. Leland, writing in the reign of Henry VIII (1509-1547), records that this good market town was mostly "maintained by smiths," making cutting tools, bits, nails, etc., and getting "iron[1] and sea-coal out of Staffordshire." Midway from navigable water on the Severn, Avon and Trent, and so able to obtain water-carried imported ore and to distribute its resulting hardware manufactures, at the canal period Birmingham was

[1] That is iron ore—fine casting sand was found locally.

MODERN INDUSTRIES

sufficiently prosperous to encourage the construction of canals, but the fact that much of this district is so elevated, so undermined and so densely populated, makes canal cutting costly, difficult, even dangerous, even if further canal construction would not interfere with the water-supply of the area's great populations. However, Birmingham lies in no danger of losing its trade: its position in the heart of England counted in the past, and while transport remains *on the ground*, the railways, successors of the canals, must make Birmingham a first objective.

The history of Sheffield is similar. The local advantages included crucible clay and water-power, together with the presence of fine grinding-stone, and fuel from Sherwood Forest. Ore from Scandinavia was easily obtained, even in Plantagenet times, this ore being especially adapted to the old methods of making steel.[1] When coal supplanted wood as a fuel here, as at Birmingham, iron-working was developed with the aid of coal, and at the expense of the Wealden industry, where charcoal was failing.

After the Industrial Revolution commercial ship-building began to decline from the ports of the south and east (London excepted), and passed to the coal-fields near the sea. The Mersey and the estuaries of Northumberland and Durham became centres of shipbuilding—the latter using Scandinavian timber. Newcastle-on-Tyne enormously increased its ancient trade in coal, and with its growing industries was enabled, in the 19th century, to absorb the hamlets of Gateshead, Jarrow and others into its suburbs, so that the town may now be regarded as extending continuously from the city nucleus along the Tyne bank to Tynemouth.

[1] The route was by the Rivers Humber, Trent, Idle to Bawtry, thence 20 miles by waggon to Sheffield.

In South Wales the flowing tide of industrialism swept over the little castle-towns, near river mouths, which discovered themselves to be well placed for participating in the productions of the great coalfield and the great industrial districts of their hinterland, thus entering into a new life on quite different lines.

CHAPTER XXII

REVOLUTION IN INDUSTRY

IT is not possible to take any definite period and say that during this time the Industrial Revolution was in operation in the same way that we can define, for example, the beginning and ending of the French Revolution. For most practical purposes, however, the Industrial Revolution may be said to lie between the dates 1785 and 1825, the one being the year of James Watt's invention of the steam engine, and the other signifying a date when modern industry and the great city had fastened their grip upon our national life.

In narrating the slight sketches of the various modern industries outlined in the preceding chapter it seemed best to follow up each separately right across the Revolutionary period to its present position, to avoid a break in the consecutiveness. But now that we have this knowledge before us it will be useful to make a more general survey of these events in our Industrial History leading to perhaps the greatest of all Revolutions.

Until the latter part of the 18th century South Britain was busily employed in many industries chiefly carried on by what was known as " Domestic Labour." This is not to say that " factories " were unknown; on the contrary, the first great factories appear as far back as the 16th century, but the labour in them was supplied by "hand." Towards the close of the 18th century a number of inventions for quicker, cheaper output were applied to the leading industries, and by 1780 these discoveries were so related to one another that *each* made it possible for *all* to work together to develop the factory and the machine. It was the discovery of a new way of smelting iron by using pit coal that made the great machine possible, and the discovery of the new uses of coal as applied to the steam engine enabled the machine to be worked economically. However, even now something more was needed before the new methods could be regarded as entirely satisfactory, the opportunity to obtain the raw material in sufficient quantities to satisfy the machine, and to dispose of the finished product. The roads were too bad—the revolution in road-making had not as yet come to pass.

At this moment, so contemporaneously with the new industrial methods that it is impossible to say which was the cause of the other—that need was met by the sudden enthusiasm for canal construction, arising, very suitably, out of the needs for coal transport. In addition events on the Continent were acting profoundly to our industrial advantage. Much of this period is covered by the French Revolution and the Napoleonic Wars; Chateaubriand was not far wrong when he stated[1] that the Continental blockade enforced by the Emperor Napoleon led us to seek oversea markets which ultimately benefited *us*, rather at the expense of France. True or not, the distant markets we were forced to seek no doubt gave an impetus to the expansion of our overseas trade which did not cease with Napoleon's overthrow.

Thus, if we are looking for causes we can find at least five out of which the Industrial Revolution may be said to have arisen: the application of a number of inventions and improved processes to leading industries; the advantages derived from steam power; the immense increase in the supplies of cotton, coal,

[1] Mémoires D'Outretombe.

REVOLUTION IN INDUSTRY

minerals and other raw materials; the greater wealth of the nation thereby gained allowing more available capital for industrial purposes; the improvement of an inland communication and in the art of navigation, foreign markets being more readily reached at a time when political and economic conditions were especially favourable to the commercial expansion abroad which followed our industrial expansion at home.

As regards the results of these recent industrial changes three points stand out prominently. The first may be better appreciated by consulting a population map dealing with England and Wales before and after this revolution. On comparison, the most outstanding features become a general shifting of the areas of greatest population from the South and East to the North and West, and, secondly, a very great augmentation of total population, so that a maximum of 100 to 250 persons per square mile in 1701 rises to a maximum of over 2,000 per square mile two centuries later.

The second point is the extraordinary change in the system of labour. As far back as the 16th century there were a few great factories, but the work done in them was handwork, requiring, proportionately to the output, very many operators. Even so, the greater bulk of the total manufactures of the country was "domestic" either for home or factory finish. The Industrial Revolution changed all this. Handicraft became almost entirely superseded by the great inventions even in such rural occupations as grain threshing, and the factory work, now the product of mechanical assistance, necessitating very few operators proportionally to the results.[1]

[1] This factor, once the cause of famous riots, is now compensated by greater output, and wider markets.

Domestic industry has therefore ceased to be the usual life of the people, but it has not been banished entirely from our midst. There exist districts in England where "cottage industries" are the usual form of manufacture for certain grades of goods. For example, in Calverton and Woodborough and the surrounding districts of Nottinghamshire knitters make up the most expensive hose on handlooms. Hand-made lace can always command a higher price than the machine-made article, and in the shires of Bedford and Buckingham hand-made lace is still a cottage industry. The same is true at Honiton, where lace-making has been carried on since its origination there by the exiled Huguenots. Even to-day the villages round Birmingham maintain a domestic industry for the manufacture of numerous small hardware goods ; tweeds are woven in the cottages of the Western Hebrides, woollen fabric produced by the cottage folk of the Shetlands, and lace and linen made in the old way in Western Ireland.

The new inventions were only slowly applied to industry—for example, it took twenty years for the power loom to supersede the hand-loom, and longer still before it was used for woollens.

In the course of the last half-century the nature of the British Industries has undergone a profound change. The early importance of the textile industries has passed to those connected with steel. But except in Staffordshire local iron is no longer smelted on the coalfields ; the South Wales local iron is not suitable for steel, and ore is imported chiefly from Spain ; for the steel shipbuilding of the Tyne, Wear and Tees, the ores of Scandinavia and Cleveland are laid under contribution. Beside this carrying of iron to the coalfields, coal is also taken to the ironfields, and the

REVOLUTION IN INDUSTRY

great industrial .populations of Middlesbrough and Barrow, in regions of vast and valuable deposits of iron (for steel), are quite off the coalfields.

Thus while the first effect of the Industrial Revolution was to withdraw the country's manufactures to the several coalfields, at the present time a certain amount of decentralization is taking place. New systems of carriage allow coal to be taken speedily and cheaply to the site of raw materials, or to less crowded districts where land and food is at present cheaper. This result, which may bring about a more equal distribution of the population of our country, is a consequence of the fourth of our great modern revolutions—the railway.

CHAPTER XXIII

REVOLUTION IN TRANSPORT: RAILWAYS

THE origin of our Railway System resembled that of our canals in being due to the necessity of providing more adequate and cheaper methods to remove coal from the coalfields, and inasmuch as the Tyne coalfields were the first to be mined in England, it is fitting that our first railroad should be evolved upon its banks.

Long before the days of scientific road-making the difficulty of removing coal from the pit to the waterway had become acute. Heavy traffic on the common roads was frequently aided by the use of wooden planks placed in the deep ruts instead of a constant in-filling of stones. But in the wet seasons this planking had a tendency to sink deeply into the mire, thereby becoming inefficient. The next step was taken by those concerned with the colliery traffic on the Tyne Coalfield, and consisted in the construction of a "surface road" of strong oak planks fastened to crosspieces underneath. Heavy coal carts moved upon four rollers as wheels, the planks being "rails" in embryo, while the haulage power of this wooden road was three times that on the rough, stone ones. About 1678 it became the custom to peg the planks to "sleepers" placed two feet apart, the space between them being filled with ashes or small stones to protect the horses' feet. This method of haulage was soon adopted by other collieries to be improved about a century later by replacing the wooden "rails" by rails of cast-iron

TRANSPORT : RAILWAYS

(1767). Nine years later still "plates" or "rails" were cast with an inner flange two or three inches high to keep the waggon wheels on the rail. This latest arrangement was known as the "Plateway" (a name not wholly out of use), "Tramway" or "Dramway,"[1]

The Sheffield iron railway was constructed in 1776, and between the years 1801 and 1825 no less than twenty-nine "Iron Railways" were opened or begun in various parts of Great Britain. Waggons or carts belonging to private owners, providing their wheels were the right distance apart to run on the rails, might use these tramways on payment of a toll or charge.

The first of these railways was constructed with the single object of conveying coal from the colliery to the canal or river in preference to extending a lateral canal from the main waterway to the colliery, but in 1801 Parliament granted an Act for the construction of what may be regarded as the first *public* railway and distinct from those serving mainly or exclusively colliery interests.

THE SURREY IRON RAILWAY

This "line" ran from the Thames at Wandsworth to Croydon, with a branch to some mills on the River Wandle whose owners were the leaders of the enterprise. The line was designed to carry "coal, corn and all goods and merchandise to and from the metropolis." Chalk, flint, firestone, fuller's earth, agricultural produce, were sent from Croydon to the Thames at Wandsworth for conveyance to the City, the return

[1] The term "tramway" is said to have been adopted from the name of Sir Benjamin Outram, of the Iron Works, Ripley, Derbyshire. A more probable derivation is from the Teutonic traem, dram, tram, a log or beam in allusion to the wooden sleepers used in the construction of the line.

load being mainly in coal (arriving by sea from Newcastle) and manure. The motive power was supplied by horses, mules and donkeys, and though the line was open on payment to carts or waggons fitted to run upon it, passenger traffic was neither expected nor provided for. The second section of the Surrey Iron Railway was the Croydon and Godstone branch, supplying the Merstham Chalk quarries.

The "Locomotive" did not follow very quickly upon Watt's improvement of the steam engine, so that those Railway Companies adopting his engine used waggons with ropes sufficiently long to haul them from one station (engine station ?) to the next.

THE FIRST LOCOMOTIVE (Origin of the N.E.R.)

The Stockton and Darlington Railway was constructed for the purpose of finding a better outlet for the coal of the South Durham coal-field. A company, whose most active member was Edward Pease, was formed in 1816, but Parliament did not authorize the making and maintaining of a railway or tramroad from the Tees at Stockton to the Wilton Park Colliery at Darlington till five years later. The engineer, George Stephenson, persuaded the company to adopt iron rails and his locomotive ("Locomotive No. 1") or moving engine which drew a load after it, and the line was opened for traffic on September 27th, 1825. On its trial trip a horseman rode a little way in front of the engine to make sure that the line was clear, and the "load" was made up of a passenger coach, named the "Experiment" and various coal waggons, some containing that mineral, and others "third-class" passengers. The usual speed of the "train" was 4 to 6 miles an hour, with a maximum of 8 on the level. The company owned fifteen waggons and at first provided only for luggage traffic, though suitable

TRANSPORT: RAILWAYS

private waggons, drawn by horse, might be used on payment of a toll. For some little time horse and "locomotive" traction were in fierce competition, horse-power being found the cheaper; but two years after the opening of the line a certain Timothy Hackworth invented an engine—named the Royal George—which required less fuel, and consequently gave a cheaper motive power. This new engine was adopted (September, 1827), upon which on this line horse-power became entirely superseded except with regard to private traffic.

The use of the railroad by private individuals as well as for the company's transport led to difficulties, especially on account of the two modes of traction employed. The impossibility of regulating this mixed traffic, the urgent need for a railroad time-table to prevent both delay and accident led the company to take the whole carrying trade into its own hands, and from 1830 onwards no more was heard of horse-power.

The line attained much popularity, but is now incorporated in the N.E.R. system.

LIVERPOOL AND MANCHESTER RAILWAY

The construction of this line resulted from the extreme dissatisfaction felt by Liverpool and Manchester traders with the exorbitant charges of the river and canal navigation companies, coupled with extreme dilatoriness in executing accepted contracts. Here, too, arose the question as to the cheapest and best mode of traction, and a competition was opened with a view to its settlement. It was won by George Stephenson's "Rocket," which showed an improvement in both weight of load carried and speed attained. It is noteworthy that part of the line was laid across Chat Moss, heather bundles being used to give support, a repetition of Metcalf's road-making device about sixty years earlier.

This latest revolution in transport met with the same vigorous opposition as had greeted the canals in their initial stages. The 15th of November, 1835, number of *John Bull* spoke of railways as "newfangled absurdities," and of those who predicted a general success of the system from the particular success of the Manchester-Liverpool Railway as "dunces and blockheads," and the early railroads were very limited in extent owing to the natural opposition of canal owners, private landowners who feared their estates might be adversely affected, of wealthy aristocrats who preferred to travel in their own carriages, and saw no reason why the poorer members of the community should desire to travel at all; and lastly, to that British prejudice and suspicion which always displays itself on the first appearance of any great innovation. Opposition was finally overcome, but by methods which revealed the venality of much of the former objection. Thus highly inflated prices were asked— and paid—for land over which the railroad had to run, and heavy sums for damages which *might*, but in fact never did, accrue. Declining canals succeeded in being bought out by the railroads at prices which only ought to have been given to prosperous and going concerns, while the opposition of certain towns to the "newfangled absurdity" was occasionally more heroic than wise—Northampton, for instance, which still suffers commercial loss through the obstinate refusal long ago of its townsfolk to allow the London and Birmingham main line to pass through it. But eventually the great profits to be made overbore all difficulties and created a "railway mania" similar to the canal mania about twenty years earlier, and

TRANSPORT : RAILWAYS

between 1840 and 1846 hundreds of Parliamentary sanctions were given annually either authorizing new railway companies or extensions of existing lines. The mania over, hundreds of small companies were amalgamated to form the Great Northern, Great Eastern, North Eastern, Midland, London and North Western and other railways.

In their early years the Railways, like the canals, suffered the penalty of the lack of uniformity arising from their separate ownerships. Most trains adopted the 4 foot $8\frac{1}{2}$ inch gauge, or distance between the centres of the two parallel lines, capable of taking the wheels of ordinary carts, and thus recalling the era of waggon transport on the railway lines. The Great Western adopted a 7-foot gauge, but ultimately laid down a double or inner rail to avoid " break of bulk " in the case of goods travelling over it and other railways. The fierce discussion raised on the subject is known as " The Battle of the Gauges," but the ultimate victory fell to the " standard gauge " of 4 foot $8\frac{1}{2}$ inches, to which the Great Western presently conformed.

The superiority of Rail transport over that of canals, rivers or roads made it possible for industries already started or those immediately consequent upon the Industrial Revolution to attain to their present proportions ; thus to this method of transport is chiefly due our modern Factory System, with its stupendous industrial populations aggregated into busy urban centres. With the advent of railways, fairs ceased to be necessary, and our country became the nation of shopkeepers that Napoleon called it. The country trader who could now obtain his stores in quantities dependent upon his speed of sale, and direct from the manufacturers or warehousemen of London, Manchester,

Sheffield, Glasgow, etc., through the large tradesman, owing to the reduced rates for quantity, reaped the greater advantage. Finally the village shopkeeper was able to satisfy local requirements, and such arts as domestic brewing, domestic weaving, meat-salting for winter use, etc., have generally vanished.

Successful ports depend much on railway connections and conversely many railways rely largely upon our import and export trade. These two factors are clearly interdependent. Of the ports that may be regarded as originating through the railways, mention may be made of Great Grimsby, now the foremost fishing port in the world (G.E.R.) ; Immingham, growing from a village with a few houses to a large seaport by virtue of the docks built on the River Humber (1912) (G.E.R.) ; Goole and Fleetwood (L. & Y.R.), Hull (N.E.R.), Harwich (G.E.R.), Bristol (G.W.R.), owe much of their present importance to the railways. Middlesbrough, not so long ago a collection of huts on a mud-bank, is now a large and important town, deriving work and wealth from the facilities offered it for obtaining coal, and sending away its great "staple" —iron ; while York, eclipsed after the last Civil War, and sunk to a quiet city little else than the winter residence of the neighbouring gentry, and centre of local amusement, by means of the Railways was brought back into close connection with English industrial life and progress.

Within the last decade, and as a consequence of the " Great War," certain changes have been made in the nomenclature and grouping of our Railways, which in 1914 were taken over by the State. An Act of Parliament, 1921, sanctioned their rearrangement in four great groups:

(1) THE SOUTHERN GROUP, amalgamating the former

London and South Western, London, Brighton and South Coast, South Eastern and Chatham Railways.

(2) THE LONDON, MIDLAND AND SCOTTISH RAILWAY (L.M.S.), composed of the former London and North Western, Midland, Lancashire and Yorkshire Railways and their local branches.

(3) THE GREAT WESTERN RAILWAY, running more or less over its old lines.

(4) THE NORTH-EASTERN GROUP, containing the former Great Eastern, Great Northern, North-Eastern, Great Central Railways ; to this group also belongs the North British and Great Northern Railways of Scotland.

CHAPTER XXIV

THE REVOLUTION IN VILLAGE LIFE: ENCLOSURES

THE mediæval system of land tenure lingered, though in a somewhat modified form, down to the eve of the Industrial Revolution. The "Lord of the Manor," indeed, is a term not obsolete to-day, though most of the rights that formerly went with the title are no longer in operation.

At the end of the 18th century, in more than half the English parishes there was still to be found the old, open-field village, with its " common lands " of arable fields, meadowland, and waste. Certainly feudal relations between the Lord of the Manor and the villagers had long since passed away, and the cultivators held their land either by lease, copyhold, or freehold, though in some manors the allotments in the arable fields belonged in successive years to different cultivators, whereas elsewhere the same cultivators might obtain the same allotments over and over again.

Steadily throughout this country, under the increasing necessity for home supplies of food, the wheat export declined, and by 1792 had finally ceased. This was the period of the beginning of the French Revolutionary wars; and the Continental Blockade, which followed Napoleon's rise to power, reduced very considerably the import of our food material from Western Europe. It therefore became necessary to effect drastic economies in the labour and time required for the production of home produce. One solution of the difficulty seemed to be a removal of the pathways leading to the different holdings in a "field,"

REVOLUTION IN VILLAGE LIFE

often bands of grass called "balks," thus bringing a larger area of land under cultivation. This remedy was suggested by Arthur Young, the Travelling Secretary of the Board of Agriculture. Clearly its introduction would pave the way for the aggregation of a number of neighbouring holdings under one owner.

For many centuries the Domestic System of Industry had existed side by side with land cultivation, and it was the ease accruing to the cultivator through this resource that was responsible for the phenomenon we call "Merrie England." At times, when work was slack, or finished for the moment, the farmer would become a weaver, for example, or perhaps his wife and daughter might card and spin. The new mill-factories at the end of the 18th century competed too successfully with the work done by this part-time farmer, and by withdrawing the industry to large cities made it difficult for him to obtain his customary livelihood at home. Two courses were therefore open to him—but as far as the land was concerned whichever he took produced the same result. He might go to town where work was plentiful, or he might stay at home. In the first case he generally sold his holding to the highest bidder, as he could not work it himself. In the second, his increased poverty, consequent on the removal of his domestic industry, and aided by the agricultural depreciation of the land due to the emigration of so much rural labour townwards, sooner or later forced a sale.

Other consequences of the new national progress were also against the small farmer. The new scientific farming of the late 18th and early 19th centuries, and the use of agricultural machinery thereby involved, required a capital or initial outlay which he did not possess, forcing him again to sell and seek work in town, or in the country as a wage-earning labourer.

This disappearance of the small farmer, or yeoman class thus accompanied the rise of the large farmer, who precisely because his farm contained so many different units desired some visible symbol of his rights and found it by " enclosing " or fencing the land he had acquired. The industrial lure that drew agricultural labour to the cities also played its part in this new system of enclosure. For those who made fortunes by industry not infrequently returned to the land to buy out the impoverished holder, and thus became great landowners themselves. It was not unnatural, perhaps, that a rich and powerful landlord, enclosing arable land for which he had paid should also enclose common or waste land over which the village had rights of pasturage and fuel, but which was not otherwise divided into holdings. In some cases the landlords might consider they had purchased the rights in the waste, just because they had purchased the holdings of the arable land, but in many others this species of enclosing was done without a shadow of right and simply to " round off " and complete an estate.

Begun as a method of necessity, and carried out with some show of justice, the operation of enclosing land eventually passed both these bounds. Where influential landlords with interests in the two Houses could persuade Parliament that the cultivation of the land, and therefore the food supply of the nation, would be increased, it became the custom to obtain—by guile and trickery—the consent of the majority of holders (generally reckoned in land values rather than in number of individuals) to the enclosing process. Certainly compensation was sometimes given, but naturally quite inadequate to the injury, and the dispossessed labourer had the right to appear before the Parliamentary Commission in London, and prove his claim—a right rarely used on account of his poverty and ignorance, to say nothing of an intentionally unsympathetic Commission. Between the years 1750 and 1810, nearly 3,000 Enclosure Acts were passed, besides a General Enclosure Act in 1801. The resentment of the labourers found vent in the last Labourers' Revolt (1830), which, with a powerful Government against it, was doomed to failure from the first.

This change in land working and ownership from the old system of small cultivators, commons and common-fields to the new, typical English system of individualist agriculture and large, enclosed farms is known as the Agrarian Revolution. Beginning just before the Industrial Revolution, powerfully influenced by that great event in our national history, it was practically complete by 1845. Its permanent effects are instanced at once in the creation of great, private estates, and the disappearance of the old English village society. As a method of furthering agriculture, it has not fulfilled its promise, and in England agriculture has steadily declined. More and more land has been given over to industry and the housing of the vast populations that the term a "manufacturing country" implies.

CHAPTER XXV

REVOLUTION IN TOWN GROWTH. CONURBATIONS

IN the Middle Ages and the period preceding the Industrial Revolution the requirements for a large town or city were comparatively simple. Leaving out of account the early *desideratum* of a wall and a castle for purposes of defence, it may be said that a town contained a church, or churches, under the shadow of which was a market, a sort of "town centre," where the main business of the region, whether commercial, judicial or legislative was carried on, including stores or warehouses for the staple or produce of the district, and upon whose premises lived the owner with his wife and family. After the close of the Middle Ages, the development of the Indian and American plantation trade gave a new impetus to town growth, and London and Bristol especially profited, becoming great warehousing and distributing centres for tea, sugar, tobacco and other foreign produce. The streets of the business part of the town were frequently named after the commodity warehoused there, such as Corn Hill, Wine Street, Pepper Street, etc. The more purely residential houses of the town were generally surrounded by gardens, though easily accessible recreation grounds were supplied by the green fields and woodlands of the surrounding district, which came right up to the encircling walls.

This simple form of town life must now be compared with the modern Industrial City. It has been shown how the Revolution in Industry enormously increased

REVOLUTION IN TOWN GROWTH

our population, and obviously, where the Industrial Machine worked to the greatest effect, there the greatest populations would crowd. The ancient towns, especially when industrialized, cannot now contain themselves within the narrow limits set by the walls; indeed to-day one no longer dreams of looking for the Green Hill outside the City Wall, but for crowded streets, docks, canals, railway lines, gasometers, cheap shops, factories, and an endless procession of trams, buses, carts, motors and preoccupied, hurrying people. In the case of the city whose modern industries are the entire cause of its rise to greatness, the spreading outwards from the centre is even of greater extent.

Clearly the heart of the Industrial City, the point of convergence of the main traffic of the district, with its atmosphere of bustle and noise, its buildings for the operations of law, banking, commerce and trade, its warehouses and offices—in short, the representation within a circumscribed area of the many interests of the complicated community—is not the place in which the merchant and the well-to-do will choose to live, quite apart from the fact that the modern crowding of so much business into a limited space puts a heavy premium upon the rent of the rooms intended for mere family occupation. Similarly, the rattle of the modern machinery, the heat of the furnaces, fumes, smoke dust, all drive the factory owner to a quiet habitation on the outskirts of the town.

Upon examination of a suitable map, it may be seen that South Britain contains large areas of territory with an exceedingly dense population. An illustration in point may be found in the "Cotton Area" of Lancashire, a district heavily threaded by railways, roads, and canals. A list of towns in South Lancashire would include Rochdale, Bolton, Oldham, Wigan, St.

Helens, Liverpool, Salford-Manchester, Warrington, Stalybridge, Stockport; Macclesfield also belongs to this same trade area or economic province. Liverpool is the great port of entry for the raw material—cotton—though Manchester, by virtue of its ship-canal, claims also to be considered a seaport. In North Lancashire, in the valley of the River Ribble system, there is another group of towns: Colne, Nelson, Burnley, Accrington, Darwen, Blackburn, Preston. Both these groups, with the exception of the port, Liverpool, are engaged in the manufacture of " Manchester goods," but owing to the slight increase of dryness, weaving takes the place of cotton spinning in the Ribble Valley, e.g., at Blackburn and Preston, while Bolton spins fine threads and Oldham (less marine) coarse ones. Rochdale, also near the Yorkshire border, has a flannel industry, Oldham and Salford in addition specialize in the manufacture of spinning and weaving machines, and at St. Helens and Widnes chemicals are made (with Cheshire salt as basis) for the purpose of dyeing and printing the cotton cloth. To Manchester, the great organizing centre of the region, the raw cotton is sent to be distributed to the localities that need it, and when the cotton has been spun and the threads woven into cloth, to Manchester the cotton returns in the shape of manufactured articles, to be exported to places at home and abroad. Twice a week, in the Manchester Royal Exchange, four thousand cotton masters from the towns of the area do the monetary business of their great industry.

This area, so full of work, would not be complete without its opportunities for recreation. To the west of Manchester and across the Cheshire border are the residential suburbs of Eccles, Altrincham and Knutsford. Further afield are Blackpool, Southport, the Isle of Man, Llandudno, and the coast of North Wales, all " Holiday Towns " serving the huge industrial population for its annual repose from labour.

It is clear from the above remarks that the South Lancashire coal-field is an economic province complete in itself, an agglomeration of towns whose separate industries, whether of mining, spinning, weaving, or dyeing, etc., are part in a corporate whole, lying, it might almost be said, on the spokes of a wheel of which Manchester is the great centre, and as one can no more think of the centre of a wheel without its spokes, so the wealth and trade of Manchester cannot be considered apart from the separate manufacturing localities to which its greatness is due.

This aggregation of associated industries, depending in part upon natural resources, and in part upon some other factor or factors such as climate or geographical position, is common to nearly all our coal-fields, and as springing into existence since the Industrial Revolution may be regarded as a modern phase of our national life. But when the various parts of such an " agglomeration " be analysed, the economic province so defined will be found to have a new significance. The case of the cotton area described above is typical. In Manchester we have the great " town centre," with its Cathedral, its celebrated Library, its Royal Exchange, its Courts of Justice ; around it, from Blackburn and Preston to Stalybridge and Stockport, from Oldham to Widnes, what are the towns but gigantic workshops, feeding the centre with their associated industries ? What is Liverpool but the gateway through which the great staple enters the district, whose residential suburbs extend across the Mersey into Cheshire? This agglomeration of towns, therefore, fulfils all the definitions of a modern Industrial City and such a phenomenon is aptly designated a "Conurbation." It has been proposed to call this industrial unit of which Manchester is the heart by the expressive name of "Lancaston" (Geddes).

The Conurbation of Lancaston is characterized by the unique "largenesses" illustrated by the following qualities of some of its component parts. "(After London) Liverpool is the first port in the Kingdom." "Preston has the largest cotton mills in the world." "Blackburn weaves more calico than any other town." "Manchester (Cottonopolis, or the Cotton Metropolis) is the centre of the World's Cotton Industry."

On the eastern side of the peninsula is another densely populated area which may be treated similarly. There is, however, no single town with the importance of Manchester, though there are many cities of the third rank: Leeds, Sheffield, Nottingham, Leicester, Bradford, Halifax, Huddersfield. There is here an economic province of which wool may be said to be the staple, and a second contiguous, mainly concerned with iron in its various forms. The first province forms the conurbation of the West Riding, the World's Wool Metropolis, and here also there is specialization in the various workshops. Thus Leeds is the head-quarters of the wholesale clothing trade, Huddersfield makes fine cloth, Halifax carpets, etc. The conurbation of the "South Riding"—a term as yet hardly in use—centres round the steel and coal of Sheffield. The local advantage of this latter place, besides crucible clay and water power, was the presence of fine grinding stone, directing the local energy into cutlery. Cleveland and Midland iron ore contain too much phosphorus and sulphur for the production of good steel, and though the Furness hæmatite (a very pure oxide

REVOLUTION IN TOWN GROWTH

of iron) is very suitable, it was and still is rather inaccessible, and high-grade ore is imported from Sweden. The blast furnaces for smelting the ore were removed about 150 years ago to Rotherham and Chesterfield.

On the Sheaf and Don only steel is produced, Swedish, Spanish or Cumbrian high-grade ore being used, here everything is "imported" except the fuel and the inherited skill. The factories of the Sheaf and Don make a "light" product with Swedish metal; but those on the Don, in addition, make armour plates, and other heavy steel goods, using for this new work Spanish and Furness ore. Here the transport factor comes in—the Don being navigable.

"Midlanton" may be regarded as a less prosaic name for that dark conurbation known as the Black Country. It is based upon the South Staffordshire coal-field, being one gigantic workshop both above ground and below. The district is described thus: "At night it is lurid with the flames of iron furnaces; by day it appears one vast, loosely-knit, town of humble homes, amid cinder heaps and fields stripped of vegetation by smoke and flames."[1] The life of the region centres round Birmingham, also the great trade centre of the Midlands. In the early days the position of Birmingham, far away from the banks of any large, navigable river, limited the weight of its articles of export and import, but as timber and iron ore were at hand, its energies were naturally turned to the making of hardware, involving either small goods such as nails, or articles connected with horse transport, such as bits, bridles, etc., its central position in the Midland Plain causing much of this kind of traffic to come its way. This trade, as we have seen, made it

[1] Lyde, "The Continent of Europe."

profitable for the canal makers to link Birmingham to the great navigable river-ways, and its central position brought added importance when the great railways were built across the country. But even with its home supplies of coal and iron, the making of heavy goods is still a difficulty where only " artificial " transport is possible, and Birmingham is compelled even in these modern times to use material whose weight is far below the labour spent upon it. Articles such as pins, pens, needles, screws, watch-springs, etc., or to deal in rolling-stock easily removed on the railway.

Round this town are a group of dependent industrial towns for which Birmingham acts as market. To the North is Stafford, engaged in that eminently "transport" industry, boot-making ; to the North-East is Burton-on-Trent, supplying the thirsty workmen of this (and other) localities with ale ; Eastward are Tamworth and Nuneaton, on a small detached coal-field, busy with the iron industry ; South is Coventry, where cycles and now aeroplanes—still " transport " industries—are made ; South-West is Bromsgrove, making nails—once only for the hoofs of horses—and Redditch, making needles. To the West lies Kidderminster, famous for its carpets, at one time getting wool from the Welsh hills, and to the North-West are Wellington and Coalbrookdale, also in small detached coal-fields. Birmingham itself shares with its three suburbs of Handsworth, Oldbury, Saltley, in the production of railway rolling-stock of first-class quality ; so also Wolverhampton, the capital of the Black Country; while at Walsall, where there is locally fine casting sand, an important harness industry is carried on.

Of this great conurbation outlying Malvern and

REVOLUTION IN TOWN GROWTH 283

Leamington may be regarded as residential suburbs. "Midlanton" is suggested as an appropriate name for this modern industrial City.

On the Northumberland and Durham coal-field is another conurbation, which might well be called Tyne-Wear-Tees-town. In this region there are three large towns, each ranged along a water street. The first is composed of a vast area of engineering and shipbuilding works stretching almost continuously from Newcastle to the mouth of the Tyne, and known in various parts of its length as Newcastle, Gateshead, Jarrow, South Shields, North Shields, Tynemouth. The second is Sunderland-Wearmouth, on the Wear. And the third, in the Tees Valley, is represented by Darlington-Stockton-Middlesbrough-Hartlepool. With the exception of Newcastle, all these industrial towns are very recent when compared with Durham, and it was the presence of coal near the surface and in proximity to sea that caused their growth and their wealth. Here, too, there is specialization in the great "workshops," and here too one deals in superlatives. "Tyneside is one of the largest coal-shipping centres in the world." ". . . is the seat of a shipbuilding industry second only to that of the Clyde," etc. The shipbuilding industry arose from the ease with which Scandinavian timber could be imported, and though the days of wooden ships are waning, still vast quantities of timber are required for the scaffolding of the "ironclads" of the Royal Navy, which are made here. The iron itself is obtained from Scandinavian and Cleveland ore. Salt, in the Tees Valley, furnishes a basis for chemical manufactures.

The above list of "conurbations"[1] is by no means

[1] This word is hardly as yet an "established" geographical term, and the names suggested by Mr. Geddes may only be provisional.

exhaustive. On the same plan the South Wales coalfield furnishes the conurbation of Greater Cardiff, northward across the English border we have the mighty one of "Forth-Clyde." Southward there is another which, without the impetus that it would seem the presence of a coal-field gives, still holds a sufficiently dense population to be known as "Greater London." Greater London has spread out widely from the city nucleus—the Tower and Ludgate Hills—engulfing old county boundaries, villages and minor boroughs, so that it may be said to be composed of parts of the counties of Middlesex, Surrey and Kent. The once rural villages of Charing and Lewisham, Lee, Greenwich (to give a very few examples out of many), and boroughs, such as Southwark, etc., have lost their original independence and become part of the modern City of "Greater London."

On the other hand, the growth of London is not surprising. Cut off by geological no less than climatic considerations from any one form of industry as its speciality, London has opportunity to be interested in all industries. Its geographical position and the relief of the country have aided London to become the focus of many ways radiating freely over the English Plain, and thus as a warehouse and a distributing centre London must share in the prosperity of other regions with which it does trade. Once started on its path of progress further increase becomes a matter of momentum. Export of the wares of other districts leads easily to a desire to export one's own district's wares, and the ease with which raw material of all kinds can be brought to London—including coal—accounts for much in the saying that "London is the largest manufacturing town in Britain." The extra population necessitated—but in part originating from

REVOLUTION IN TOWN GROWTH

—these numerous commercial activities, does much to account for the building over of the former waste or agricultural regions between the City and the outlying villages and small towns. Once reached by the "feelers" from the great City the advantages to these "engulfed" places of a closer union are obvious. Perhaps it is not such a sad operation as some geographers would seem to suggest—that of taking the Ordnance Survey Map of the London district, and of calculating the number of small, self-satisfied villages which have lost their ancient independence in becoming a corporate part of the world's most important City!

Before closing this account of the Historical Geography of South Britain, a few words should perhaps be added concerning the possible approach of a new Revolution comparable to that of the growth of the great Conurbations.

In a previous section we dealt briefly with the parcelling out of the land into suitable administrative units. But these ancient counties of England and Wales, whose roots go back to the Anglo-Saxon Heptarchy, no longer represent autonomous districts looking to a central town as rallying point or head. Right down to the middle of the 18th century, England was pre-eminently agricultural and pastoral, but to-day it is as pre-eminently industrial and commercial. The new conditions of living are tending to break up old historic associations and to develop fresh ones, so that—especially in several of the great conurbations—large districts in one ancient county may look to some city in quite another as the pivot of its whole industrial life and development. In other cases a man's work is in one county and his home life in a second—conditions which bring into his regional patriotism different and sometimes quite conflicting enthusiasms, ill-calculated to foster historic traditions either in existence or in the making.

Apart from this, many of the capitals of the ancient counties are now of small importance in comparison with the newer towns. Sometimes a remedy has been found in creating a new county, and it is not so long since a generation of schoolchildren repeated unquestioningly " Middlesex, London on the Thames," and even to-day there are adults who will scarcely credit the statement that the capital of Lancashire is neither of the wealthy and populous cities of Liverpool and Manchester, but almost forgotten Lancaster on the Lune!

Already the boundaries of the ancient counties are being attacked on the ground that they divide groups of people industrially or commercially united, or that changing geographical values have made the one-time useful and appropriate barriers to-day of none effect, and many of the historic " Shires " no longer quite coincide with the present " Administrative County " which carries on the work for which they were formerly created. The Administrative County of London, for example, embraces parts of Kent, Surrey and Middlesex; and the boundaries of " Leicestershire " are not coincident with the Administrative County of Leicester.

It has been suggested that these anomalies may be avoided by sweeping away all historic and modern divisions and redistributing the surface of South Britain into regions more closely bound together by the circumstances of their present life. This would involve the creation of new administrative units which might be called " Provinces." In King Alfred's time an effort was made so to choose the boundaries that no part of the " Shire " was beyond a day's journey of the shire town. With the modern facilities for rapid travelling a three or four hours' journey would bring much more distant localities into connection with the "Provincial" capital; and consequently England and Wales could be reasonably divided into thirteen or fourteen provinces, in place of the fifty-three present counties. Whether these enlarged divisions should have a species of "Home Rule" as formerly had our northern counties, under the Council of the North, or whether London still be regarded as the centre and metropolis of *all* English life is a problem which must be left to the future.

THE END

INDEX

Abbeys, 95, 96
"Abbey" Towns, 206, 207
Act of Union, 134
Adulterine Castles, 131
Agrarian Revolution, 275
Akerman Street, 58
Alabaster, 165
Ale-Wives, 169
Amber, 40, 48
Ancient Woodlands, 146
Angles, 60-66, 70-73, 90, 112, 113, 216
Anglo-Saxon Churches, 100
Armada, 32
Artificial Harbours, 198, 199
Avebury, 20, 24, 24f, 33, 35, 40

Barons' War, 130
Barrows, 36
Bath Stone, 165
Benedictine Order, 95
"Bishop" Towns, 207
Black Death, 162
Booklands, 124
Boroughs (Berghs, Burghs)—
  Danish, 67, 122, 190, 202
  Military Places, 67, 67f, 122, 122f, 123, 201-203
  Parliamentary, 121-123, 203
  Royal, 202, 205
Brewing, 169
Bridge Chapels, 99f
"Bridge" Towns, 201
Britons, 37, 45, 48, 49, 61-65, 72, 89, 110, 112-114, 157, 212
Broad Heads, 35-37
Bronze Age, 21, 24f, 34-44
Brythons, 37, 38, 46
Burgesses, 122-124

Calico, 166, 242
Cambridge University, 186f, 209
Canals, 78, 234-241, 251, 256, 257, 260, 268, 269, 282
Cantii, 44, 62, 104
Car Dyke, 150
Carron Iron Works, 252, 253
Castles, 81-84, 132, 134

"Castle" Towns, 84, 201, 203-205, 258
Cathedrals, 94, 95, 95f
Cathedral Cities, 206
Catuvellauni, 44
Cave Man, 13, 14, 15f
Celts, 31, 33, 36-40, 44, 45, 61, 61f, 65, 106, 113
Chalk, 163, 164
Chapels-of-Ease, 210
Chase (defined), 147
Church Cities and Towns, 206
Cinque Ports, 134, 178, 193, 194
Cistercians, 96, 97
Cloth Assize, 174
Cloth Industry, 166, 171-178, 242, 243
Cloth Towns, 247, 248
Cluniacs, 95, 96
Coaching Era, 230
Coal and Coal Mining, 49, 159-161, 235, 236, 241, 249, 250, 253, 254, 257, 260, 262, 265, 270, 280, 282-284
Common Lands, 128, 272
Companies, 181, 182
Conquest of Wales, 133, 134
Continental Blockade, 262, 272
Conurbations, 280-284
"Convent" Towns, 207
Copper, 34, 49, 55, 157, 162
Cottage Industries, 262
Cotton Industry, 242, 243
Counties—
  Administrative, 286
  Ancient, 79, 103, 109, 109f, 111, 112, 285, 286
County Palatine, 106, 113, 115, 132
County Towns, 205, 206
Crown Lands, 127
Crusades, 218

Damnonii, 48, 104
Danegeld, 181f
Danelaw, 66, 67, 69, 202
Danes, 60, 66-70, 73, 76, 84, 101, 105, 110, 112, 114, 143, 205, 215, 216

Deforestation, 147, 148
Deneholes, 164, 164f
Devil's Ditch, 107
Diocese, 89-94, 113
Discovery of the New World, 216
Dissolution of the Monasteries, 88, 101, 124, 224
Dolmen, 24
Domesday (Book), 83, 107, 109-111, 157, 162, 163, 166, 204
Domestic Industries, 172, 178, 188, 204, 254, 259, 261, 262, 273
Drift Man, 13, 14

Earthworks, 31, 32
Ecclesiastical Orders, 95-97
Economic Province, 279, 286, 287
Eleanor Crosses, 165, 165f
Enclosures, 274, 275
English Nomenclature, 52f, 54, 54f, 69, 70, 71, 73, 74, 74f, 146, 147, 150f, 151, 153, 201
Eolithic Man, 12, 13
Episcopal Province, 93
Ermine (Erming, Irming) Street, 56, 57, 145, 205
Erse, 36, 37
Exports, 48, 49, 179

Factory System, 172, 178, 259, 269
Fairs, 146, 183-188, 208, 210, 213
Fens (Draining of the), 97, 150-152
Fishing Industry, 254-256
Flemish Weavers, 133, 146, 173, 182, 197
" Ford " Towns, 200, 201
Forest, 80, 106, 107, 110, 142-147
Foss Dyke, 150, 209, 213
Fosse Way, 54, 57, 58
Free Men, 119, 123, 124
Freestone, 164
French Revolution, 259, 260, 272
Fuller's Earth, 165, 166

Gaelic, 36, 37, 68
Genoa Trade, 186, 219, 249
Glass, 48, 99, 169
Goidels, 37, 38
Gold, 36, 39, 49
Goths, 59, 88
Great North Road, 51, 57, 76, 78, 82, 211, 223
Guilds, 177, 181, 182
Gypsum, 165

Hadrian's Wall, 46, 47, 57, 81
Hardware, 262, 282, 283
Halls (Cloth, Guild of, etc.), 172, 182
Hanseatic (Hansa) League, 180, 186, 194, 249
Harrow Way, 42, 43
Hermits, 99, 219
Hide, 117, 118
Hog Ward, 120, 121
Holiday Towns, 279
Huguenots, 177, 249, 262
Hundred, 117
Hwicca Saxons, 64, 92, 105

Ice Age, 12, 14-16, 22, 25
Ichnield Way, 41, 53, 57, 58, 78, 185, 205
Imports, 48, 179
Industrial City, 276, 277, 279-283
Industrial Revolution, 244, 257, 259-263, 269, 272, 275, 276, 279
Industries, 157-189, 242-258
Inroads of the Sea, 135-138, 198
Iron, 35, 37, 40, 41, 48, 49, 55, 157-159, 179, 186, 252, 253, 256, 256f, 257, 260, 262, 270, 280-283
Iron Age, 21, 35
Iron Industry, 99, 143, 147, 148, 157-159, 214, 251-254, 257, 260, 262
" Iron " Villages, 159, 160
Itali, 26f
Ivernians, 23, 35-37, 61f
Ivory, 48

Jutes, 60f, 62, 63, 91, 104, 143, 216

INDEX

Kaolin, 251f
Kent's Cavern, 18
King's Highway, 211, 212
" King's " Towns, 122f
Kingdoms (Anglo-Saxon), 62-65
Kits Coty Hole, 24

Lace, 262
Lake Dwellings, 20, 31
Lead, 39-41, 49, 55, 157, 162, 163, 186
Leather, 169, 170, 177
Long Heads, 23, 23f, 36
Long Waggon, 228
Lords Marcher, 132

Mail Coaches, 230
Manor, 79, 119-121, 272
Manor Village, 118-122, 125
Manx, 36, 37
Marble, 165
Market Cross, 189
Markets, 188, 189, 208, 210
Market Towns, 208
Marsh, 148-153
Mediæval Ecclesiasticism, 88
Mediæval Towns, 192-208
Megalith, 24
Menhir, 24
Merchant of the Staple, 171, 172, 196
Merrie England, 273
Metal Working, 167
" Minster " Towns, 207, 208
Monasticism, 97
Monastic Towns, 100, 101
" Monk " Towns, 208

Neolithic Man, 12, 13, 17, 23-33, 35, 61f, 138
New Forest Exiles, 112, 114
Norman Castle (defined), 83
Norman Castles, 81-84, 132
Norman Conquest, 75-84, 93, 110, 112, 118, 119, 122, 139, 143, 181, 205, 206, 210, 213
Norse (Men), 60-66, 68, 69, 112, 114, 217
Norwegians, 66, 68
" Nun " Towns, 207, 208

Old Road, 41-43
Old Sea Dyke, 150

Oolite, 41, 165, 246
Oxford University, 209

Palæolithic Man, 12, 13, 15-17, 22, 23, 26, 31
Palatine Provinces, 106
Paper Making, 249
Parish, 126, 224, 272
Parish (Civil), 125f
Parish (Ecclesiastical), 94, 124, 125
Parish Churches, 94, 101, 102, 124, 125
Pearls, 39
Pele Towers, 112
Phœnicians, 161
Picts, 36, 46, 112, 114
Pilgrim's Way, 42, 185
Piltdown Skull, 18
Pit Dwellings, 32
Plantagenet Castles, 134
Plantation Products, 276
Plaster of Paris, 165
Ports, 172, 192-200, 270
Pottery, 48, 167, 168, 236, 250
Potteries (The), 237, 251
Prehistoric Buildings, 20, 24, 31-33
Prehistoric Religions, 27-29
Prehistoric Remains, 19-21, 23-25, 35, 138
Prehistoric " Roads," 40-43
Primitive Man, 21
" Priory " Towns, 207
Provincial Capitals, 202
Purbeck Marbles, 165

Quarrying, 99, 163

Railways and Roadways, 78, 199, 230, 239, 240, 263-271
Reformation, 165, 175
Religious Holdings, 127
Revocation of the Edict of Nantes, 177, 249
Ridgeways, 32, 40, 41
River Improvements, 232-234, 250
River Ports, 195, 196, 199-200
River Towns, 200
River Transport, 211
Road Making, 225-228, 260
Road Repair, 99, 225, 226

INDEX

Roads (Prehistoric), 40-43, 53, 54, 57, 58, 78, 185, 205
Roads (Roman), 48, 51-58, 67, 77, 78, 109, 205, 209, 210, 233
Road Transport, 210, 211
Roebuck's Blast Furnace, 252, 253
Romans, 31, 36, 45-59, 80, 157, 160, 161, 163, 168, 209, 216, 252
Royal Forests, 145-147

Salt, 49, 166, 167, 186, 210, 234, 278, 283
Saxons, 53, 54, 59, 60, 62-64, 70-73, 82, 84, 90, 91, 104, 105, 108, 112, 114, 143, 164, 216
Saxon Shore, 53, 59, 61, 66
Scots, 84, 112-114
Sea Ports, 192-195, 197-199, 212
Shipbuilding, 148, 159, 178, 249, 257, 283
Shire Making, 79, 103-116, 286
Silk Weaving, 177, 249
Silting, 139-142, 198, 199, 233
Silver, 39, 157, 162, 163
Slates, 164
Spinning, 242, 243
Stage Coach, 228, 229
Stane Street, 56, 56f
Staple Industries, 171
Staple Ports, 172, 196, 197, 200
Staple Towns, 172, 208
Steel, 253, 280, 281
Steel Age, 21f
Stephenson's Engine, 267
Stone Age, 12-34, 168
Stonehenge, 20-24, 24f, 33, 35, 36, 40, 42
Synod of Whitby, 92

Teutons, 38, 60-74, 164
Textiles, 243-249
Thames Castles, 82, 130
Tiles, 168
Tin, 40, 41, 45, 48, 55, 157, 161, 162, 180
Town (Classical), 274
Town (Mediæval Development), 121
Towns (in Classification), 84, 100, 101, 122f, 172, 200-208, 247, 248, 258, 279
Trading Towns, 208
Treaty of Westphalia, 180
Tumulus, 28
Turnpike, 43, 223-225, 230, 231, 237
Tweeds, 262

Vandals, 59, 88
Venetian Trade, 167, 172, 179, 186, 195, 218-220, 249
Vikings, 60, 68

Wapentake, 117
Wars of the Roses, 130, 131
Waterways, 232-234
Watling Street, 53, 54, 56-58, 67, 77, 78, 109, 145, 205
Watt's Steam Engine, 243, 253
Welsh Border Castles, 82, 132
West Country Cloth, 176, 176f, 232f, 245-248
Woodlands, 143
Woollen Trade, 98, 99, 166, 178, 244-249
Woolsack, 171
Worsted, 174, 243-245

For Product Safety Concerns and Information please contact our EU representative GPSR@taylorandfrancis.com
Taylor & Francis Verlag GmbH, Kaufingerstraße 24, 80331 München, Germany

www.ingramcontent.com/pod-product-compliance
Lightning Source LLC
Chambersburg PA
CBHW050626300426
44112CB00012B/1670